On the Edge of Darkness

On the Edge of Darkness

CONVERSATIONS
ABOUT CONQUERING
DEPRESSION

Kathy Cronkite

Doubleday

New York London Sydney Toronto Auckland

PUBLISHED BY DOUBLEDAY
a division of Bantam Doubleday Dell Publishing Group, Inc.
1540 Broadway, New York, NY 10036

DOUBLEDAY and the portrayal of an anchor with a dolphin
are trademarks of Doubleday, a division of Bantam
Doubleday Dell Publishing Group, Inc.

Book design by Jennifer Ann Daddio

Library of Congress Cataloging-in-Publication Data
Cronkite, Kathy.
On the edge of darkness : conversations about conquering
depression / Kathy Cronkite. — 1st ed.
p.   cm.
1. Depressed persons—Interviews.   2. Depression,
Mental.   I. Title.
RC537.C77   1994
616.85'27—dc20   93-29956
                                                    CIP

ISBN 0-385-42194-X
Printed in the United States of America
March 1994

1   3   5   7   9   10   8   6   4   2

First Edition

For the children

Acknowledgments

I have aimed to make this book as useful to as wide an audience as possible. To the extent that I have accomplished my goal, I am grateful to all those who helped, who shared their stories, who read, who transcribed, who filed, who edited, who watched children, who encouraged, who listened, who hugged, who believed. My husband and children put up with an awful lot, and each day they gave me the grace that allowed me to go on. I love them deeply. Special thanks to Richard Pine, Paul Beutel, Casey Fuetsch, A. John Rush, M.D., Lyn Phillips, Ph.D., Marion Coleman, Ph.D., and Dennis Wholey, and deep gratitude for editorial advice, persistence, perspective, and perspicacity, but most of all friendship, to Kevin Phinney.

Contents

On the Edge of Darkness

Prologue

April 1991

I'm afraid the black dog has really got me. Churchill's image of despair suits me better than "the black hole." A black hole just swallows you up. Would that it were that easy, to sink down into darkness, as if sleeping. But this dog, this dog! It crouches in the corner of the room, waits for me to make a move. Or lies at the foot of the bed, like a shadow, until I try to get up.

Growls, and will not let me up.

I go nowhere alone; he is at my side. He stands between me and any other, while I'm looking good, staying calm, smiling to disarm his ferocity.

Little things overwhelm me: I can't find the mate to my sock. I break the yolk of the egg. The doorbell rings while I'm on the phone. I can't cope with the little things while he's there.

I have a lunch date.
I cannot see how to get dressed for it.
The dog stands in the way.
I can't figure out where to put the baby down so he's safe,
so I'm holding him in one arm while I prepare to bathe him
in the kitchen sink. It isn't clean. I can't find any cleanser. I
want to cry. I am a terrible mother because I can't bathe the
baby. I am a terrible housewife because I can't find the
cleanser. I am a terrible household manager, because maybe
there isn't any cleanser . . .

I walk outside, it's the first day of spring, sun shining, breeze
wafting, birds singing—so what? My baby gives me one of
those dazzling you're-the-only-one-in-the-world smiles—so
what? My best friend calls with good news, my boss gives me
a raise, my husband cooks my favorite meal—so what? None
of it touches me, nothing makes me smile. I'm one beat off,
one step removed from all around me. I don't shower, brush
my hair, or make the bed. I wear the same clothes night and
day. I cancel appointments, or just don't show up. I call in
sick to work. I don't answer the phone—it's too much work to
put on the game face and sound normal—though I'm very
good at it, up to a point. Sometimes I actually feel ill, or just
off, or chilled. Curling up under all the covers with my
softest, snuggliest jammies on—doesn't help. There are things
that should be important, things I need to do—pay bills,
attend a business dinner or a child's school play—but I can't.
The simplest decisions are overwhelming and reduce me to
tears—how much to tip, what to buy for dinner . . .
And when I drive, the dog rides along, and I think, "If I
just turn the wheel—now—it would all be over."
I pass the crystal shelf and see myself shattering the
precious glass and running a shard across my wrist.
The dog and I stand a moment too long in front of the
cabinet staring at the Drano and thinking "I wonder what
would happen if I drank it?"

Although I am no longer suicidal, as I write this the weight is still on my shoulders, the stone sits in my stomach, my face wears a tight mask. I don't give in to it. I keep myself moving, the battle invisible even to those closest to me.

But now, at least, I know what's dogging me. I know this will not last. I am not going to die. I am not going to feel this way forever. The world is not crumbling. I am not crazy, or bad, or lacking in faith or in discipline. I have a disease. It's called depression.

1

The Dog and I

For Sir Winston Churchill, depression was a "black dog" that tormented him throughout his life. His wife said that after the failure of the Dardanelles Expedition in 1915, he "was filled with such a black depression that I felt he would never recover."

I didn't need a failure as large as the Dardanelles Expedition. For me, tenth grade was bad enough.

I didn't know about the dog back then, but he was there, crouching in the shadows. I missed classes because I would break down crying on the back stairs and be unable to stop. I cut myself with razor blades, not in an attempt to die, but in an effort to release some of the emotional pain by focusing it in physical pain. I withdrew from my friends. I took drugs in an effort to feel okay at least some of the time. I felt like a failure. Yet, here is what was written in my yearbook:

> *It's always such a joy to see your smiling face in the*
> *   halls . . .*
> *Though I don't know you very well, I'd love to have a*

cheerful friend like you . . .
We sure had fun this year, didn't we?

My pain was mine alone; my mask of normalcy, almost seamless.

And although I have only dim recollections of my earlier childhood, I wonder if the dog was there even then. My report card always seemed to read "She does fine work *when she applies herself.*" "A grade A student *when she wants to be.*" Was I in fact a lazy, self-indulgent pupil? Or was I even then only periodically capable of doing the work, at other times fighting internal demons?

I see snapshots from my later life with depression: As a college student, putting a DO NOT DISTURB sign on my dorm room door and not emerging for days at a time; as a young woman, struggling to establish a life on my own, a thousand miles from home, lying on the floor all night thinking that the pain I felt was mere loneliness, thinking that if I could just hang on till sunrise, I'd be okay; as a professional, slogging through what felt like waist-deep mud each morning to make it to the office, to give everything I had just to get the job done; and most recently, as a wife and mother, with children to be nurtured, plumbing to be repaired, errands to be run, and a marriage to be salvaged amid the desperation of emotional illness. Most of my life I fought the anger, the pain, the hopelessness, the irrationality, the hyper-emotionalism, and the apathy that drove off lovers, ruined my self-esteem, and brought me to the brink of suicide more than a few times. I didn't know it had a name; I didn't know it could be stopped.

In actuality, depression is one of the disorders most successfully treated by psychiatrists, but if you call it what it is, a mental illness, you conjure up images of Bedlam, of maniacs running uncontrolled or lunatics gibbering on the sidewalk. Despite *Newsweek* cover stories, many people don't know that the pain in which they live may be an easily treatable condition. It does not mean that you, or your afflicted loved one, is evil or weak, or lazy, or nuts. Full-blown clinical depression is a real disease, like diabetes or heart disease. It is not under the control of the person who has it and not amenable to a do-it-yourself approach, but professional help *is* available and can change your life. *Many successful, competent men and women have succeeded in life in spite of debilitating depression.*

It can happen to anyone, at any time, and it takes many forms. It may be a lifelong problem or a transitory response to a particular crisis. Some people experience only one episode in a lifetime; others live through it many times, or continuously; while others sweep from exhilarating highs to debilitating lows.

The costs of depression are great: Estimates range from $16 billion to $45 billion a year nationally in direct services and lost productivity. But the most painful costs can't be quantified—lost relationships, lost self-esteem, lost lives. Depression cuts across all social and economic strata. Though rates are highest for those between twenty-five and forty-four years of age, neither the very old nor the very young are exempt. During any six-month period, about 3.5 percent of men in the United States and almost twice as many women *that we know of* will experience depressive illness. That's 24 million people.

We have an idea of how many people have it, but we may not know if our best friend does. Like alcoholism ten years ago, or cancer a decade before that, no one talks about it. We are ashamed.

What causes this disorder? Is it an illness, a weakness, a syndrome? Causes are still being researched, and there appear to be several. Genetics may predispose an individual to depression, which may then be triggered by an event such as a death or other loss or trauma, by physical illness, hormonal imbalance, certain medications, or even developed personality traits.

Like the causes, the "cures" are various and not well understood. The prescription for conquering depression is not cut and dried. All too often, sufferers are told to "pull themselves up by their bootstraps," an admonishment rarely given to other medical patients. "Take a walk; do something for others; get up and get going," exclaim so many of the articles in popular magazines. It may be excellent advice for the blues or even a mild depression, but it is frustrating and painful for those with more serious illnesses. Such advice serves only to increase self-blame as the depressed person "fails" to heal him- or herself. "Big D" depression, the real thing, the involuntary chemical imbalance, can't be walked away, or overcome with good thoughts, or treated with self-help manuals.

Nor is medication the only answer. Prozac, a relatively new antidepressant, received considerable attention in the media—first, as a powerful new medicine, later as a dangerous, violence-inducing drug*—demonstrating that although various medications can be a miracle for many, they are no solution at all for others. Some people can't tolerate the side effects of certain antidepressants. Pregnant women and nursing mothers should refrain when possible from taking drugs. So how do sufferers cope without pharmacological intervention? What techniques have they developed to help them make it through the day? What tactics have they found just to survive from moment to moment until the black dog departs? And what if it doesn't?

It's not always easy to take the first step back to health. First, we need to know that there is a problem, that not everyone lives in this black pit that seems normal to us. Second, we must overcome the inertia of melancholia, the apathy and hopelessness that is part of the disease and that keeps us from seeking help. Third, we must overcome our own internal fears of being "crazy" and of the stigma of mental illness ruining our careers, our friendships, and our entire lives.

Once we seek help, we still have to hope a correct diagnosis is made and a correct treatment prescribed. For some of us, the next hurdle is overcoming the fear of the treatment itself, which is often just a fear of the unknown.

I remember so vividly leaning against the kitchen counter staring at the prescription I'd been given, in an agony of indecision, scared even to get it filled. On the one hand, I was hopeful that maybe this would be the answer, maybe now the pain would stop; on the other, it seemed too simple, and I was fearful of being medicated. What would it do to me? How would I feel? Would it

---

* These later studies claiming that Prozac induced violent behavior have been discredited.

slow me down? Make me feel groggy or stupid? Would it dull my senses, or my imagination? Would I still be *me*? My dear husband Bill gave me a hug and said, "Hey, if you don't like the way it feels, we'll find another solution."

For many, the word "normal" connotes "boring, ordinary." But you can't imagine how wonderful "normal" is to someone who hasn't experienced it before. When I drop a glass and it shatters on the kitchen floor, I say "Ooops!" or maybe even "Shit!" but I don't collapse on the tile in tears moaning "Oh, god, I'm so stupid! I can't do anything right!" And I don't have to schedule every moment of the day in fear that if I stop moving, I won't be able to get back up again.

Often, in the early stages of depression, I would pile more work, more projects, more commitments and activities on my schedule, afraid that if I sat down to catch my breath, inertia—that is, depression—would overcome me. I read later and later into the night, knowing that when I finally turned the light off, sleep would not come. Sometimes I'd pace the house in the dark or stare at late-night television, or simply wrap myself in a blanket on the couch. I saw the world through dark-tinted glasses—my house was a wreck, my children monsters, my marriage in trouble, my body fat, my wardrobe ugly, my work without merit, and on and on. "I can't stand this, I can't stand feeling this way," I thought a million times, but I would have been unable to define what "this way" was. I labeled myself "irritable," "cranky," "bitchy," but the feeling was "out of control."

And I took drugs. "Self-medicated" is the trendy euphemism. I took uppers, mostly, to counteract the lethargy. Someone once said a depressed person on uppers approaches the energy level of normal people. I would make myself stay up round the clock for days. Then, when I did sleep, I was able to sleep hard.

There were other symptoms that I never imagined were connected to the depression until the depression was gone and, magically, so were they—the bad dreams, the morbid fantasies and "daymares" that I thought everyone had. Images would haunt me of dismemberments, fiery death, Armageddon. What-ifs spun through my head: What if my husband were killed in a car crash? What if the freeway collapsed beneath my child's school bus? The entire scenario would play itself out, in all its grim detail.

I started seeing a therapist when I was seventeen. He was the first of a dozen. Each was helpful, in his or her way; each assisted me through trying times, helped me toward greater self-knowledge, and in many cases offered true friendship. But of the twelve, eleven failed to diagnose or treat my disease. When I was prospering financially, I saw doctors and shrinks from New York's Upper East Side to Beverly Hills, but the man who put me on the path to wellness was a pastoral care counselor who charged on a sliding scale. For the relative pittance of ten dollars a session, he saved my life. It was he who noticed the pattern of my behavior and suggested I might want to be evaluated for depression by a psychiatrist. A few weeks later I had a prescription in my hand and was about to discover what "normal" felt like.

When my depression first was diagnosed, I felt both relief and shame—relief that my condition was real, had a name, and possibly a cure; shame that I was afflicted with a mental disorder. I still felt I should have been able to rise above it, to use my will to overcome it on my own, and that my inability to do so was proof of my weak nature. I kept the diagnosis and my condition a secret from all but my husband and family, at first.

In the spring of 1990, *U.S. News & World Report* featured a cover story on depression. I was stunned to read a sidebar interview with Mike Wallace describing his bout with it. I was overwhelmed by his courage, and it empowered me to admit that depression has been a part of my life. It was as though the windows were thrown open on the first bright, clear, spring day, to know that someone whom I respected and admired, who has achieved so much in his profession, who had so much more to lose through his candor than I, was able to talk about his problem without shame and to seek the help he needed without fear. For me, it was the start of a journey of discovery and acceptance, a journey that advanced through the writing of this book and that continues today.

You may feel that your life has little in common with the perceived glamour of Joan Rivers's or Rod Steiger's. You may be right. But depression is a great equalizer—the pain is the same, the floor is just as hard when you fall, and whether your window overlooks Malibu beach or a brick wall, all you see is gray. My family, and those of the celebrities in this book, may have had all the resources you can imagine—financial, social, educational—yet I lay on the bed week after week unable to call for help. Too often, when we did reach out, our calls still went unanswered. Nowhere is it more true that money can't buy happiness than when you're standing on the edge of a cliff and down is the only conceivable direction.

This book will look at what depression is and what it is not; what it feels like, how it is treated and mistreated, and what it means to the individuals suffering from it, to their families, to professionals, and to you and me. The main focus is on moderate, unipolar major depression, not on the small percentage of the severely ill, the chronically hospitalized, the psychotic, or on those whose depression is amenable to self-help therapy, such as exercise or meditation. It is not intended to be comprehensive, but will answer some of the questions you may have. This book is not so much a "how-to" as a "how it is," less a book about causes than effects.

In part, this is a book about courage—the courage that it takes to get out of bed when nothing in life seems worthwhile, the courage to seek treatment when you may not even know what that entails, the courage to speak out publicly when it could mean the end of all you've built in your life.

Most of all, this is a book about hope. If your spouse reaches the end of his or her patience, if you feel intolerably alone even when surrounded by friends, if you look down into the injured faces of your children and feel only rage, or if your treatment fails and you have to start over, you may feel frustrated and discouraged. But even if you don't believe, have faith. There is help, there is hope.

Hope starts with a spark of recognition that what you are

struggling with has a name, depression. It is fanned with stories of people who have found ways to heal themselves and it bursts into flame with the realization that a great breadth of healing options exists and that, with perseverance, even the darkest corners of despair will be illuminated.

2

It Takes One to
Know One

I have known Mike Wallace and his family all my life. Even when I was young, he was one of those rare grown-ups who seemed to take me seriously. Still, I never dreamed that as an adult, I would interview him, one professional to another. I was honored that he would be so candid with me and was struck by similarities between our illnesses. Mike Wallace helped me to clarify the goal of this book. For the first time, I had the experience of recognition, that illuminating moment when you realize you are not alone. I saw that in spite of our differences, we are part of a community of survivors of depression, with the capacity to offer great support one to another. At the same time, this interview revealed the diversity of experiences that are depression and reminded me that my experience is not the experience. And it was a cocktail party conversation with Mary Wallace that awakened me to the importance of addressing the spouses' point of view.

Since the article about Mike in U.S. News & World Report *planted the seed that became this book, I sought him out for the first interview. Mike and his wife, Mary, welcomed me in the driveway of their expansive new house on a bluff in Vineyard Haven, Martha's Vineyard. On a beautiful, peaceful summer day, he and I sat overlooking the sailboats in the harbor, the view broken periodically by the massive ferryboat to the mainland of Cape Cod. Author William Styron and columnist Art Buchwald have their summer homes nearby, and the three men and their wives are close friends.*

Mike Wallace

I didn't know what was the matter with me. All I knew was that I was feeling lower than a snake's belly. I was on trial in the Westmoreland suit* and that goes to your gut, that goes to your heart. Mary was living with me at the time; we were old friends. She used to go to the court house with me every morning—we'd get up early and go to court and sit there, and I heard myself called dirty names over and over again for five months.

The first three months were the plaintiff making his case. I'd pick up the paper every day, and they were saying "Cheat, liar, fraud," et cetera. After a while I began to feel that way; you suddenly say to yourself, "Well, yeah, they're right."

I still didn't know what it was. I thought I was just down. I remember we used to go to restaurants, and I'd say "Everybody's pointing at me, the cheat, the fraud, the fake." You really believe these things! Astonishing! I had pains in my arms and a kind of weakness in my legs. I would be asking questions in an interview, and suddenly I wouldn't be able to hear the answer, or think of the next question. My mind was on a completely different plane. I had no memory, no powers of concentration. If you asked me questions about a newspaper column I'd read two minutes before, I wouldn't have been able to answer. Mary saw what was happening, but I wasn't willing to acknowledge it.

I couldn't sleep, and because I couldn't sleep, I started taking

---

* General Westmoreland had sued Wallace and *Sixty Minutes* for libel in connection with a story about Vietnam.

half a sleeping pill, then it went up to one sleeping pill, and then if
I wasn't sleeping, I'd take another. And I was feeling lousy all day
long.

When the opportunity came to go on assignment to Ethiopia,
it seemed like a good way to get away from the trial for ten days. I
thought, "Maybe this will change the way I feel. Maybe I'll be
able to sleep. Maybe I'll feel better." Although it was such a joy to
be away, the trial was never off my mind, and you can run, but
you cannot hide from this damned disease. With the jet lag, and
the exhaustion, sleeping in fourth-rate hotels in a Third World
country, and a bug I picked up, I became even more vulnerable.

When the trial recessed for Christmas, we went away to St.
Martin. I'm a tennis player; Ivan Lendl was down there, and he
was practicing. I couldn't watch. I kept looking at the water and
thinking "Oh, boy, that's very tempting." I think everybody
thinks of suicide at one time or another during his or her life,
wonders about it. You get to the point where you say to yourself
"Hey, that would be a wonderful. That would kill the pain in a
hurry." I knew I was in trouble. Still didn't know what I had.

When we got back, I was in very, very bad shape. I had a
doctor, who had been my doctor for fifteen years. Why he did not
know, to this day I don't know. He's a wonderful doctor; he just
missed it. Mary felt that he should have known and started to
treat [me for depression] a lot earlier. I wound up in the hospital
for what we called exhaustion, and I *was* emotionally, physically
exhausted. But really, it was depression. While I was in the hospital, I was feeling so bad, he said, "Why don't you talk to the chief
of psychiatry? Maybe you'll find something." The chief of psychiatry came in and said, "You're suffering from clinical depression.
Not a deep, deep depression, but you have all the classic manifestations of a clinical depression."

I was grateful to have some kind of diagnosis. The mystery
was over. I said, "You're sure? That's it? I'm not losing my mind,
I'm not cashing it in, there isn't some tumor back there?"

He said, "No, we'll take CAT scans, we'll take all the tests, but
no. As a doctor I'm reluctant to say that I know exactly what it is
without doing those tests, but I can virtually guarantee you that

you have a classic case, not a very deep case, of clinical depression." And I . . . heaved a sigh of relief.

The doctor said, "First, we're going to start you on a drug to arrest it chemically. It will dampen the pain in your arms and your legs, and it'll also put a floor under your depression, so that we have something to work with. Then we'll talk." I talked to him for about an hour a day during the week I was in the hospital. After I got out, I just went on talking to him.

I went back to the trial, and sat there, and it's a funny thing, the psychiatrist didn't know anything about television, and nothing about the news, and had no real idea who I was, but he learned very quickly. He studied it. After about two or three weeks, he said, "All right, we've got to get you ready to testify. Because you're afraid of that." He was right. Because suddenly the fellow who asks the questions is going to be asked the questions. "And then we have to get you ready to lose, because you believe that if you lose, you lose everything, that your life is worthless." And I really did believe it.

In any case, the psychiatrist began to talk to me about myself, and about my mind, and about my spirit, and about what I had done. He started to not psychoanalyze, but give me psychiatric understanding of what was going on. When he gave me material to read about depression, I suddenly realized that one out of every ten Americans has suffered from this disease at one time or another, and that my symptoms were classic, and not mild, but by no means deep. I suddenly realized that my friend Styron and my friend Buchwald had been going though the same thing. But I still was ashamed. So nobody in the shop [CBS] knew. I was trying to do my job, go to the trial, talk to the doctor, et cetera. And not let anybody know.

When I first had it diagnosed, you know something? I don't think I thought about the public reaction. I was so sick, that I didn't give a damn about what the public thinks. Tell 'em, you know, I have trouble enough. But I didn't want to lose my job because of it; I didn't want to get off [Sixty Minutes] because of it, suddenly to be replaced and have people asking why. I am sure that is one reason that I never came forward and said to our producer, "Hey, Don, I've got to quit." I didn't even tell my individual producers, and Barry and I have been working together now for twenty years. The people at CBS knew I was acting strange, not characteristically Mike Wallace. They saw a lack of confidence, a lack of healthy aggressiveness. I wasn't as engaged as I ordinarily am. They knew I was really being carried by my producer.

I remember we were doing a piece about airport security in Chicago, and going through one of the tunnels, I felt dizzy, spacey. This was before I went to the hospital. I used to look up walking along, and the sky would shake. I had a kind of buzzing in my head all the time. A kind of nauseating light-headedness. But I just didn't want to acknowledge what was happening to me.

I never even talked to the kids until after I came out of the hospital. Once it became open, we all talked about it. The only one who really knew at the time was Mary.

I just did not want people to know of my vulnerability. I was ashamed. It was a confession of weakness. For years, depression meant the crazy house. As I look back at it, it just seems damned foolishness. Really, really damned foolishness. Which is one reason I talk about it now.

Finally, two days before I was to testify, I was down rehearsing my testimony and getting prepared for cross examination with a battery of attorneys. And the lead attorney came in, and he said, "There's a possibility, maybe one in ten, that Westmoreland is going to pull out." I had tried to convey "Oh ho! Wait'll I get on that stand, and I'll hand you your head," but the fact is I had no desire to testify. And I wouldn't have been very good. By this time, I was taking the drug,* and the drug made me dizzy. And the drug dried me up. And my hands shook. The side effects wouldn't look good on the stand. By the time the afternoon was over, a period of four or five hours, they came up and said that he'd pulled out. In return for our saying that we believed him to be a patriot. That was it. Didn't have to retract a word, and didn't

* In most cases I have omitted naming people's medication because prescriptions that work for one person may not work for another, and side effects that are severe for one patient may be unnoticeable to another.

have to pick up a penny of his expenses, so in effect we won. Immediately I felt great. I mean, I felt better, but I still had all the other manifestations.

By this time, I was going to a doctor about three times a week, and then I cut back to two, then back to one. But my doctor said I should stay on the drug for six months after I began to feel pretty good. Under normal circumstances, I hate to take aspirin, let alone drugs, so after two months, two and a half, three, I said, "Hey, I feel great." I could feel some aftereffects, but basically, I felt the cloud had lifted, and I was on my way back.

I said, "I want to quit [the medication]."

The doctor said, "Well, I don't think it's a good idea. You're doing it against my advice, but if you feel confident . . ." Anyway, I quit. Mary and I were staying up here [in Martha's Vineyard]. We went down to Nicaragua to do a piece, and I remember the first day after I came back, playing tennis, I fell, with my wrist under me. I could feel the crack, the smash. I had really split it.

Within twenty-four hours, I was deeper in depression than I had been the first time. All of a sudden. Why? Mortality, old age, the fact that I had gotten off the drug? I had all of the manifestations, all over again. Everything. The pain in the arms, the pain in the leg . . . Astonishing. Back to the doctor. He didn't say "I told you so," but . . . And this episode lasted longer, and there was no proximate reason beyond this. I used to walk home from the appointments, and think, "Jesus God, will this ever lift?" Thinking, you know, "Should I quit? Should I . . . ?" I doubted myself all over again, all that mindless garbage. So, this time I stayed on [the drug], talked to him, and little by little, it lifted. It took somewhere between three and six months to lift. I gather it is not unusual to have recurring experiences.

That would have been in '85. The effects of it diminished, and diminished, and diminished, but you know that you've had it for a couple of years. At least, I found that is true of me. I don't know that you're ever back totally to normal, because you're always looking out the corner of your mind, thinking "Is it laying over there someplace?" And every once in a while, you say, "Ooh, wait a minute, is this the depression coming?" but then that's it. It passes. Bill [Styron] and Artie [Buchwald] and I talk about it a great deal, and compare notes. We're each other's support network.

I still take [a very small dose of] a very, very mild antianxiety, antiwhatever. The last two summers, I tried to kick it. After a while, I began to get those warning signs of depression, and I said, "It's not worth it."

I think that I'm probably evener of disposition now than I used to be. I guard against excess, or I try to anyway, in my dealings with people. And with myself. Of course that may be a function of age, but I'm probably a little kinder—I know there are those who say that's a snare and a delusion—but I'm a little more moderate; I am more forgiving. To some degree, I guess, it's taken a little of the edge off my reporting, and by that I mean the abrasiveness of my reporting. That may be not just the disease, but also the whole experience of the trial. You see what it does to other people, and what it does to you, when you are the object of that kind of inquiry. I don't think that it has changed me, it just made me moderate everything a little bit; I'm a little more careful, I think, of life. I really don't know why, except that the ocean is out there as an option, someplace in the back of your head.

So I've learned, don't get into fights. Don't get into fights. Cool it. That's the single most important thing for me, because that's when I suddenly feel some of the symptoms. If you have a point to make, make it, but don't get in a fight. For me anyway, depression is caught up with anxiety. When I came out of the hospital, there was some wild man who kept threatening me with exposing something, although I never understood what it was that he was going to expose. I'd pick up the phone and hear heavy breathing and a voice saying "I have this record" and so forth. Suddenly, when the phone rang, it was as though a light was going off or an electric shock was going through me. And when people coughed very hard near me . . . Look, it happens. It's like an elastic band that has lost its elasticity—now when you pull it, it doesn't snap right back, it stays out there for a while. So what I try to do is not test the elastic too much.

It's good for a depressive to talk about it; it helps you. You bring it to the surface, and it gives you a kind of cleansing. Not forever. Styron has made a career out of talking about it. But I think it's useful to talk about it, because it remains a mystery to so many people, and it remains verboten to so many people to talk about. If somebody has suffered it, survived it, and gone on about his business, and people know that, then it's got to be useful.

People who don't know [what depression is], who say it's self-indulgence, sound callous, but it's not callousness born of indifference; I think it's callousness born of ignorance. That kind of ignorance we've got to get rid of, and little by little I suppose, we will. You say to them, "It's a pity you don't know. I'm sure that if you knew, I'm sure that *if you knew*, not only wouldn't you say that, you'd try to help in one way or another."

If you have a friend who is depressed, be patient. Be patient. Check in. Listen. LISTEN. Just say "Um-hm, um-hm." I couldn't believe it that Artie did it with me, and I did it with him, but what he did with Styron was incredible. And he's done it with others, too. But he's that kind of soul. And I think it's good for *him* to do that. So what can you do? Patience, listen, reassure, reassure. You look at a scratch on your hand, you know it's going to heal; you *know*. Why do you know? Because you've seen it so many times. Little by little, it heals; it knits, and it's better. Maybe it leaves a little bit of a scar. So you take that on faith. I'm saying, do the same with the soul, or the head, or the mind, or the spirit, or whatever it is. It is going to get better. So go see the doctor, find out about it, find the drug that will help.

Let people know that 95 percent of people who get it get over it. The effect of it can be reduced by pharmacology and, I believe, talk. Simply get yourself to a doctor who understands that, and if your doctor doesn't understand that . . . just get yourself some help. Get yourself some help.

In closing, I asked Mike the interviewer's classic last question: "What would you like to say that I haven't given you the opportunity to say?" He shook his head, made a gesture of completion, and said to me knowingly, "It takes one to know one."

3

What Is Depression?

"My boyfriend's out of town, I'm so depressed."

"I hate rain. It's depressing."

"I don't want to go out tonight, I'm too depressed over my haircut. Call me tomorrow."

One of the great misunderstandings people have about clinical, or medical, depression stems from the colloquial use of the word to mean less than happy. Everyone has felt pain; everyone has felt grief. Those are part of the human experience. Fortunately, not everyone knows the depth of anguish that takes over your life when depression rules.

According to the *Random House Dictionary*, the fourth definition of depression is "emotional dejection greater than that warranted by any objective reason." It's not a bad starting place. To some, "depression" can sound ordinary, inconsequential. To others, it may sound scary, even bizarre, but in fact it describes a range of conditions.

"After a loss, or a major disappointment," explains Frederick Goodwin, M.D., director of the National Institute of Mental

Health and an authority on depression and manic depressive illness, "it's normal to feel sad, tearful, to lose interest in things, to see the glass as half empty, to question your ability to do anything well. A parent after the first confrontation with a teenaged child, a writer who can't come up with a story, a student who receives a failing grade, may all experience difficulty sleeping, or a change in appetite. The difference between that and clinical depression rests on three questions: How many symptoms have been experienced? For example, tingling in the limbs, heaviness in the chest, serious inability to fall asleep or to stay asleep, appetite changes that result in weight loss or gain.

"Second, how long have the symptoms lasted? After the worst disasters, the loss of a spouse, or a child, you would expect to lose interest in things around you, to lose interest in sex, to think more slowly, to move in a haze, but you would expect gradually to pull out of it. The pain wouldn't go away, but it would interfere less with your life as the weeks passed. But with clinical depression the symptoms go on relentlessly, week after week, month after month.

"That brings us to the third criterion: How much do these feelings interfere with your normal functioning? Can you still care for your children? Engage in social intercourse? Hold a job?"

As Dr. Goodwin tells us, the experience of depression exists along a continuum. Some people stumble on through life but with no real joy. Some, while suffering serious depressive symptoms, fulfill only the day's most urgent requirements—a journalist who can't complete basic hygienic functions but appears each morning at the newspaper; a mother who can't conduct a simple social exchange but keeps her children fed and clothed. Others are incapacitated.

The current diagnostic criteria published by the American Psychiatric Association contain two principal categories of mood disorders, bipolar and unipolar, or depressive. Sufferers in the first category alternate between two poles, the highs and lows of what sometimes is called manic-depression or manic-depressive illness. With unipolar disorder, people experience only the lows.

Manic episodes are characterized typically by an elated, expansive mood, although irritability may be exhibited instead. Judgment and behavior are impaired to the extent that normal relationships, occupations, or social activities are disrupted significantly. At least three of the following symptoms occur:

- inflated ego, all things seem possible, great schemes are envisioned with a conviction of success;
- incredible energy, with little sleep required or taken;
- verbosity, a need to keep talking and talking;
- racing thoughts;
- distractibility;
- agitation or increased participation in projects and activities;
- reckless involvement in self-gratifying pursuits with a potential for harm, for example, shopping sprees beyond what is affordable, sexual promiscuity, precipitous and unwise business ventures.

In a manic state, a person may believe that he or she has special abilities, knowledge or power, or a special relationship with a famous person or even God. Other symptoms include delusions of being controlled by thoughts or external forces. Such catatonic symptoms as loss of speech or total lack of physical activity may be exhibited as well. When symptoms are less severe, without serious disruption of usual activities, hypomania is diagnosed. The occurrence of both hypomanic, but not manic, episodes and depressive episodes may be referred to as bipolar II.

Depressive episodes comprise a depressed, hopeless, or apathetic mood (including loss of interest in things that previously gave pleasure, such as hobbies, sex, social relationships) that lasts most of the day, nearly every day, for at least two weeks, and that is a change from previous behavior. (In children and adolescents depression may appear instead as irritability.) In addition, a number of other symptoms must be present, for example:

- significant change in appetite or weight;
- disturbed sleep patterns;
- observable agitation or slowing down of movements and physical activity;
- constant fatigue or lack of energy;
- feelings of worthlessness, low self-esteem, self-blame, guilt;
- difficulty thinking, concentrating, or making decisions;
- recurrent thoughts of suicide or death.

As with mania, delusions and hallucinations may occur with depression, although here the themes may be of death, disease, guilt, or punishment. Physical symptoms are often manifested, such as headaches, stomachaches, tingling or heaviness in arms and legs, and fainting.

Both bipolar and unipolar disorders have chronic forms (called, respectively, cyclothymia and dysthymia) that last for at least two years in adults, one year in children and adolescents, with asymptomatic periods of relief of no more than two months. Fewer symptoms are required to make a diagnosis of cyclothymia or dysthymia, but they must have lasted over a longer time.

Originally, I had planned for this book to discuss unipolar depression only. The less common condition, manic depressive illness, or bipolar disorder, seemed much more extreme, and frightening—more like a "real" mental illness. I thought of it as an entirely separate problem.

The first medical advisor I talked to, Dr. Goodwin, vehemently set me straight.

"Bipolar disorder is treated as separate when, in fact, it is not. It is one part of the spectrum of mood disorders. The unipolar depression that is recurrent has a close relationship to the bipolar form. That is, those patients are more likely to have a family history of manic-depressive illness, more likely to have an early onset of the illness, more likely to have multiple episodes and more likely to require maintenance treatment. The description of 'bipolar' is more precise; 'unipolar' covers a wider range."

Jules Feiffer

I've been depressed for most of my life until a few years ago, but it always seemed to me that there were reasons for it. I could always trace it back to a cause or two or three or seven or twenty-five. There are real reasons in the course of a day, or a week, or a month to be down. Now how do you separate depression from when there's an authentic reason not to feel good? Maybe I haven't been depressed. Maybe I was simply sad.

I always considered myself, as far back as I can remember from the age of three, four, five, certainly by five, just being in a low-level depression, where I often had to fight to function. Some of the worst times were in my twenties and thirties. I hated being a bachelor and I hated all my bachelor years, and I hated having to do what I had to do to have a sex life, which often was to become a different person than I was to get girls to go to bed with me. There wasn't a moment in those single years I look back on with any kind of pleasure.

For reasons I understand in some ways and in others I don't, the older I got, the more energy I got. I'm not that person anymore, not that I don't feel depressed and I don't feel angry or upset. There are moments when I screw up in the kitchen, or I'm opening a can of cat food and cut myself on the can and it throws me into this violent rage where I thank God I don't have a gun in my house or I'd blow my head off—just over the top. And then it stops.

The difference is getting into a marriage that is my first good one, and having a much happier life, and feeling for the first time in my life as if I have a family. While my older daughter and I had a lot of precious time together, without a wife there was never a sense of family, a sense of belonging. I've always been very reactive against families, not having liked my own very much. Never wanted a family, had contempt of families. Break them up, get rid of them, they can't do any good. Suddenly, I found myself quite contented. God knows there are problems, and there is rage and there are all the feelings that one has that go with tight relationships, but there is a very solid linkage here that I never ever experienced in my life, not with my parents and not in my first marriage.

Lewis Judd, M.D.

There are increasing gradations in [depression], which may be on a continuum. There is major depression, which is clearly and easily defined: one is having dysphoria, intense sadness and blueness for two weeks, plus four or five symptoms of depression. There is dysthymia, which is a much more protracted, long term, lower-grade depression. There is minor depression, which would describe someone who has had a couple of weeks of depression and dysphoria and maybe two symptoms of depression, possibly three. Another syndrome that I've been working on is subsyndromal symptomatic depression. This, I believe, includes a very large group of people, maybe somewhere upward of 8 or 9 percent of the population, who are experiencing symptoms of depression but do not qualify for the diagnosis of dysthymia or major depression. The description of minor depression would subsume large numbers of these.

A depression diagnosis is based on the length of time one has the symptoms and the accumulation of numbers of symptoms. We're finding that significant numbers of people in the population only have one, two, or three symptoms of depression. That would not qualify for a diagnosis of minor depression, yet these people may have significant disability. We believe that is an extremely important, underrecognized public health problem that we are moving to study very quickly.

We know there are a lot of them. We know they would not be recognized or treated in the standard clinic as depressed. But we also are aware that many of these sufferers are very disabled and in all likelihood will benefit from treatment. They're the ones that go in for a vitamin shot or who say "I have low energy, I feel kind of blue, I don't feel up to snuff, I don't feel up to par, I've felt this way for quite a while." They may have problems with eating. They may have problems with sleep. They may have problems with thinking, or they may be plagued by thoughts of death and dying. All those things are in the depressive spectrum.

Are these people on the way to developing a major depression, and if we intercede early will it prevent that? At this point, we believe the answer to both questions is yes.

Judith Belushi Pisano

Sadness is part of it, but you can be sad without being depressed. Depression is deeper and more encompassing. You could be sad and still have a joy for life. But that gets covered up when you're depressed. A truly depressed person even seems pulled by gravity more. You can see it in the way they stand. Everything is just harder. It's harder to get up, it's harder to care about what you eat. You can be sad and have a good meal. When you're depressed, you have to force something down.

A. John Rush, M.D.

Depression can kill you, yet this is a treatable condition. It's treatable, and yet two-thirds of cases aren't even diagnosed. That's incredible.

First, you have to see it as an illness and then get somebody to make a diagnosis. The physical tests don't matter very much. In spite of all the tests that are driving up health-care costs, most of the time 80 percent of the diagnosis is still based on an accurate history. Ten percent is in the physical [exam], and 10 percent is in the laboratory tests.

If you come into the emergency room, and you have chest pain that's whipping down your left arm, and you're sweating all over the place and you're nauseated and you throw up in the emergency room, and you're forty-five years old and you're a male, smoker, and your father died of a heart attack at age fifty, let me tell you, you're having a heart attack. The doctor may not find that the EKG is abnormal, because it takes a few hours or a day to go abnormal, and the enzyme tests, which are blood tests, may not go up for a couple of days. You don't say to the person "Well, you have a normal EKG. Why don't you go home?" You say "Come right into the intensive care unit. We're going to keep an eye on you. I think you're having a heart attack." You made the diagnosis with no lab tests.

So the notion that lab tests are so critical in medicine is just not correct. Most of the time the history is the clincher, and most of the time people with depression will tell you all the symptoms, and they will say "They come and they go, either completely away or partly away, and it started at this time." They can often remember their first episode of depression. It's pretty clear. The diagnosis consists of taking a very careful history, usually from the patient, also helpful from another person who knows them well, the husband or parent or child or somebody. Then you've got to make sure that they don't have some known cause for depression, such as anabolic steroids. Kids that are taking these things for building up their muscles need to know that they can cause a pretty big-time depression, even psychosis. Other medications, such as some blood pressure medicines, can cause depression, not in everybody, but in some people.*

Medical causes include thyroid disease, adrenal disease, brain tumors, and early dementia, but the vast majority of depressions is kind of like "essential" hypertension, meaning that we don't know the ultimate cause.

Diagnosing depression depends on the person and the way they come in. If you have a person who is over age fifty, who's never had a depression before and has a negative family history, and now experiences a big depression, you're going to work up and do these tests for more medical disorders, because people

---

* Depression may be a side effect of reserpine in up to 15 percent of patients. See appendix 3 for other medications that may cause depression.

over fifty are at a higher risk for these medical problems, and these medical problems may cause depression.

If you have a twenty-two-year-old person who has had two prior episodes, starting at age fourteen, with a positive family history of depression already, who otherwise has no particular complaints, not bleeding from anywhere, not seeing double, whose physical exam is normal, who looks like he has just plain old standard depression, then you don't need much in the way of testing at all. Maybe a blood count, maybe a thyroid test, but if he has no symptoms of thyroid disease, you're more likely to have a false positive thyroid test than you are to have thyroid disease.

Maybe 10 percent of depressions have some underlying medical cause. Substance abusers, alcohol abusers—heavy, heavy users or in withdrawal states—can develop a depression. If they stop drinking or abusing, it goes away. The treatment is to treat the substance abuse.

Then you have other psychiatric disorders, people with anorexia nervosa, bulimia, obsessive-compulsive disorder, panic disorder. Sometimes they come in with at least some depressive symptoms, but those other symptoms are so clear you can see it. You treat the anorexia, put them back into a well-nourished state, the depression goes away in 90 percent of the cases. So you treat those other psychiatric conditions first, and then if they still have the depression, you treat that.

Then we have the rare, but not too rare, situation in which someone close to a person dies, and the person has a grief reaction, but it stays around and is crippling, and it is beyond normal grief. It may be a major depression, which should be treated.

When people still have the symptoms of major depression two months after the loss, they may well have the disorder. If they have symptoms of major depression that are really incapacitating even before two months [have passed]—they're not just feeling lousy, they're not functioning—they've got major depression. If they're psychotic, they have hallucinations or delusions, that's beyond normal grief.

Most of the people who have a clinical depression following a loss are people who have had a prior history. It's perhaps a vulnerability issue. People come with vulnerabilities, and then something happens to them.

Part of the reason these illnesses haven't come out of the closet like a "real medical disease" is that people confuse being mildly upset or being in a lousy situation with having an illness, although it's fairly easy to tell which is which.

It is not normal to have recurrent spells of major depression, period. It doesn't happen to most people. It shouldn't happen to most people. It won't happen to most people. So if you have recurrent episodes of major depression with five of the nine symptoms, you have an illness. It's guaranteed. It's very important for people to separate that from "Oh, you know, I don't feel so good," or "I've got to pay my taxes and I feel disgruntled and I can't buy a new car." If two-thirds are not diagnosed and in treatment, we are underdiagnosing it.

The danger is that when a person goes to see the doctor and tells him or her all the symptoms of major depression, the doctor will say "Well, what's been bothering you?" Anyone who is depressed has everything bothering them because their outlook is so negative that if they win the Publisher's Sweepstakes, they don't think about the profit, they worry about paying their taxes. They get depressed if they win, they get depressed if they lose, and they get depressed if they're not playing the game. They're sad all the time.

So when you ask someone who is depressed "Tell me, do you know why you're depressed?" he or she will give you a laundry list, and it's because of a colored view of things. The illness makes these people see things negatively. Everybody has stresses. Stresses may precipitate an episode of illness, but there is more to it than simply stress. Most people with the same stresses don't get a clinical depression. So it's stress plus a biological, psychological, or genetic vulnerability.

We used to say "Tell me why you're depressed," and if the person had an answer, we'd say "Oh, that's a reactive or exogenous depression." If the patient said, "I don't know why I'm depressed," that was endogenous depression.

One is supposed to be caused by your neurosis and bad things happening to you; the other is caused by a bad brain. That's no longer the case. We don't have any reason to think that's true. We have good reason to think it's not true.

If you ask most people with most illnesses, at the time they got sick, what was going on in their lives, and you just keep interviewing them, you will find life stresses. I'll guarantee you, unless they're under general anesthesia, they've got life stresses. That doesn't explain anything in terms of causes or treatment choices. For example, if you have stresses, do you need therapy? If you don't have stresses, do you need medication? No, it doesn't mean a thing.

It has to do with the signs, the symptoms, what does this illness look like, and that's what tells a doctor how to respond. The issue is how long are they ill, how badly are they ill, how many symptoms do they have, are they getting suicidal? For example, most people with a grief reaction do not get suicidal or have hallucinations. If you start hallucinating after someone close to you dies, see a doctor. You're sick. You have an illness. The precipitant may have been the stress; the condition that is precipitated is an illness. That's the key.

Question: Is my depression biological or psychological?

Answer: It's always both.

Here's why: The brain is the organ of the mind. If your mind isn't working correctly, your brain can't be working correctly. This is absolutely key. It sounds strange to say, it's so simple. The brain is the organ of the mind, so when you think, when you feel, you're not doing that with your spleen; you do that with your brain.

The evidence that life stress only plays a small role in the course of these illnesses would argue that these illnesses are "real" illnesses. Life stress doesn't do them any good, but it doesn't explain everything; people have an underlying biological/genetic proclivity, and with or without the stress, they get the illness.

Everybody has bad days, but if your thinking is screwed up, if your motivation is abnormal, if your mood is off the wall, if your emotional state is clearly abnormal and it stays that way, that means your brain can't be working correctly, because your mind is not working correctly. The brain is the organ of the mind. So the mind is the psychology, the brain is the biology, and whenever one goes bad, the other goes bad, so all depressions are biological *and* psychological. It is so closely interactive that it's the issue of the first cause: Which came first, the chicken or the egg? I don't think that we know enough about any of these illnesses to say which came first.

Once things start to go bad, they snowball. They get worse right away. Your biology is not great, you don't have too much interest, now you're not sleeping, now you're not eating, now you're also not functioning. Now you're blaming yourself for not functioning; now you're guilt-ridden for not functioning because your brain isn't working, your mind is telling you it's all your fault, and you can spiral into the thing, making it worse.

There is no evidence that bipolar disorder is caused by a stressful life. The disorder is genetic, so that offspring of people with bipolar disorder that are raised in an adoptive family get the same rate of bipolar disorder as if they're raised by their own mom and dad. It's clearly a genetic illness.

With a genetic illness, you can have episodes of worsening precipitated by stress. For instance, thyroid disease runs in families; diabetes runs in families. Stress sometimes precedes the onset of the expression of those illnesses that are rather genetic.

You know a lot of heart attacks are due to high cholesterol, which is a genetic disease. Guess when you have your heart attack? When you're stressed. Does stress cause heart attacks? Well, sort of. It can be a precipitant, given the vulnerability.

The same is probably true for recurrent major depression. There is some evidence that the first or second episode may be more likely precipitated by stress, but as the illness becomes more recurrent [and is not treated], it takes on a life of its own. The longer you have had the illness, the less relevant life's stresses are. Stress may increase the earliness of the onset or be an antecedent to the episode that's coming up, but [without treatment], you might well have had that episode anyway.

On the other hand, you can really throw yourself into a disaster if you're chronically stressed out. You can either get hives or ulcerative colitis or ulcers or thyroid disease or heart attacks, or you can have depression, dealer's choice, genetics' choice. Stress may play a role; it's just not sufficient to account for the fact that a person has the illness. It's one of several risk factors.

For example, for first-degree relatives, like children of a parent who has had major depressions, a single episode may not bestow any extra risks, but recurrence does. Then you're looking at people with, say, a 12 to 15 percent chance for recurrent depressions in that individual. In the general populous, the risk is probably about 4 to 6 percent for recurrent forms. Females are at greater risk than males, by two to one. Boys and girls are at equal risk until they hit puberty, at which point girls have a two-to-one hit rate. In the geriatric age group, men and women are a bit more equal, according to some studies. You can't prove that isn't because the women with depression killed themselves and never made it to be old, but assuming that didn't happen, then you could argue that, gee, that's after menopause, and so the female reproductive system may carry some "vulnerability" to this problem or the male's reproductive hormone, testosterone, carries some "immunization" to it. We don't know.

Now, of course, there are other sociological considerations. Some suggest women are in subservient roles, or oppressed by society, and consequently develop more depression. Where it's been looked at across developing, or developed, countries, it seems the ratio holds up. It doesn't seem to matter whether it's in Sweden or in France or in Germany, Japan, the United States, or Brazil. The bottom line is we just don't yet know why women are at greater risk for major depression. For bipolar disorder, though, men and women are equally affected.

Jane Doe

[Jane Doe is the pseudonym of a Washington, D.C. professional whose fear of exposure is explained in Chapter 6.]

When I would go into a clinical depression, it had different manifestations than just my normal low-grade dysthymia. You would never know how you would wake up. You couldn't just say "Oh, well, I am just having a blue day" or, as some people call it, "a nightgown day." That might be the beginning of six months or one year of horror, of feeling worse and worse and worse and worse. And nobody understanding the loneliness of it. Because people who have never experienced depression cannot imagine what it feels like, the hopelessness. Nothing helps you to feel better. Nothing. The ordinary things of life—a movie, a good meal, company, a walk, a beautiful painting—make you feel worse because they enhance how detached you are from the real world, how much I wasn't able to partake of the banquet in front of me. There is a great line from *Auntie Mame:* "Life is a banquet, most people are starving." I use it all the time.

The clinical depression is tearfulness and a morbid kind of hopelessness, where it really, really interferes with your life. A lot of fatigue and sleeping. For me, it was overeating, for some people it is not being able to eat. Dysthymia is just feeling blue and miserable and depressed all the time, as the world understands depression. Constant, my entire life.

I was born with it, clearly. The depression manifested itself very, very early when I was two, three, four, five. It was explained away. I was rambunctious. I was the middle child. I was the only child my father liked, and my mother hated me for that. It was an immigrant family with many other dysfunctional things going on.

When I was five, they thought I had rheumatic fever so we moved from New York to Arizona and to California. Every day I would get a fever. I used to wake up at one o'clock in the morning, which was the hour that I was born, with a blood-curdling scream. I am convinced that all this was the early manifestations of the brain chemistry. It was early signs of depression.

I had very horrible childhood and teenage years. When I was a teenager, I was identified as the sick one, which often happens to a middle child. They sent me to a therapy group, which was a bunch of twelve-year-old girls who thought they were lesbians. I had no idea what I was doing there.

I had good reason to be depressed with the terrible things happening around me in this family. Then I got married to get out of the house. I used geographic escape all my life, escaping from the problems, from the bad feelings. I was a crisis junky, liking the highs, being terribly afraid of the lows, being able to run on adrenaline. I quit the TV network and I went to Paris. I could have been Barbara Walters earning eight million dollars a year today had I stayed. Instead, I went off to Paris and stayed there for six years. I drove from Paris to India. I spent six months in India. I had a devastating case of hepatitis. What they don't tell you after hepatitis is that it affects your thyroid, which I already have chronic problems with, and that you have two years of real depression afterward. I came back to the States and hibernated in New York for almost five years. I had a little hole-in-the-wall apartment with rent control that was really a tenement. I did some freelance projects in the Middle East. The rest of the time I would come back and be depressed.

One time I had just come back from a trip to the Middle East and was still a little jet-lagged a day or two later. I was at home and I had a panic attack. I was absolutely sure that I was going to go insane, going to die. Many people lose their cognizant side when they are in a panic attack. I never did; I could always describe it. I would call people up and say "I am having a panic attack." They would hear me sound perfectly normal, but inside I was gripped with total terror. The walls would be closing in, even if I were in a wide open space. It isn't fear of anything. It is just fear, unnamed fear. Then the fear of having another panic attack, the anticipatory anxiety, brings them on more and more.

As is often frustrating to nonmedical people, there is no one right answer to many of the questions I posed to these experts. I found at least two major approaches to depression, the psychological and the biological. Frankly, the bias of this book is toward the biological. Some sufferers would rather not think that something is physically wrong with them. For me, however, viewing my dysfunction as a physiological disorder helps to mitigate the blame and self-loathing that are part of the disease. It is evident that the depressive bouts I experience have no proximate cause, that they arrive as regularly as menses, that I have had them almost as long as I can remember, and that my diet, sleep, and exercise patterns affect the course of an episode. To me, these facts and the expert opinions of doctors such as John Rush and Frederick Goodwin are conclusive. Yet for some kinds of depression, the solutions are found not in medicine but in psychology.

Stephen P. Hersh, M.D., F.A.P.A.

Psychiatrists such as myself who are trained in pediatrics as well as child and adolescent psychiatry have a different view of humans; better, I think. I think we're better therapists, too. We tend to see issues of depression somewhat differently because of the more intense training about the whole life cycle.

I have simultaneously a romantic and unromantic view of illness. The unromantic view is that we're not much different from the sea sponge: a chemical and electrical system of collaborative, highly specialized cells. There's no such thing as a thought without a cascade of physiological events that are basically, again, chemical and electrical events. And there is no such thing as an experience of the organism, any part of it, whether it's a gas bubble in your belly or a teacher telling you you're a jerk, or your parents abusing you, without, also, a cascade of physiological events and associated thoughts and feelings. So, I see us as a wondrously complex system.

It is hard to deal with all the variables at once. The different researchers get involved with their particular area and they say, like the six blind men, "Uh-huh, that's the whole elephant." They oversimplify it. I understand it and forgive them, but that's what they're doing.

First of all, the experience of depression in the most generic way is universal. One can not go through life without having had some experience with the feeling state of depression, and the associated changes in behaviors, like those outlined on the Beck inventory*—the relative loss of interest in things and people, being more irritable, that kind of stuff.

* An assessment tool for diagnosing depression.

So, the state of depression is part of life, but then there is a clinical syndrome of depression, where the state of depression has become a pattern and is interfering with a person's functioning and capacity to use one's own resources and to relate to oneself and the environment.

Some people clearly have a biologically, genetically based vulnerability to a mood disorder. There's no question about that. Similarly, some people have a vulnerability to develop migraines or stomach ulcers. Depression is just one of the possible variations on a theme. In considering depression, you have to ask "What kind of depression?" If you're talking about a single episode of depression, then you're probably talking about circumstantial, environmental, psychological responses. If you're talking about serious, chronic depression, then I think it's developmental or repressed developmental traumas and experiences combined with a biological vulnerability that push most people into a depression. That's why the right kind of psychotherapy combined with other things, not necessarily medication, would help so many people.

In most people with a biological vulnerability who experience over time the appropriate combination of traumatic events, the vulnerability is going to transition into an expression of the disorder. The most extreme event would be bipolar disorder, which is a whole spectrum in itself. Researchers in the bipolar disorders are certain that environmental and life experience do influence significantly how much the disorder is expressed in individuals and, if they're on medication, how well the medication helps.

The other extreme is where people get depressed from life events, such as reaction to a loss, or in the period of recovery from the flu.

Recovery from the flu is one example of depression where its origins are purely physiological, rather than because your mother didn't love you. (I'm using that as a cartoon, if you will, to make a point.) People will get the flu, be ill for a week, and then recover. In that recovery period, whether they notice it or not, there is a relative depression: They're more irritable; they're more tired; they're not interested in things; they cry a little bit more easily; things don't taste so great; their energy is down, their interests not so sharp. They have mastered the infection but the transient depression is a response to their recovering from this virus that has challenged their system. Infections are physiological assaults that induce transient depression; chemotherapy can do it, too.

Life events also may cause depression for particular individuals, whether it is a loss, or a loss of control, where they don't see themselves gathering control back. This is an example of a psychological cause of depression. Or the person who was emotionally abused, put down all the time, may end up with some form of dysthymia, a chronic low-grade depression and poor self-esteem. That is an example of a developmental experience producing depression. In all those situations, you may have as the major cause a psychological, or psychosocial, or psychosocial-developmental series of events.

Chronic depression may be one clinical expression of an unrecognized posttraumatic stress disorder. Such individuals often come in with multiple physical complaints, often chest or cardiac, but the evaluation does not find any "real disease." It may have to do with the combined losses and loss of control that they suffered and the meaningfulness of these losses in their lives, even if they think they've handled them. To all external appearances, of course they did. But some of these people who didn't have a history of depression before, find that three months or six months or twelve months [after a traumatic event], they have become depressed and just can't shake it. Anything that is importantly disruptive and disorienting to the individual, that creates a serious dissonance with their expectations of how things are supposed to be can cause PTSD—prisoners of war; Vietnam veterans; rape victims; chronic abuse within the family, whether it's physical or emotional or sexual. In a surgical situation, or a car accident, depending upon how they're handled, what the person hears [while semiconscious or anesthetized] also can create posttraumatic stress disorder scenarios.

Internalized anger, rage, and not being able to express anger is clearly a dynamic in some people. It's amazing the number of people who when you ask them about being angry will say "Oh, no, I'm never angry." "Annoyed" might be the strongest word they'll ever use. Anger may not have influenced how they function up to a certain point, but then they'll come to a change in their lives and depression will take over. Anything that makes a human being unable to express and know how to make use of normal emotions and reactions makes that person, in my mind, vulnerable to depression.

There are different people and different types of depression. The problem is that in our culture everybody wants a real simple series of headlines to explain something. Life isn't explainable that way. People are complex mosaics and if you shift the pieces around, the pattern changes. Sometimes it changes in a way you hardly notice it, sometimes it's terribly significant, depending upon which piece you're switching and what the mosaic is.

Each person is born with a certain kind of capacity to interact with the world. Some people go through things that make you think, "Jesus, what are they so upset about?" Yet they will get seriously clinically depressed. It depends on their complex combination of vulnerabilities influenced by biology and life experience and temperament, the kind of personality that they come into the world with. The expert nurse in the neonatal nursery can take you around and tell you about the personalities of the newborns, and they generally are accurate. So, everybody who gets raped doesn't become dysfunctional sexually, and burdened with a chronic depression. Everybody who goes into a prison camp doesn't become dysfunctional or chronically depressed, et cetera. Some do, some don't, and that's why [psychiatry] is always such a wonderful, exciting profession. The variation on the theme is infinite, from my perspective.

I firmly believe that we will continue to document that no matter what the cause, whether it's physiological cause, like the flu, or it's psychosocial-developmental cause—you still have biologic changes within the organism that are common to all forms of depression, such as shifts in neurotransmitters and hormones. You can assault the person physiologically, making those changes, and then the resulting experience is depression.

The responsibility of the healer or the clinician, or the psychiatrist or psychologist, is to look at that individual and to get a good family and developmental history, and history of the illness itself and other intervening factors. Then he or she must decide whether this is primarily a biological-based depression, or primarily a psychosocial and developmentally based depression, or a special mixture of both; and then determine what the treatment plan should be. The etiology should influence the decision in treatment, not as the total decision-making factor, but it certainly should influence it.

Joan Rivers

All I want to do is lie in bed. I don't talk to anyone, I don't answer the phone, I just retreat. You feel that it's all over, that everything is over, that you can't get up, you can't pretend, you can't deal with anything and you don't want to deal with anything. And you don't want to hear anybody else's cheerfulness.

The worst time is the morning, when you wake up and it's still there. At night, finally you manage to get to sleep and you sleep, well or badly, you dream or you don't dream, and then when you wake up in the morning, it's all back. That, to me, is the worst part of depression. You feel like there is no point. You're out of control; you're out of control of your life, and you're out of control of your emotions, and you're out of control of everything. It is a terrible, terrible frustration, and weakness, and depression.

One very low time for me was after my husband's death when I had gone out with some friends of his to dinner. It was just wrong, I know that. I was down and they were the wrong people to be with. I had them drop me off at the bottom of our long driveway. I didn't even want them to take me up to the house.

I couldn't wait to get home, it was so awful. I went halfway up the hill, and I just couldn't walk the rest of it. I sat in the driveway saying "I can't, I just can't, I can't go up, I can't go down, I can't." Like an idiot for two hours on the driveway in my heels and my stockings. And then you get up and you go on.

How do you get out of it? I don't know. But you do . . . I'm very lucky to be able to sit and talk about it. But nobody understands it, nobody gets it. If you say to someone "I sat in my driveway for two hours last night," they think, "What were you sitting in your driveway for?" Except people who have been there.

John Kenneth Galbraith

Anybody can have a depressing day, I do regularly. But I don't identify that with a real continuing [Churchill] type of black dog, which I certainly have had. It's just deeper and worse, and persists.

Occasionally if I have something that I don't want to do and I feel depressed about it, I revise my life to accommodate to it, or sometimes go and see my doctor. But I don't consider myself really subject to it. I think of three episodes out of my life, that's all. That's something I would particularly emphasize; I'm not a depressed person. My normal existence has been calm and reasonably pleasant.

William Styron

Sadness is a component of depression. You're not happy. But it's a much more intense emotion then mere sadness. It's sadness that has become intensified into excruciating pain. Sadness is there as a kind of shadow. To me, sadness is characterized by just a general melancholy feeling about a life, a kind of sense of regret, a sense of disaffection in the life, in the absence of happiness. But depression is significantly more intense than that. It's pain, real pain.

It may be that some people are constitutionally so developed in a certain way that they don't really understand. They have never been touched even by the slightest bit of depression. So this real profound depression eludes them as a concept. I think that they erect barriers against the possibility, against a willingness to try to empathize with this thing in other people.

Rose Styron

Sure, they called it depression. And they called it melancholia, and they called it craziness, and they called it all sorts of things. We knew that we had moved from one doctor to another doctor, we knew that they were giving him tons of pills, and that they were calling it depression. But as Bill is quick to point out, the word "depression" semantically means different things. We weren't aware of the depth of what it was or exactly what was happening. He really hadn't slept for ages, he would fall asleep and wake up and so forth, but he doesn't remember the way it actually happened.

He had been in bed staring at the ceiling for a couple of weeks. He had been hinting at suicide. The doctor had said, "He doesn't need to be in the hospital. Just don't let him out of your sight." So for days and days I had been right there with him, and our daughter Polly would come and be terrific and relieve me.

That night he was so totally wound up. It was around supper-time. Polly and I were both sitting in the bed with him, when he grabbed hold of Polly's arm and started to say things to her which made her very unhappy. She looked at me and mouthed, "Go downstairs and call the doctor. Put him in the hospital." So I called the doctor, while Polly was there with him, and said, "We can't watch him any more. Please get him into the hospital tomorrow. I'll take anything you can get as long as it's tomorrow." Polly and I talked to Bill about going to the hospital, and instead of the old stuff, saying "I don't want to go; I'm not going to," he said, "I want to go. I think I should go to the hospital, as soon as I can." We got through the night and he left the next morning. It was his decision, which was great.

The first indication of a problem was that he was upset about his work and he was upset about his health. In six or seven different ways he was determined not to do things that would normally give him or us pleasure. He withdrew socially.

We were supposed to go on a wonderful and long-planned sailing trip around the Mediterranean with some dear friends. The whole thing had been set up for a long time, to coincide with his sixtieth birthday. And he precipitously said, "No, I'm not going to do it." There was nothing I could do to persuade him to go, and there was no reason given. It wasn't a matter of the work, which wasn't going well anyway. That was the first clue that he was really feeling lousy about himself and about everything. The second was actually on his sixtieth birthday when he said he didn't want to celebrate, and that was fine because I didn't either. But some very close friends of his, like Willie Morris, who lives in Mississippi, persuaded me that even if he said he didn't want a party, that there had to be some kind of celebration. We arranged that Willie and Peter Matthiessen and George Plimpton and just a dozen of his close friends would come up by plane to have lunch and tennis and swim and sit around and shoot the breeze, and then they'd go back. But when they arrived, he was horrified. He pulled himself together for the day, but everybody was aware that it wasn't this incredible occasion that we had planned. After everybody went home, he didn't want to see anybody for a long time.

So we had a very difficult summer, in which he felt that he had more and more disparate physical things going wrong with him. The doctors couldn't really confirm any of this, so it seemed like extreme hypochondria to me. We had all known Bill to be a hypochondriac from way back, so it seemed just an extreme form of it. Then when we were all sitting around here one night, someone began to talk about [a benzodiazepine that he had been taking], and how bad it was. When he looked it up in his physicians' desk manual, he read that it shouldn't be taken for more than a month or so, and it shouldn't be taken by people who are sixty, and that there were all kinds of side effects. He'd been taking it for two years.

He stopped like that, because he has terrific willpower. He stopped smoking like that, too, and he stopped drinking that way. He went into what I thought was withdrawal symptoms—not sleeping, being frenetic, and so forth. Friends tried to convince him and me that it was withdrawal from alcohol, which he had also stopped cold. It took awhile into the fall to realize that this was something a lot more than withdrawal that was going on.

Toward the end of the summer and into the fall, he began to talk to me about how he felt, because he was scared, and I think he didn't understand what was happening. We talked about his going to some kind of retreat or rehabilitation place for a little while; he absolutely didn't want to do that. We became very close as he talked a lot about how he felt, but as time wore on he got crazier and crazier. He got more and more into it, and he became obsessed with himself and the way he felt and the fact that everything was going downhill and that he was never going to come out of it. He didn't want to go to a hospital because he thought maybe that meant he would never come back.

He began to remember things about his family and all the troubles that they had had, uncles who had been in veterans' hospitals and never come out, and another uncle who I think was an alcoholic and had died there. He began to dwell a lot on the fact that his mother had died when he was just approaching adolescence, and started talking about her and about the family in ways that I had never heard before. Some things he told me, I decided he was making up, because I'd been married to him for close to thirty years, and I'd never heard any of this stuff before, and it was quite bizarre. It's not bizarre as far as other people's family histories go, but it came so out of the blue that I just decided it was all part of his paranoia and self-doubt. Well, it turned out that it all was true, and that there was a big genetic component in it that he had never faced before.

His doctors absolutely insisted that he go on with his regular routine. If it hadn't been a year when he was being given many awards and asked to make many speeches, and the grand reading at PEN* and the accepting of that award at NYU [New York University] and the accepting of an award in Paris and so forth, maybe there wouldn't have been so much of a strain. He made all

* Poets, Playwrights, Editors, Essayists and Novelists, a literary organization.

these superhuman efforts, and I went with him to do it, being more and more discouraged and horrified, though some of the things that happened were really comical. Like the time I made the mistake of taking him to a special poets and writers performance of the Big Apple Circus, and we sat in the front row, and he completely freaked out. They were funny, but they were funny and serious.

I'm sure it's in his book, but maybe it's not presented comically, but when he got the del Duca prize* in Paris, he went through all sorts of shenanigans. He forgot that with the prize went this grand luncheon with all the old and staid members of the French Academy, [given by] Madame del Duca, who was the widow of the person who [originated the prize], and who had now inscribed Bill's name in marble in one of the big halls of Paris. So he accepted the award, got through that, and she said, "Now we're going to lunch."

"I don't want to have lunch," he said.

"You don't want to have lunch!" she said.

"I don't want to have lunch with you. I've gotten my award, I'm going out to lunch with my publisher." Of course the publisher was dying because the publisher didn't want to take Bill to lunch, Bill was supposed to go to this grand honor for him. We finally got hold of him and shook him, though the woman had now flounced out, and we said, "You have to go. You have to understand this is part of it. Don't you remember it was on the invitation?" So finally he went back and said to her that he would have lunch, but we had a very stiff lunch. They presented him with a huge [cash award], which he said he would give to the French hospital, making the grand gesture. He didn't know what the hell he was saying. But he did it. Then we went out to dinner with his publisher at a restaurant, and he lost the check. So by nine o'clock in the evening, the publisher and the publisher's family and I were all on the floor under the table, and so was Bill, hunting for the check that we knew was lost somewhere in the restaurant. We finally found it, but the whole behavior was so

* The Prix Mondial Cino del Duca, a French award for literary achievement.

crazy all day long and then all the next day and the next day. We finally got him home and pretty soon thereafter he went into the hospital.

Rod Steiger

Early on I started to get suicidal thoughts. Then I started to get thoughts of doing away with my wife and myself. I called a friend of mine, a psychiatrist, and said, "You'd better get over here." I had enough sense and willpower to think that clearly. I said, "I'm going to give you my shotgun, get it out of the house. I don't want to have one of these impulses be so strong that the next thing, we're the headline in the *National Enquirer*, 'So-called Star Blows Family Away.' " After I got rid of the gun, I locked myself in the guest room downstairs at night, and I wound up with burning sensations and clawing my skin and pounding on the wall for three days, scaring my wife to death.

It's difficult for the public to realize how powerful the mind is, and how much pain the mind can give you. When you're depressed, it's as though this committee has taken over your mind, leaving you one depressing thought after the other. You don't shave, you don't shower, you don't brush your teeth. You don't care. The one thing I did do, I still ate a little bit. But I didn't have much of an appetite. I know a lot of people who say they didn't eat at all.

You have moments when you're locked in an ever-increasing terror that seems to be running all over your mind and your body. You begin to doubt your sanity. But you remember the things that frighten you that you thought of the most, and that is hurting people that you love. When you're depressed, there's no calendar. There are no dates, there's no day, there's no night, there's no seconds, there's no minutes, there's nothing. You're just existing in this cold, murky, ever-heavy atmosphere, like they put you inside a vial of mercury.

You don't want to communicate. You don't care about anybody's opinion. If Jesus, Buddha, or the Little Prince came down

and said, "What are you doing? I command you to get up!" you'd
say "Fuck you. Who do you think you are? I don't want to get
up." So that's the self-pity part.

The terrible thing about the depression is that it's like wel-
coming the thing you fear most, knowing at the same time it may
be a living death, knowing it's your enemy, but you care so little
you still open the door. You become like a semimobile statue. You
move a little bit, and when you stop, you stop for a long time. You
sit on the couch for seven hours and maybe you move a little and
then go back for another four hours. Friends would come over—
one man went to pieces in front of me, crying, yelling at me "Rod,
for Christ's sake, do something! Don't just sit there!" And men in
our society usually don't show that much love.

Depending on the size of your ego, there's something about
yourself you may not like, and part of the depression is as though
you're punishing yourself for something. There's a reason you let
yourself sink into the excrement. Your sense of self, your appreciation for yourself, your respect for yourself, disappears completely. It certainly isn't that your mind goes blank. On the contrary, when you're depressed your mind beats you to death with
thoughts. It never stops. You wake up in the morning, all of a
sudden you get that feeling like your head got three times heavier
in one split second. Sadness is a good part of it, but there's also
self-pity. And anger. And fear. There is the fear of waking up and
having to start another period of being awake with the depression.
Many times the thought goes through your head, "Well, if I take
enough pills maybe I won't wake up, I won't have to start again
right away with that." The word that keeps coming back is heaviness. I wake up, boom, it hits me, like they put me in a suit of
armor that's too heavy.

The I-don't-care part of it is amazing. My wife threw little
parties, tennis parties, everything. I sat there and knew everybody
was politely trying not to have me see how sick they thought I
was, and being jaunty jolly trying to talk to me, like everything's
all right, and I could see in their eyes that partial fear, sympathy,
puzzlement. And you don't care. You don't care. You don't even
talk to them. You're just looking, not even seeing. Your attitude is

"What the fuck are you gonna tell me? Are you gonna tell me I'm sick? I know I'm sick. So what?"

There's this little bit of anger in you, too, because you hurt, because you know you're not whatever is called normal. They ask you simple questions. "You should care for yourself," they say.

And your answer is "Why?"

"Because you did all this," they say.

"It isn't enough."

"Your wife loves you, your child loves you, we're worried about you."

"They don't understand," the tired voice says. That's the wallowing in self-pity. "They don't understand." Finally this fatigue gets to a point where you get so tired that your last ounce of health says "If I go any further, I will die, no matter how long I stay alive on this earth." Something makes you start to move back, if you're not too sick. If you get to be too sick, you may never come back. You just get tired of being tired. Tired of not caring. But it takes years. It took me four years, then a year and a half off, and four more years.

It's like a fine mist enters through the pores of your skin, over a period of months and then maybe years. It may take a week, three weeks, it may take three months. But it's growing and it's not stoppable without help. Your chemistry is changing. You don't know. Until one day somebody says "What's wrong with you?" in such a way that you hear the screaming in their voice. No matter how softly they say "What's wrong with you?" their tone has such truth in it that you say "My God, something's wrong." It has nothing to do with language. It has to do with that incredible tone of voice that is trying to say "I want to help you."

Pat Love, Ed.D.

I've been a psychologist for ten years, but I didn't wake up to my own depression until about two years ago, because I am not classically depressed. I have a lot of energy. I get a lot of things done.

I'm highly motivated. I don't sit around moping, and I don't tend to have a negative attitude.

Then I read somewhere about some atypical signs of depression, like sleep interruption, like reactivity, overreacting and hypervigilance, and morning depression, and seasonal affective depression. I woke up one morning and realized that I have the money that I need; I have a great profession; I have two healthy children, grandchildren, a husband, friends. I travel all over the world. So why don't I feel happy? And then I realized, I have felt this all my life. I could always find things wrong with my life. Who can't? "It's my relationship. It's because my son's in Germany. I'm not out of graduate school. I need more . . ."

There came a point in my life where I literally had it all. And I thought, "There's nothing left to blame it on." I remember saying to my therapist at the time "I'm depressed." There was a little shame in that, but when I finally said it, it was like "Oh!"

The way it affects me is that I have a gloomy outlook on life. The best way I can put it is that life doesn't excite me. It puts a negative slant on life for me. It's not how I think, it's how I feel. I am a positive thinker, and when you feel negative, it's just like if you have a throbbing toothache, it's difficult to think positively. It's not an attitudinal problem. It's a biological problem.

Anger turned inward—guilt—is a form of depression, but that's not what I feel when I feel depressed. I know what that feels like. When it is anger turned inward, after I figure out what I'm angry about and talk about it and do something, I feel better. I do believe that feels like depression, but I've been at this long enough that I know the difference. This is like having a really bad hangover. It feels almost like a physical residue of a drug in my tissues.

I wake up in the morning and my body says, "What is the point?" Have you ever taken sleeping pills, or too much cough medicine? It's in your cells. It's not in your mind. My body feels gloomy. But when you feel that way, the inclination is to start thinking that way.

Another one of the symptoms was the reactivity, like over the issue of stepchildren, or financial strain, like being unable to get my husband on the phone, paranoia-type things, instead of being able to say "Well, wait a minute, now what's the logical reason that this is happening?" It's like a dumping of adrenaline in your system when certain old triggers get pushed.

I was depressed for the first time when I was first married. I was about twenty. I was depressed, but the doctor didn't call it that. He said, "The problem with your life is you don't have anything to worry about. Today is going to be like next Tuesday, and like the Tuesday after that. You don't have to worry about money, or anything else. You need to have a baby." That's what he told me. I was that impressionable that I believed him. Once my children came along, I was so busy, I didn't have the luxury of thinking about it. Then once my kids were in school, I started back to school, getting an associate's degree, and a bachelor's, and a master's, and a doctorate. So those tasks covered it up. It was only when I had the luxury of time, and had done everything, that I thought about it.

The first thing that drove me to therapy years ago was that as long as I was busy I was fine, but when I'd lie down to rest I'd have an anxiety attack. I resolved the workaholism and then was left with the depression. I remember being in withdrawal around the workaholism; the anxiety that came up around cutting back my work schedule was really scary. We self-medicate through the hyped-up adrenaline we get pumping by running around trying to do everything. It catches up with you in life. Or I just got to where I didn't want to do that any more. You don't have time for the quality of life.

If I were to stay in that state, I would just give up, I guess. And I think there is a fear that I will give up. A part of me would like to go to bed and just sleep it off.

In many ways, it's a luxury to complain about what I complain about. I know that if I didn't have discretionary money to spend on prescriptions, I could live like this, and exercise, and do other things to mitigate it. It is a luxury to be able to treat it. For me, it's not debilitating. It just taxes the quality of life, and I want to live it as well as I can.

4

Black Dog, White Dog

Although affecting only about one percent of the adult population, one of the most extreme, most disruptive and most painful forms of depression is bipolar disorder, or manic-depressive illness. Like other types of mental illness, bipolar disorder can express itself mildly or severely. At times, the highs seem almost appealing. During my struggling-young-actor years in Los Angeles, I dated a man who would stay up all night long, for days in a row. During those nights that I stayed up with him, the power of his enthusiasm as he paced the room, arms waving, voice soaring, describing his next project, would sweep me along in heady exuberance. He would find all the money he needed to produce the movie, to sign all the stars; he sang the score, described each camera angle. Then he would drop out of sight, for days or for weeks. As far as I know, none of his vast, exciting, magnificent projects ever got off the ground.

None of our gang knew that his behavior was typical of bipolar disorder. Although I haven't seen him since, I still wonder if he ever got

the help he needed to harness his great mind and creative gift and to
allow its expression in deed.

Barbara Parry, M.D.

If you look at who gets manias and who gets depressions, it's the
women who get the depressions and the men who are more likely
to get manias. Women tend to be more predisposed to getting
depressions and having just little manias (hypomanias) what they
call bipolar II. Sometimes when people have hypomanias, they
feel great. They may have a few spending sprees and their spouses
may be upset. Usually the hypomanias don't get them in trouble,
they don't have to be hospitalized, but I think an astute clinician
who gets a good history would pick up on it. Whereas the men
who get the manias really go berserk and do all kinds of destructive things.

Kitty Dukakis

I don't remember any of this "less than" kind of feeling of not
measuring up until after I stopped taking the amphetamines. The
first episodes started that fall, just a month after I was off the
drugs, and repeated themselves every year in the fall. One year I
started as early as August, and it would last until February or
March. I would wake up one day and it would be over. People say
it must have been gradual, and the answer is it wasn't. It started
quickly and it ended quickly. The last time, September 1989, I
was unwilling to admit it was happening. I was sober at that point,
and I was unwilling to admit that I had a problem with the depression. I didn't want to give any credit to that depression, because I didn't want it to continue happening. I kept thinking if I
ignored it and didn't talk about it, it would go away. It was ludi-
crous thinking. I was sober and I still got depressed, so one thing
has nothing to do with the other.

During the down periods, I would not want to talk on the

phone. My dad, who was a very effusive, effervescent kind of person, would just go into tailspins because he'd call and I'd have the phone unplugged. I'd come out of it in six months, and then go through one of these whirling dervish periods. I would wake up one day and the sun would be out and I'd be myself again, or feeling good, as I used to say. It was not unlike the feeling I had from taking amphetamines. It was a high. I shopped more, spent more money. I was interested and engaged. I had an enormous reservoir of energy for everything. My judgment wasn't great, because I would take on more than I could handle, but I also felt as though I needed to make up for that six-month period when I was just so down. I was driven, beyond my control, but also I would think about having not done very much for a long time.

It was six months up, six months down. No in between. I went through almost eight years of that.

I think there were times the kids didn't want to bring friends home, because my behavior embarrassed them. It's a hard thing to admit right now, but it's reality. I can't do anything about stuff that happened yesterday, but I can look at it and be honest about it.

When we went to [my daughter] Kara's graduation, it was an up period. I was tense, I was at the edge of my seat. Kara shared the award for the most outstanding student. I was really anxious about that, because her sister had gotten the same award three years before and I knew how competitive she was. At the time I kept thinking "She's got to win that award." What I should have done was to prepare her for and help her to deal with the possibility of not winning it. So there was a tension in the auditorium during the ceremony. When we went into the cafeteria for refreshments, [my husband] Michael was busy talking to people, and it annoyed me that he wasn't with Kara and myself and the other kids. I said something really ugly and nasty to him that he claims other people heard. I didn't think anything of it. But I think Michael noticed it more than Kara did. I wouldn't think of what I was saying, and although I prided myself on being sensitive, I was terribly insensitive of people closest to me.

My son John was out of the house by then, but as time went

on I think the girls would just get disgusted. I think at the time their attitude was "There goes Mom again: She's taken to bed, she doesn't want to do anything, she's not much fun to be around. I'm not going to ask her for help with anything in my life. She can't even handle her own life." I just didn't care.

I took several trips to Thailand to help refugees get out and I did some good things. I also did stuff with the press that I would never dream of doing today. One person in the program had very faulty judgment. Today I would tell him to go to hell, but instead I allowed myself to be manipulated by him and to be used as a conduit for what he felt was the right thing to do for refugees. And I insulted people. I wouldn't dream of doing that today.

It was during the summertime so it was a high, up period for me. I'll never forget the wife of the ambassador to Thailand at the time was Sheppe Abromowitz. Just a wonderful woman. She invited us to the embassy, but when she met me, her greeting was like ice. She was reacting to something I had said about her husband in the paper. That is an example of the kind of judgment lapse. Saying inappropriate things at inappropriate times. By the time the brunch was over, we were friends.

Impatience is a big part of it. I'm not the most patient person in the world now, but I'm miles ahead of where I was. My patience level was zero during those up periods; I was just so biting. There was no balance.

I don't know how I went through that campaign in the fall months of '87. I remember slogging across the country in a depressed state, getting up at six or six-thirty in the morning, and going all day long, speaking six or seven or eight times a day. How did I do it? At times you do things you don't think you can. Other times I'd cancel events, as I did when I was drinking. Most of the time I would manage to get up and smile and do not a good job, but a reasonable job. I couldn't have cared what the reporters asked me, yet I did it. Part of it is societal expectations, part of it is what you've been brought up with, that you have obligations and you have to follow through on them. Part of it is the fear of being found out if you don't, and so you do what's superhuman under the circumstances—and getting up and being on stage in the context of an almost lifelong depression is superhuman. People might say "Well, then you didn't have a chemical depression." Bullshit I didn't. Toward the end I couldn't get up. I just physically couldn't.

John Kelsoe, M.D.

A characteristic part of mania is that manic people feel great. They are on top of the world. At least for a while. At the later stages, they are very unhappy and miserable. But in the early to middle stages of it, they are having a ball. They don't think they need help. It is very important to try to get them into help as early as possible, which is difficult because they don't want to go.

After I start seeing a person with manic-depressive illness, I bring the family in as soon as possible. I sit down with that patient and the family and say "I want you as the patient to give permission to your family members to call me whenever they feel necessary, because they are the ones who are going to see the very early changes that you may not be aware of, when you are just starting to get a little enthusiastic and sleeping five hours a night. Then we can probably treat it as an outpatient."

What typically happens is that these folks will say "Nothing is wrong with me," and they will wind up in the most florid stage of mania and end up hospitalized. They will crash into a terrible depression afterwards that can last as long as a year. They will go through that two or three times before finally it sinks in that they don't want to go through this again. That is when they will begin to learn to recognize the signs themselves and they will begin to trust that family member when that family member says "You are not right."

I learned more about the ravages of severe bipolar disorder when I met with Susan Crosby, widow of Lindsay, one of Bing Crosby's two sons who died by suicide.

Susan Crosby

When [people are] on that manic high, they are superhuman. They don't feel pain; they can do things they never would have done before. Those fantasies that people have about the doctors showing up with a syringe and knocking the guy out, that doesn't happen. I saw five different guys who could not hold [my husband] Lindsay down, and he was five foot seven. In the mania, there was a lot of violence, too. He became very violent, because he didn't see things as they are. I used to call Lindsay "macho man," because everything became very macho.

The delusions of grandeur are really bad. They spend money they don't have. They're so up there, with so much energy, that it's beyond what's humanly possible. That's why most people think they are on drugs or something. They go for days on end without any sleep and still function, to a point. And then the crash comes.

In Lindsay's case, the devastation that he would feel about what had happened when he was in a mania would compound the depression that followed. When he was in the high, everything was at rapid speed, even his sexual drive, so he would pick up an awful lot of women. Then he would crash and he didn't know why he had done it, and he didn't even know who they were. Girls would call all the time, often saying they were pregnant and wanting money because it was Lindsay Crosby, of course. I even had parents of some of these broads call me and ask me please to get out of the way so their daughter could marry Lindsay. It was strange, the things that people would do. And the Lindsay they dealt with was not a nice person to know. That always would amaze me, why they wanted to spend time with him [when he was in that state]. If that's the only side of Lindsay that I'd ever seen, I would be horrified.

When he came down off the high, Lindsay would be so humiliated and so embarrassed when he heard the stories about his behavior, if he could have crawled into a hole and just disappeared, he would have. Lindsay himself was a very moral, caring, honest man, and this was like hearing a nightmare about himself. So on top of physical and emotional exhaustion, he was depressed. He'd become immobile. Couldn't function, period.

It almost sounds like schizophrenia and a split personality, but there's a difference between this and the schizophrenia that I've seen in my family.

A. John Rush, M.D.

Although schizophrenia and bipolar disorder can look similar when the patient is in a psychotic state, they are absolutely different diseases. They are not close. They are different in biology, in how you treat them, in treatment response, in prognosis, family history, in every way you can think of. They are about as distinct as arthritis and diabetes.

And yet there has been a history of misdiagnosis. An international collaborative study that was done between the U.S. and the U.K. found that in the United States through the 1960s and until about the early 1970s, people here were [more often] diagnosed as having schizophrenia, while people in Britain were [more often] diagnosed as having manic-depressive illness, and it had to do not with the British being different from the Americans, it had to do with the criteria that we were using to diagnose this.

When somebody has a severe psychotic depression or is manic and, during the manic episode, becomes psychotic, which is very common, those people can look as "crazy," so to speak as a person who is psychotic from schizophrenia.

They don't make any sense; they hallucinate; they hear voices, sometimes even see visions, but voices are more common. They can be delusional, think people are after them, and so on. In the recurrent forms of depression, about 15 percent will have psychotic symptoms of the severe kind, and they tend to repeat from episode to episode, so if a person has had a psychotic episode, the next episode also tends to be psychotic. That doesn't mean it's not treatable. It's just treatable with a different approach and different kinds of medicine.

Many but not all persons with schizophrenia classically have a course that's gradually deteriorating, so they have psychotic episodes, and they get well, but they don't get quite as well as they were before.

Now, people with psychotic depression or bipolar illness, when they get into one of their episodes, can be devastated and unable to function, but when they're not in the episode, they can be entirely well. They walk; they talk; and they enjoy themselves, with or without treatment. It's an entirely different disease.

The good news is that since bipolar disorder is easier than major depression to identify and to study discretely, much more research is proceeding at a more rapid pace. New medications and perhaps even treatment on a genetic level are just around the corner.

5

Effects on a Career

*In hiding our battles with depression from public scrutiny, often we fear
not the reactions of our families and friends but the repercussions our
disclosures might have on our professional lives. Although it may appear
that artists have greater license than the rest of us—that actors, for
example, are expected to be a little loopy—as Rod Steiger tells us, that
ain't necessarily so. Any of us might well wonder "What will the boss
think?" Those in the public eye also must wonder "What will the public
think?"*

*At the time my depression was diagnosed, I hosted a radio talk show
three hours a day, five or six days a week. Although I told my producer
and trusted friend about my illness, I swore her to secrecy, afraid that if
others knew, I might be fired or at least my dependability would be
questioned. I was afraid the listeners would have less confidence in me,
that co-workers and social acquaintances would treat me differently if
they knew, that they'd pussyfoot around me, afraid to upset this unbal-
anced person. I also feared that I might be passed over for positions
involving public affairs or added responsibilities or stress, even though I
had performed well every day, every year, through all my secret ups and*

downs. When I left the station a couple of years later to mother my youngest boy, I took my secret with me.

Jim Jensen

I came back from seven weeks at [a residential treatment facility in Minnesota] in October of '88, and I immediately went back on the air, because I was feeling fine. Everybody said, "How great you look, good to have you back." Signed the same contract, same money. Nothing changed. "Still your station," that kind of thing, you know. Then the Valium withdrawal set in. Oh, Christ. I would walk through Central Park to go to work and I'd have to sit down five or six times because I couldn't get any breath. And the pain, and the depression, and you just sit there wondering "How can I go on? How can I go on the air?"

It was discipline. Years of doing the job. Night after night I'd get through it. I was sleeping three to four hours a week. Finally I got desperate. I was having a terrifying panic attack, and I called a friend from work and said, "I have to go to a hospital." He came in the middle of the night and he took me to the hospital. [The station] sent me out to the Midwest with the words "Get well and come on back." Then when I was in the midst of it, deadly depression, fighting for my life, he came out there, my friend, and told me the company had taken everything away, including my job and most of my salary.

I couldn't go anywhere else. My name was wrecked because of the [publicity about my abuse of] cocaine. But after a couple of months, [the station] assumed I was getting better. They knew how valuable I had been. And the mail was pouring in. In twenty-five boxes of mail, none of it was unfavorable. It was all "When is Jim coming back?"

The viewers knew there was a depression problem; they knew about the coke; and they were totally forgiving. Unbelievable. The stigma is within the industry, not from the public perception. Most of the stigma I gave myself. I was ashamed of myself. "Come on back," they said. "Here's your office and a new Sunday broadcast." During the week, I'd come to work, sit in my office every day, just do mail and read the papers. Nobody would talk to me. Five days a week. Nothing. People would come in and say hello, but not a manager. They never came back once to find out how I was doing. Then came the Ellis Island dedication, and they wanted me to go to Europe to do something for that, and then the [Persian Gulf] war and an assignment in Israel for that. I know as much about Israel as I do anything. It's my beat. And I did some of the best reporting I ever did in my life.

I want to be fair to the company, though. They did come up and take away my pay, but they could have fired me. While I was in the hospital, I kept saying to myself "If you straighten yourself out, the door is ajar. The door is not shut," so when I got better and proved myself sane and sober, and able to do the job, they opened the door and let me back in.

When people see you're making an honest effort, most of them are cheering for you. When I first started to come back on the air, people on the street would drive by and give me the thumbs-up—garbage truck drivers, bus drivers, cops. It was like someone putting an oxygen mask over your face when you're suffocating. Like someone holding your head when you're sick. Like someone putting their arm around you when you're scared to death.

I got everything back. The company has confidence in me now. Now if I take a sick day off work, nobody looks at me crossways.

I saw [my friend] at a party and he said, "You're still the best." I'm sure he didn't enjoy the plane ride out to Minnesota. He was doing his job.

I would tell companies, be a little patient. If you don't throw a drowning man a life preserver, he's going to drown. Now, when he gets back on deck, he'd better behave.

The miracle of getting over depression is that if people give you half a chance, you can come back.

Judith Belushi Pisano

In the first few months after John died, I was doing T-shirt designs for James Taylor. I couldn't concentrate. I'd be working and then I'd start wandering, pacing, but I wasn't aware I was. One time, when I stopped, I was standing at my secretary's desk wondering "Why am I here?" I was looking down at the desk, and there had been a heart on the desk where John had written "JJ and JB."* The heart was in indelible ink but the letters weren't, so that the initials had disappeared. I found myself looking at this, and thinking it was just like my life—the heart was still there, but the initials were gone.

I left work. I just thought, "I can't do this stupid job. Who cares about these shirts anyway?" A friend called and wanted me to see *E.T.: The Extra-Terrestrial.* Though I didn't really want to go, I thought, "What the heck, I'm going to sit here or be there, I might as well go there." As we were leaving the movie, I saw a T-shirt that said, "E.T., Welcome Home," I thought, "Oh! You could do, 'J.T., Welcome Him, Just a Terrestrial.'" And it did give me a sense of accomplishment when it all worked out. It was a simple job of sorts, and yet it caused me so much trouble, and then had a successful conclusion. I was very lucky that I had friends who pushed me [into doing the job]. We need to push ourselves, and sometimes we can't, and others can help push us.

William Styron

I was totally unengaged from my work. The depression consumed the mind and body so totally that you can't think of anything else. You can barely *read* a book.

---

* Judith Jacklin was her maiden name.

Rose Styron

I realized how bad Bill's crisis was when I was in Budapest in late October with a group from PEN. We were about to go over the border into Transylvania, in Romania, in search of a couple of writers who were in deep trouble—both literary and human rights. We had been briefed; people were prepared to meet us on the other side and take us through to see what we had to do. From all the stories and the briefing I realized that I might be incommunicado for a couple of weeks, so I called home. Bill had not been well at all, but when I had left, he was going up to Albany for a speaking engagement, and I went off to Budapest, assuming everything was okay. But when I talked to him on the phone, I realized nothing was okay.

He had been so supportive of all the work I'd done in [the human rights organization] Amnesty International. I was often away from home for a couple of weeks doing things, and he had always encouraged me to do it. Now he was saying "I wish you wouldn't go to Romania, and oh, you think you might not be in touch?"

"Would you rather that I come home?" I said.

And he said, "Yes, please." That was so unusual for him that I figured that he must be feeling pretty bad. I thought about it for three or four hours, because so many other people were involved in this whole chain of events. Then I asked the others if they would go without me.

I really stopped work entirely for months, and even though of course I went back to it, I don't think I ever went back as full time as I had been. And once he got better, we were having really such a good relationship that I didn't want to push it away.

Jules Feiffer

One thing that helped jolt me out of this black self-regard was when I was about seventeen and working on one of my first cartoonist jobs. A friend of mine working in the office, whom I was endlessly running to with one problem or another, said, "How come you're funny about so many things and see humor in everything, but you don't see any humor in yourself?" It was like a bolt of lightning. Suddenly the truth of that struck me so strongly that it turned me around. I started seeing my situation as less grim and more funny. I realized that these complaints, though real, were not all that serious.

I had deliberately set out for myself a high risk career, where the chances of success were slim, and where I had to learn that rejection and even contempt by people whom you depended on to make a living was more likely to happen than not. The things that I love to do most are the things that are least likely to find an audience. It's a life of constant pleasure in the work itself—more than pleasure, ecstasy, euphoria. It's just great joy to do what I do. And then, the result is almost always doomed, and somewhere along the line you have to deal with that, and then you have to keep dealing with it, and keep finding reasons to go on doing it. One of those reasons being, well, you know, after all, I chose it. Nobody made me do this. So I must be doing it for some reason. Other than that I enjoy being kicked in the head.

From my middle twenties on, when I found satire as a form (which was in the Army), I was generally healthy about my work. I began enjoying difficulties and discovering there was a pleasure in solving problems rather than letting them defeat you, and enjoying challenges, and that when something was tough, rather than discourage me it would enliven me. I saw it as a chance to outfox the problem. Come up from behind. Surround it. So it gave me a sense of greater and greater competence, and with this competence came self-confidence. Also, getting famous along the way doesn't hurt. That gave me the courage to write for theater, something I never would have done if I hadn't been a famous cartoonist already.

Whatever depression I feel today doesn't feel chronic the way I felt as a little boy, as a young man, through my entire first marriage, and through many of the years after that. I've got bad days, bad weeks. When my last play got panned and closed and it was my best play I felt literally crazy, in a wild rage for months. I felt insane, unwired, unhinged. But I also knew that I would come out of that, and I have come out of it.

The way that manifested itself was by drinking a lot, not during the day because I've never been a day drinker, but at night. We went to Italy afterward with friends. Unlike real depression, God knows I took pleasure in the food and took pleasure in the drink, and took pleasure in the art. In the course of feeling rotten, and feeling suicidal, and feeling that an important part of my life was over, I also was having a wonderful time. I was enjoying my friends, enjoying what I saw on walls everywhere, frescoes, paintings, and enjoying just about everything that went down my mouth, and enjoying the walks I took in the Tuscan countryside.

When you're a child and you get depressed, or when you're a young person and don't have anything to compare it to, it is scarier because you don't know that it's ever going to stop. But I knew that it would stop, and that as bad as this was, and as legitimately angry, embittered, and depressed I was about my theatrical fate, I knew even then I was overdramatizing it, and that whatever my bitching and moaning, I'd get back to writing another play sooner or later. And whatever my bitching and moaning, there would be a time when I felt happy again.

Rod Steiger

Actor Rod Steiger discusses the effects of his depression on his work on F.I.S.T. *and* January Man, *both directed by Norman Jewison.*

I thought that no matter how sick I could be, there was one thing I could do, and that was act. Now I realize I didn't have as much control as I thought I had. I was acting in a fog. I looked all right, I sounded all right, but I was walking through, and I'm not known for walking through anything.

Your mind's off; you don't have the objectivity; you don't have the necessary intellectual command. Your responses are a bit crooked. And you don't know it. With my ego, even though I was in the clutches of the disease, I thought, "I'm acting so well they don't know I'm depressed." I thought I was getting away with it.

I was obviously more afraid of public failure than I was of the depression. Even with whatever I had left to work with, and maybe twenty, thirty years of experience, I was so terrified. I had a very good friend of mine come over at five o'clock in the morning to sit in the den with me and go over that day's scene. Yet when I'd be riding in a limousine to the set, I couldn't remember it at all. I went berserk trying to find ways, to find associations, that would help me remember. What terrified me the most was that these are trial scenes. I'm used to paraphrasing and improvising. You can't improvise, "On January 16th, 1972, you were in Seattle, at Mr. So and So's house, is that true, sir?" So where I have this gift of improvisation that might have saved my ass, I couldn't putz around here.

That was my first depression. It lasted about four years. I worked a little bit. Not much. Nothing that anybody would want to see or remember: Italy, Argentina, Israel.

I didn't have to audition. I had to go to work though. But listen, that's nothing. I'm one of the small group of people who could afford financially to be depressed for ten years. How does a person get up and go to work at civil service, or an insurance company, or a garage, or a shoemaker shop, feeling probably worse than I did, because they've got to pay the rent? If they don't get out of bed, there's nothing for the family. These people I bow humbly before. I don't know how they do it. How do you carry that weight to work?

Just before I was on my way out of depression, I did a picture called *January Man*. I was just beginning to feel again, to have healthy emotions. Enjoy the taste of food, enjoy the look of the sunshine, enjoy the touch of soft skin, enjoy the warmth of the kiss, enjoy all those things that you take for granted until you've been depressed. I had a scene in which I was supposed to get angry, and while I was filming the scene, whatever power I had as an actor came back all of a sudden. I unconsciously celebrated the return of full feelings to my life in front of the camera, and went so overboard in that scene that it's ridiculous. What I did had nothing to do with the acting. I was celebrating the fact that I could feel something strongly again. I'm sorry it happened that way, and that didn't help my career at all. But what happened that day was a major breakthrough for me. I could feel again the things that I knew I had to feel fully in order to perform, and I overdosed with the feeling. Also, I was so angry about the time I had lost in the depression. Everybody watching me didn't know what the hell was going on. The funny thing about it, even though I was condemned for overacting in that scene, I never thought of it until this minute: That was a true, honest, angry human being.

For a while I couldn't get a job with any of the major studios because my acting was off. I couldn't understand it. I'm still having trouble today getting a first-class picture in this town. Now my problem is also my age, plus whatever damage my depressive behavior did, plus in the decade that I was half alive and half dead a new generation of younger executives has gotten into power. Recently I went to talk to this guy about work and he said, "Can you do a southern accent?"

I said, "Well, I did in *In the Heat of the Night*. I did a southern accent pretty good. I got an Academy Award. Did you ever see it?" He said no. He was thirty-five.

I don't know how much the depression has hurt. I have no idea.

Everybody used to call me "Rodney the Rock." Used to be a cartoon character in the papers called "Rodney the Rock." Now they can call me "Mr. Steiger, the Marshmallow."

Norman Jewison

I remember Rod coming out of the depression. Boy, that took a long time. He was really down. It was even worse when we did *F.I.S.T.* But I knew when he came out of the starting gate, when the lights came up, he'd be fine. When he was going do his first scene, with Stallone, he was sitting all by himself, and he looked worried. I went over and I sat with him. He doesn't remember this. I've never seen anyone so depressed, and so insecure, from someone who had always been very secure, who always knew where he was going as an actor and a person. He was playing a senator that was after Hoffa. It was written from the transcripts, and testimony, and I sat with him and he said, "Norm, Norm, I'm worried about my goddamned lines."

I said, "I have enough confidence for both of us. Don't worry about it." Three hours later he was doing the scene, and he was right back. He didn't know it, but he was fine. He still thought he was giving less. He gives a very good performance in the film, some very interesting scenes.

Barbara Parry, M.D.

People who are depressed tend to plod along, doing their jobs. I remember treating a woman who was in real estate and had a menopausal depression. If you're in the lab and you're not having to interact with people, it's not so much a problem, but [it's harder on] people who are in advertising or real estate, where they have to go out and sell themselves. It's not that they shouldn't have the job, they should just get treated for the depression. It's not just in the workplace. A woman who has depression, who is trying to raise children, is going to have a very difficult time.

Lewis Judd, M.D.

Often depression can be treated without many people on the job even being aware of it. But if someone was going to lose his or her job or were about to be fired, or was fired, one might want to consider intervening. Maybe even with the patient's permission, have the clinician talk to the employer, to say "Look, this person is suffering from depression. It's the reason they haven't been functioning very well. They may be missing some time from work right now, but they're currently under treatment, and within a few weeks or a month or two, they will be back to their old selves." I would like to believe that it is a realistic approach to things. I think that most people are fairly enlightened and when confronted with information like this, will acknowledge it, although you could find someone who will react negatively.

Let's say the supervisor is a run-of-the-mill supervisor, well meaning, nice person, but totally unaware of what depression is all about. What he might see is an employee who does not seem to care as much about the job any more, who seems more remote and unavailable, less friendly. The level of productivity of that worker drops off, and despite counseling from management, it seems to continue to get worse. He might even see an employee who begins to self-medicate with alcohol or something and that adds to the problem until the worker can't do the job any more. Despite repeated interactions, if the individual is unable to respond, he or she might end up being fired or moved to another job or demoted. Employers need to be very sensitive to this issue. They should be alerted that in all likelihood they're dealing with someone who's depressed, not someone who has suddenly or gradually become a bad employee, that it is treatable, and that they ought to urge and promote treatment for that individual.

6

Overcoming the
Stigma and
the Shame

Two women represented in these pages, and many other men and women who declined to be interviewed at all, are still fearful about what effect public knowledge of their illness would have on their lives. Many remember all too well the disappointment of Senator Thomas Eagleton's resignation from the Democratic vice-presidential race in 1972, precipitated by the revelation of his electroshock treatment for depression. Some, like Jane Doe, talk candidly at cocktail parties about their illnesses, but they can't bring themselves to go on the record. People who will trumpet their stays at the Betty Ford Clinic won't admit their battle with depression. What is more surprising, however, is the number of men and women who are willing to go on the record. Twenty years ago, I don't believe any of them would have. Twenty years from now, I hope treatment for mental illnesses will be as accepted as treatment for substance abuse is today.

Rod Steiger

I have been opening my mouth in newspaper interviews since I've been feeling better the last three years, and businesspeople around me are quite hysterical. It might have damaged me to some degree in the profession, I don't know. Across the country, one in five has a mental disease. It's about time we began to talk about this thing: It's a much better cause than politics. In the words of Gertrude Steiger [sic], "A disease is a disease." I certainly don't intend at my age to shut up about anything. And I will not have people condemned for a very human ailment.

Jane Doe

I love L.A. because it is irreverent. It is marginal. People talk about feelings there. The whole holistic lifestyle is a common topic of the conversation. Half the people I know out there are the artsy-craftsy types. They are all taking something. Out there I would feel differently about discussing it publicly. Where I live, in Washington, D.C., I am already marginal. I don't fit in here at all. I am an outspoken, strong, ethnic woman, and I am irreverent. Even New York is different. It is a cosmopolitan, energized place. This is a sleepy little village inside the Beltway. It is a company town; the U.S. government is the company. Everybody is in the company, servicing the company, or trying to find out what the company is doing.

I loathe Washington. I really loathe it. What Truman said is absolutely true: "If you want a friend in Washington, get a dog." People don't have feelings here, and they don't have problems. And they don't have disease. And they don't have depression. And they don't have sadness.

It is a town that is in total denial. Alcoholism is still acceptable. Every bar, every lunch, every dinner is based on power, on what you can do for me, what I can do for you. It is not "Gee, what are you doing? Come on over, and we will talk about our-selves." I used to think that it was me. Then a friend who is a very famous journalist here for many years, an Episcopalian, very WASPy, told me that it is the nature of the town, to be cold and distant and impersonal and unsupportive.

I remember when Bud McFarlane attempted suicide. It had been all over the front pages. I saw him in a meeting a week later. He came in a little late. We were all sitting around the table, and he sat in a corner. And I said, "Hi, Bud." He is not a friend of mine. He is not somebody I admire. But at the break, I went up to him and said, "I am sure that your psychiatrist has told you that it is business as usual. This is probably the hardest thing you have ever done, but you will look back at this as a period of growth. I am really glad you are here." Then I said, "Come on, let's go get something to drink." As we stood there, people whose careers he had made in the White House signaled him from across the room; they would not come up to him. Then it came time for the dinner. I could see that he was absolutely paralyzed, so depressed. The medicine wasn't working yet. So I brought him next to me. The chair on the other side of him stayed empty until the very end. It was so tragic, so sad. It was all Washington people. To this day, when this man sees me, a mile away, he comes running. A little touch of humanity in a very cruel town.

I have taken it upon myself now to educate people. When they say "Oh my God, you are so thin. You are so this, so that," I say "Yep, Prozac. I have finally arrested a lifelong disease."

And they say "What did you have? What is that?"

"Depression. It is called dysthymia."

I am not ready to do that publicly, but I say that all the time.

Norman Rosenthal, M.D.

I don't think people with depression can all be lumped into the same category. Some people whose depressions are not incapaci-tating could do a wonderful job at just about anything. Others are so badly affected that it is hard to hold any job. When you are dealing with such a huge range of symptoms and capacities, I would be loath to make any blanket proscriptions.

Lewis Judd, M.D.

Depression is a very, very treatable disease, and if managed right, these individuals can live extremely normal lives, and I can't think of any job or position that they could not hold.

John Kelsoe, M.D.

I think that it is a mistake to say that people with manic-depressive illness should never be in air traffic control, period. You answer these questions by asking "Well, how would you feel about people [being in those jobs] who have heart arhythmias or diabetes or something that could conceivably result in their having problems at some point?" How do you make that decision? Should people with epilepsy be able to drive? Well, that depends on how well controlled their epilepsy is. The issues are exactly the same.

Jane Doe

Whether it should be or not, society's not ready for a person who has had depression to be president, because there's a stigma. A recovering alcoholic who had had thirty years of sobriety also would not get elected.

   After someone has arrested the disease, he or she should have the chance. If he starts drinking, you kick him out.

William Styron

To be honest, I would wonder whether it would be wise to have a president who quite possibly would fall into the kind of depressive state in which he might be incapacitated at certain periods. It would not be a good thing to have, would it? Yet Abraham Lincoln is a very good example of a man who managed to deal with it. My basic inclination is that there should not be stigmatization of a person. If a person has had a bout of depression, even a severe major depression, that should not disqualify him from being able to function, as president or anything else.

Lewis Judd, M.D.

If Senator Thomas Eagleton were on the ticket today, his mental health history would not be the problem that it was then, but I think the public's reaction would not be terribly enlightened either. I have no confidence that we'd have a perception and attitude across the board in the U.S. about the true nature of mental disorders. We just don't. We tend to want very healthy people as our leaders. We're on the way, we're making progress, but we're not there yet.

John Kenneth Galbraith

I was very much involved in that whole Eagleton episode. There was the usual journalistic feeding frenzy on that issue, and if George McGovern had just stuck with Tom Eagleton, as George Bush stuck with what's-his-name, it would have been all over in a week or two. George [McGovern] just succumbed, shouldn't have done it. But I was responsible for his getting Tom Eagleton.

I never knew about Eagleton's problems. I suppose I would have mentioned it, but I didn't know about it. If Eagleton had been on lithium, no one would have known about it, but shock treatments have a sort of definitive aspect. Well, nobody would have electric shocks anymore. It's a form of therapy that's partly disappeared, hasn't it?* Well, if Danny Quayle had had it, I would think he was better, wouldn't you?

Rona Barrett

It's one of those taboos of the early days. I'm not sure that younger generations feel the same way or have the same information as people of Mike Wallace's generation or my generation or your generation. The first thought was always that if you had this dark cloud over you, maybe you were crazy. In the early days, if you were crazy, what it really was saying is that your family gave birth to a crazy person, and therefore [the stigma] went on to them, and they were ashamed. It was like divorce; people didn't get divorced because it became a stigma on the family that they didn't produce so-called perfect people. The same thing is true about depression and the inability to understand that it is a chemical imbalance for many. And for many, something quite different.

Norman Rosenthal, M.D.

I think there is less of a stigma with Seasonal Affective Disorder than with other types of depression. People empathize with being part of the animal kingdom. They empathize with hibernating bears and other kinds of animals that change seasonally. It makes one feel more a part of nature and less a separate entity from the rest of nature. It would be nice if other conditions were equally

* Recently a target of the same antipsychiatry group that tried to discredit Ritalin and Prozac, ECT, or electroconvulsive therapy, is viewed by some doctors as the safest, most effective treatment for depression and by others as a treatment of last resort. Almost all respect its potency and efficacy.

destigmatized, because these are not things that people choose. These are things that are part of who they are.

Rose Styron

The most important thing is that everybody talks about it and everybody knows how many other people there are. So many, many, many of our friends who thought they were isolated have been through this and now come to tell us that they too have been depressed. Even the doctors made Bill feel there was a stigma, which is just horrifying.

We were both so ignorant about depression. We really had no insight into it at all. Neither of us had ever been to a psychiatrist. We were not the kind of people who read much psychiatric literature. We knew about the history of poets and painters and so forth, because they are so prone to mood swings and depression. But it was in historical context, and it was other people. We hadn't known it among our friends, because we lived out in the country or in Martha's Vineyard. [Both places] were removed from those centers of science and trouble, so we just didn't have that kind of contact with it. When it started to happen to Bill, there was an immediate recognition of what had been happening all his life, and what had probably been happening to other friends all their lives, which we hadn't understood as real clinical depression. Within a year before and after Bill's experience, we had four other close friends, all of an age, all men, who went through something extremely similar. At that point we began reading everything we could lay our hands on.

William Styron

You do feel somewhat disconcerted by having an illness that is taking possession of you in this way, which is so bizarre. You're suffering from a mental illness. You've been trained most of your life that you're not vulnerable that way and all of a sudden it's

happening to you. So there's a great deal of confusion and per-
plexity about this. But I didn't feel shame. You feel shame only
when you've done something that you're derelict about. I had
enough awareness to know that this was not my fault. I felt laid
low. I felt demoralized, and helpless. But I didn't feel shame.

I was pretty enlightened, if I may use that word, from the very
beginning. I never made it a secret. I probably bored people by
overemphasizing the fact that I was suffering a very severe mental
seizure.

It would lessen my sense of a person's integrity if I learned
that he or she had suffered from depression and had hidden it. I
honor or respect whatever personal reasons they had for that, but
I would feel far more respect for people who fully face up to the
fact that they have had an illness and tell the world. I think it's a
matter of responsibility, because the illness will continue to be
stigmatized as people try to hide the fact that they've had it.

Traditionally, people have had fear and repugnance for mental
illness, that somehow it's spooky. I read about a poll recently
which found that [almost] 50 percent of American people, Mr.
and Mrs. Frontporch, believes that there is a moral incapacity in
depression. Only 50 percent, on the other hand, is aware that it is
a mental illness to which no moral stigma should be attached.*

James Farmer

There was no stigma as far as I was concerned. There would have
been a stigma had I gone to a hospital. "What? Farmer in a
psycho hospital? He's crazy?" There would have been that sort of
stigma. "He had a nervous breakdown?" I was at the point of a
nervous breakdown. Or maybe it *was* a nervous breakdown. I

---

* In a recent National Institute of Mental Health study, 25 percent of the respondents had
experienced depression, 26 percent had observed it in family members, 43 percent felt
depression was a reflection of personal weakness, and 11 percent wasn't sure whether
depression was a matter of personal, character, or moral weakness or a health problem. The
concern is that if people don't believe that what they have is an illness, they won't seek
treatment for it.

don't know. I don't know what the psychologists or psychiatrists could say.

A. John Rush, M.D.

Doctors are still reluctant to make the diagnosis because they, too, feel like "Oh, you must have done something wrong. How did you get yourself into this pickle?" which sort of means the patient is to blame.

What it really is is a psychiatric illness. Do you want to call it a brain disease? That's a neurological illness. If you have heart disease, that's cardiac illness. If you have bowel disease, that's gastrointestinal illness. If you have joint problems, that's arthritis or joint disease, or orthopedic problems. But when you say "My mind and my brain are affected badly," it's not okay to call it a psychiatric illness. It's okay if you have a neurological disease—Parkinson's, Huntington's, urinary incontinence, a busted spine because you got in an auto accident—but once you move up to the higher cortical areas, now you don't have a disease any more; now you have "trouble coping"; now you have "a bad attitude"; now you have "a mental disease."

It's as though we believe that this part of the brain, the most important part for humans, is immune to disease. You can't have any disease up there. The soul has moved from the heart to the mind, and people don't want to hear "My brain can go bad, just like my mind. That doesn't mean I'm weak, it doesn't mean I'm incurable, it doesn't mean I'm insane. It means I've got a disease and somebody had better treat it."

One of my friends says "Depression? Hell, boy, that's wimp disease." Wimp disease? Oh, yeah, it's wimp disease. And I guess the ultimate wimp kills himself. Unfortunately, because it's more often a women's disease in adulthood, people say "Oh, that's women," and "Oh, they have all those hormone problems." It's almost a thing I would suggest you don't put in the book, because they say "Oh, those women. You know, they have their spells."

It's demeaning because it's a women's disease. Baloney. It can kill you, and, in fact, it kills more men than it does women.

Barbara Parry, M.D.

It's disturbing to me as a physician to know that here's a depression and the probability is that I can treat it so easily, and these people's lives could be so much better, but they're reluctant to see a psychiatrist, or to get into treatment because they think it's some kind of moral failure or something. Those are attitudes coming out of the Dark Ages, as far as I'm concerned. People are afraid of things they don't understand. Not treating a depression is like not having a broken leg fixed or not treating a pneumonia.

Lewis Judd, M.D.

There is a stigma, even within the medical profession, against mental disorders. At best, doctors feel that they're complicating features of the so-called medical management of a patient. At worst, they don't even see them, they ignore them. We have not done a great job in training physicians to recognize mental disorders and to be comfortable treating them.

Kitty Dukakis

When I think of mental illness I think of people who are schizophrenic, who are psychotic, who can't function in society, people with whom you and I wouldn't want to spend much time. That's probably one of the reasons that more people don't come forward and get the help that they need. I hid it, but other people who are mentally ill, in the other categories, can't put up a veil and hide it, and that's the only difference between them and us. The tragedy is that so many people, in particular people in highly visible positions, don't get the help that they need because of their concern about what the public will perceive. Children of politicians, children of Hollywood people, children of well-known broadcasters, children of anybody who is publicly visible are at high risk for not getting help, for untreated mental illnesses. I don't think they get [ill] any more than anybody else, but I think they're not treated as much as other people.

Mary Jones

It does not seem to me that anybody who has lived to be thirty-five with any intensity at all can have failed to realize how thin the line is between sane and crazy. Defining mental illnesses as illnesses has been one of the best things this society has accomplished so far.

I am convinced that within twenty years scientists will have discovered a great deal more about the minor chemical imbalances in the brain that produce various forms of insanity. In fact, one reason I'm opposed to the death penalty is that we execute many people whose problem is not that they're vicious, their problem is they're sick. I think that [eventually] we will be regarded as barbarians.

Pat Love, Ed.D.

I'm real open about it because I don't see it as any fault. I compare it to diabetes. You're not embarrassed about having diabetes. It's like being right-handed or left-handed; it's part of the genetic structure.

I asked a friend of mine, "Do you want to be interviewed about your depression?"

She said, "I'd rather be interviewed about my incontinence."

Although I have been in and out of therapy since before I knew how to drive, I only recently answered affirmatively on the driver's license form that asks "Have you been under medication or hospitalized for a mental, nervous, or emotional condition within the past one year?" What will the consequences be? Well, I probably won't be able to buy a handgun, but I doubt I'll want to anyway. Other than that, I don't know. It scares me to wonder, but it is, after all, who I am. We can't afford to be cowards. To stay silent is to perpetuate the pain, for us, for our children, for all those who suffer now, in silence.

7

Substance Abuse

Amphetamines, cocaine, marijuana, Valium, psychedelics, and alcohol. I tried every mood-altering substance to which I had access, anything to take me out of where I was, to make the bad feelings go away. I was looking for something that would make me feel normal. My need seemed different from most of my peers'. I didn't really care whether they were using or not, although I certainly remember pleasant occasions of social use. (I remember some horrible ones, as well: crouching on the floor of the kitchen in self-imposed darkness, my friends trying to convince me there were no sirens or bombs; believing I was floating in outer space held to earth by a narrow tether; the sun hitting the back of my neck like a sledge hammer—and for years not being able to expose that skin to direct rays without fear of re-creating the "trip".)

My use escalated each fall and spring, and somehow, each time I neared the brink of addiction, I stepped back. Was it self-preservation that prompted me to quit when I did? Or was it because the depressive episode had passed?

I never was in danger of being committed to a facility for the treatment of substance abuse. Had I been, I have no reason to believe

that my underlying depression would have been diagnosed or treated. I
would like to say that has changed by the 1990s, but judging from the
stories I hear, it has not.

Kitty Dukakis

It started in September and got worse and worse. In October I
spoke four or five times in different parts of the country. I did
okay, but I was really depressed. People said, "Well, you shouldn't
have done so much." Whether I had kept my speaking engage-
ments or not, the depression would have continued. With an
organic kind of depression, there doesn't have to be a trigger. I
remember Jane Scovell, the woman with whom I wrote my [auto-
biography], trying to get me to meet with her, and I kept cancel-
ing meetings. Then one Monday I wanted a pill or a drink, because I had just been lying in bed doing nothing. I couldn't get up
and get dressed, but I couldn't sleep either. I went into the bathroom, and I opened the medicine cabinet. The rubbing alcohol
was there. Had it been Valium or vodka or anything, I would have
done the same thing. I drank a swig of it and it was horrible. I can
almost taste it now two years later. I remember looking at my
face. I had lost a lot of weight, and I looked awful. I took another
swig and I got into bed, and I guess I passed out. I woke up in the
hospital.

I stayed in the hospital for five days. It was hideous. I realized
that this had been broadcast all over the world. There were reporters camped out. Other people could do what I did, and *have*
done what I did, and nobody pays any attention. I was mortified.
I've learned since that shame destroys the ego, and let me tell you
I had it in spades. Then I went to the Deaconess Hospital, where
they had a depressive unit. In your wildest dreams you can't imagine the scene when I walked out on the hospital floor. People
looked comatose. All the women on the floor were practically
eighty, and in terrible shape. I refused to participate in anything, I
was in a back room, and a dear friend stayed with me that first
day. They kept using the word bipolar with me. I didn't realize

that they were talking about manic-depressive disease. I stayed there for a couple of weeks and then was a day patient, coming back and forth. I stayed sober for a little bit.

During that six-month period after drinking the rubbing alcohol, I started drinking other substances in the house. Hairspray, nail polish remover, anything I could get my hands on. Clearly, I needed more help, and I didn't want to go anyplace in Massachusetts, which was ridiculous, but I didn't. So I went to Four Winds.* They did the best they could, but my alcoholism needed to be treated at the same time and it really wasn't. I went to some meetings on the grounds and off the grounds, but psychotherapy was not the answer for me. And they tried all kinds of medications.

Kara was coming back from Spain on the twenty-second of December, and she and Michael came to pick me up. I had talked them into letting me go home for Christmas. Big mistake. I have never been through a more difficult three days in my life.

I got through Christmas. We had the whole family at the house and the kids helped get the meal together. How we did it, I'll never know. I remember having terrible apprehension before I got into the house, and I should have gone right back. I should have. The one thing that the psychiatric hospital did was to provide a safe haven for me. I managed not to do anything destructive on Christmas day. Michael had done all the shopping and had everything in the house. I remember the day of my birthday, December 26. I said, "This is my birthday, I can do what I want to do." So I stayed in bed all day. It was horrible. I only got up to drink anything that I could get my hands on. The next day, the twenty-seventh, Michael had to go into the office, and he asked Kara to help get me ready to go back to the hospital. I got into bed and refused to get up. They practically dragged me into the car.

Back at the hospital, they had people with me twenty-four hours a day for two days. They were sure I was suicidal. I was not, not in the traditional sense. I was killing myself, and I thought

* A psychiatric hospital in Katonah, New York, with an alcohol and drug abuse program.

about death periodically, that it would be easier if I weren't alive, but I don't think I was truly suicidal. I don't think I had the courage to do something like that. Anyhow, I got back there and it was just more of the same. I learned how to play backgammon, and I also made a very good friend who has remained a good friend. They let me go in January. I lasted for two weeks. I was still just as depressed, and went back, and was there another three weeks. I was just as depressed when I left as when I entered. I got home in March and started drinking. I put a kerchief on and a beauty mark on my face and sunglasses to go to the liquor store. I used to hide the alcohol in a laundry basket. I would drink myself to sleep.

Jane was trying to work with me. I sit here and I can laugh now at how awful it was, but I don't know how she handled it. I had no interest in working on the book. I had no interest in it, I couldn't care less about what was going on. Finally, Michael told my sister in early May to bring me a quart of vodka, that we had to have it in the house so that I wouldn't drink other things. He didn't know that I had been drinking vodka for three or four weeks, but I was and that gave me license just to go crazy. The last time I drank, I finished that quart of vodka within a thirteen- or fourteen-hour period. I mean, I just went nuts, passed out for six or seven hours. The next day I was on a plane on my way to [a treatment center in] Alabama.

A young woman, younger than my son, who was a counselor in this program came into the room I was detoxing in, and looked at me and said, "You're a mess." Which I didn't realize they said to everybody.

And I said to myself, "Who the hell does she think she is telling me I'm a mess?" And I was. I was an absolute mess.

The next day I met with the general practitioner, the physician, and he said to me, "Has anyone ever suggested that you're manic-depressive or bipolar?"

"Are those the same thing?" I asked.

"Yes," he said.

"A lot of people."

"Well, that's what you are," he said, "and you need to be on lithium." I was there for a month and started the lithium when I got home. And I've been on it since. And I have been free of depression since.

I have a double problem because I've got an alcohol problem, too. Lots of people who are bipolar, or who are unipolar, don't have the problem with alcohol. I've got to treat both of them and be responsible for both parts of my being, a predisposition toward depression and a predisposition toward alcohol abuse.

In my experience and those of people I've talked to, when you're depressed and you're an alcoholic, you will reach for something to blot out the pain. You want to sleep, and you don't want to face the pain, and it compounds the depression, because alcohol is a depressant.

Treatment is complicated because alcoholics lie when they're in denial, and so you don't let the psychiatrist know what you're doing. You really must be treated by someone who has experience and training in the disease of addiction, even somebody who is himself or herself recovering from the disease of alcoholism. I'm back at school now, getting a certificate in counseling, and probably 90 percent of my class is recovered. You don't have to be recovering to take that step, but I think it adds a dimension to your understanding.

Bill W. and Dr. Bob started AA in 1935, over fifty years ago, and in those days it was thought that any kind of mood-altering medication [would cause problems]. There are still old-timers around who feel that way. But one has to separate mood-altering drugs from medications. There is a difference between mood altering and response to an organic chemical problem.

There are still places where people who have been in a twelve-step program more than twenty or thirty years feel strongly that you cannot take any medication, period. I think it's shortsighted. If I were to come up against that, I think I would just keep my own counsel. I'm doing what I think is right, and other people's response to that is irrelevant.

John Kelsoe, M.D.

When we admit somebody with alcoholism and depression onto our unit, what we ideally would like to do is just wait. After they've been sober for three or four weeks, often the depression begins to clear. On the converse side, those who are depressed are sometimes inclined to drink and that may exacerbate their depression. On a clinical, practical basis, we're always trying to guess is it the depression causing the alcoholism, or the alcoholism causing the depression?

Clearly, alcoholism has hereditary components to it. No doubt an aspect of the predisposition to alcoholism is genetic, and there is at least some report now that a gene that is involved in that predisposition has been identified, although it's kind of controversial. And depression is hereditary. So then you also have the interaction, nongenetic, between alcoholism and depression in that alcoholism can cause depression. They occur together very commonly and this is an area in psychiatric research that is finally being studied, that of co-morbidity: people who have more than one diagnosis.

William Styron

Alcohol was a central factor, to the best of my knowledge, in my depression. I believe that many people who are by nature depressive, or have a depressive bent, use alcohol throughout most of their lives to, paradoxically, alleviate the depression. I think, if you're not an alcoholic, you use alcohol as a kind of medication to keep your demons at arm's length. But all of a sudden I was unable to drink. I developed a severe intolerance to alcohol. Instead of alcohol making me high, euphoric, or giving me a mild sort of buzz, it did the opposite. It brought me down. It began to act as the depressant it really is, accompanied by nausea. All the potent magical things that it used to do disappeared.

This happened as I arrived on the Vineyard in the summer of that year, 1985. So I stopped drinking. It was quite amazing to me that I was doing this thing to my body. I was never an alcoholic, but I think I was an abuser of alcohol. I had been drinking with some heaviness most of my life. And all of a sudden I was no longer able to drink. In the absence of this mood bath, as I call it, that I would have every day in the evening, now I had a new experience of not having alcohol there to give me that sensation of euphoria. And that allowed the depression to crowd in on me. During the period between June of 1985 and my plunge into depression in the next fall and winter, and my recovery the following spring of 1986, I didn't have a drink. I didn't have a drop of alcohol, except once or twice, which were reckless sort of experiments which I shouldn't have done, and which put me into tailspins. One single drink would just give me a horrible reaction, both physical and emotional. When I recovered I began very tentatively to drink again, a little white wine in the evening, sometimes a beer for lunch. But I swore off hard liquor forever. That's an indication to me that I'm not an alcoholic, that I've learned to control it.

Jim Jensen

When you dissociate yourself from society, that's a self-destructive act. And I look back on other things along the way, and see them as self-destructive. Ultimately of course cocaine is self-destructive. I never was a drinker, never been drunk in my life. Never did anything wrong. Never got fired ever in my life. Did well in the Army and the Air Force during the war. But I must have been looking for something. When I went to a party where there was cocaine, I said, "Who needs it?" At that time everybody thought it was nonaddictive. It was a toy. Like a vodka tonic or something. I tried it. Didn't like it. Sometime later I tried it again. Didn't like it. The third time I tried it, I didn't like it. And the fourth time I tried it, I did. Now, if somebody offered me food, and I didn't like it the first time, I'll be damned if I'd try it three more times. Subconsciously, some part of me was looking for something.

Now I'll tell you what happened when the cocaine finally connected. All of a sudden, for the first time in my life, I felt like I belonged inside my own skin. I felt like me. I said, "Jesus Christ, I've been trying to feel like this since I was a kid." In other words, comfortable with me. I didn't feel alienated from myself. Of course, that's what sucked Freud into cocaine. He thought it was a panacea for depression.

It felt good to be comfortable with myself. I didn't have to pretend. My palms didn't sweat. I thought, "This is cheaper than doctor bills and twice as fast." One time at the beginning I went with a group of guys to Florida to watch a Jets' playoff game, and on the way we stopped in the Bahamas for a few days. We went out for dinner and there were some ladies and we were dancing. I like to dance but I'm very shy, and if I can't be as good as Arthur Murray or Fred Astaire then I feel I shouldn't be on the floor. But I do like to dance. And that night, high on cocaine, I danced. I had the time of my life. I was telling stories, listening to people, and I felt comfortable. I didn't feel shy, didn't feel stupid or didn't feel awkward. I didn't feel like I felt when I was a kid. When I was a kid, I thought I was tall, gaunt, gangly, awkward, dumb. There was nothing but skin and bones. I thought I was the ugliest, dumbest kid God ever made. A friend of mine said, "Jesus, I have never seen you like this in my life." He said, "You were having such a good time. You were so much fun." I didn't have the heart to tell him.

I remember going to my room and, in an almost prayerful mode, saying, "Why can't I be this way without this crap? Just with my own resources." See, what the cocaine allowed was all the inhibitions, guilt, and rage to drop away. That's the allure of the shit.

But it doesn't stop with that. Because you never ever re-create that same feeling that you had that first time, and you've got to use more and more and more and you never get back. It takes on a life of its own. Then it controls you. And when you fall off cocaine, there's a depression. And depression was the main cause of it all.

I could have been arrested, I could have been in jail. I was daring. "Fuck you" is what I was saying to the world. "I dare you. I dare you to do something to me." Remember, I came out of the Midwest, Lutheran background, where everything was a sin, including breathing. You bet I wanted to be punished.

Frederick Goodwin, M.D.

The genetic connection may not be about addiction and depression. Instead, the connection may be a disturbed reward system in the brain. In the case of drug addiction or alcoholism, the reward system must be stimulated chemically and immediately rather than diffusely by experience. In order to derive pleasure from an *experience*, one has to work at it, whereas alcohol and drugs can short-circuit all that.

All behavior requires some motivation. Motivation involves an individual making a connection between the behavior and some reward or benefit to the person—getting something he wants or avoiding something she doesn't want. In depression, those reward mechanisms don't appear to work normally, so that a person may lose all capacity for pleasure, by disconnecting the pleasure from the activity. If he ordinarily gets pleasure out of listening to music or interacting with his spouse, depression can wipe out the connection. He doesn't feel any relationship between his actions and feeling rewarded by them, so either he'd be shut down and not do anything, or his activity would be aimless: pacing around, wringing his or her hands, moving and rearranging things. A lack of motivated directedness is central to what happens in depression.

Addicts to alcohol have a very restricted voluntariness. They've lost the capacity to make a conscious choice, very much like a very thirsty person who discovers water will drink it whether it's dirty or not. Powerful biological needs like pleasure and thirst overcome the normal judgments and restraints.

It appears that some of the same chemical mechanisms in the brain that relate to alcohol addiction and cocaine addiction also involve depression and manic-depressive illness. Clinically, it is very important to understand this. If someone is clinically depressed or manic depressive and currently using alcohol or drugs, you have to treat that first. You have to get them detoxified, off the drugs or alcohol, before you can evaluate if they have a real depression underneath. Likewise, if a person whom you're trying to treat for addictive disorder also is depressed or has a history of manic-depressive illness, that has to be addressed or else the treatment for the addiction will have even less chance of succeeding long term. It's difficult enough even if you do treat the depression. It requires a tremendous amount of help and work by the alcoholic not to go back to drinking, and most alcoholics will fall off the wagon quite a few times before they are able to conquer it. Conquering it is that much more difficult if there is also a depressive disorder that is not recognized and not treated.

We've also looked at the sequence of the development of all the disorders. It appears that at least with regard to drug addiction, often the drug addiction is preceded by manic-depressive disorder rather than the other way around. From a probability perspective, if you have a depressive or anxiety disorder in adolescence, the likelihood of developing drug abuse in your twenties doubles. So this means that a very potent method of substance abuse prevention would be early detection and early treatment of those adolescents.

Mary Jones

It occurs to me that part of depression, which is identified with low self-esteem, may be in equal amounts high expectations of yourself. I think perfectionists and those with perfectionist tendencies must have real problems with it. When you turn out to be merely human, it is devastating. So, many alcoholics drink in an effort to self-medicate against depression, which, of course, is absolutely the wrong thing to do.

When I would try to explain to people my experience last time I sobered up, I would tell them about a famous painting traditionally called *Nightwatch in Amsterdam*. It was painted by Rembrandt. It's a scene of a bunch of seventeenth-century gentlemen on the wall of a fortress keeping watch during some battle. For hundreds of years, it has been assumed that it was a night [scene], because it was so dark, until they cleaned it about ten years ago. To everyone's amazement, it's actually a day portrait. That's what it's like when alcoholics stop drinking. Everything is still there, the wall is still there, the kids are still there, all the same people are still there, it's just a lot lighter than you thought it was.

Coming up from the depths of depression or addiction, the world indeed looks lighter. In the aftermath of substance abuse, a lot of work remains to be done to put one's life back together. But if a loved one is recovering from addiction and still sees the world through dung-covered glasses, depression may be shading his or her view. Don't just assume it's a result of the addiction; get help for the depression. Be especially vigilant for suicidal ideas. Keep on being as supportive through the recovery from depression as you were through the recovery from addiction.

I still wonder: If I had never been depressed, would I have taken drugs? And, if I hadn't taken drugs, would I have survived the depression?

Skeptics wonder if antidepressants are addictive—they make you feel good, don't they? You have to come off them slowly, don't you? Sounds like an addiction, doesn't it? But as Dr. Goodwin tells us, "In order for a drug to be addictive, it has to act very quickly. A drug that doesn't have any effect on you for several hours, or several days, like an antidepressant, really has little or no capacity for addiction because you do not associate [pleasure with] taking the drug."

You might think if antidepressants take me from depressed to normal, a few more might take you from normal to high, but they don't work that way. In fact, if a person who was not depressed took them, they most likely would just put him or her to sleep. Antidepressants don't make you high. They don't even make you happy. They simply take away the depression.

8

Love's Labour's Lost: Susan Crosby

One of the most dramatic stories I heard while writing this book was that of Susan Crosby, who spent twenty-four years, some of them married, with Lindsay Crosby, who had a manic-depressive illness. Their long love affair ended when he put a gun to his head and killed himself. For Susan, one source of great pain in her husband's illness was the violent macho personality that would overtake him in his manic phase. The Lindsay that Susan knew and loved was a gentle and caring man.

Lindsay won my heart by buying me a beautiful mare named Bonnie Sue for my birthday. She was my escape through many of these tough times. I would get on her bareback; she would take me places and bring me home. A Rolls-Royce I would not have cared about, but this mare, a black mare with white stockings, was just perfect. She got really sick, and it's funny, because when the same thing happened to one dog we had that was so special, Lindsay couldn't handle it and I had to put him down. That was

really tough, but with Bonnie Sue, I couldn't handle it. I just was
in pieces. Lindsay did it, and I can still see him to this day. He
loaded her up, and he took care of putting her down, and then
he fell down crying so hard. I really felt his love for me as much
on that day as any day, because that was so hard for him.

Lindsay was my best friend actually. He started out as a real
buddy. I wasn't in love with Lindsay at all although we hung
around together all the time. Then one day he said, "You know,
I'm really in love with you." He was just so good and so comfortable and he was there and I could be as silly as I wanted, or
plain as I wanted.

Lindsay's illness was seasonal. In the spring, he would go into
the mania. That took about three months out of the year—going
in, being in it, and coming out. It happened once a year and then
the rest of the time we did normal, suburban, family-type things.
Lindsay was a baseball coach for [son] Kevin, and soccer coach
for [son] Chip. We went to school functions. He was very attentive. He was an incredibly good husband. He did things that
weren't done in those days. He would do the dishes, and vacuum
the floor. He would watch the kids more than I did. I don't like
to get up in the morning. Lindsay always took the morning duty.
Loved to garden, loved to be rather quiet. And he loved me
unconditionally.

During the two and a half years we lived together before we
got married, we'd go out and party and run around and stuff like
that—it wasn't real sedate, so his behavior didn't seem abnormal
at the time. But in 1969 after I had our first son, I started notic-
ing his behavior was really strange. I had gone to Palm Springs
with my mother right after Lindsay, Jr. [Chip], was born, and
when I came back, Lindsay had the house full of people. He had
a huge party going on, and he didn't think there was anything
wrong with that. The conversation was strange, and there were
women who were in my closet wearing all my clothes, using all
my things.

This behavior seemed really out of the blue. It startled me,
because now we were a family, with a baby, and the rules should
have been different. I screamed at him to get the people out and

he couldn't understand why I didn't come in and have a drink, and party with the people.

But I knew something was very, very wrong. Something was more wrong than just a party or somebody just drinking or somebody just having a good time, more wrong than a lot of people just stopping over and visiting. It was very different from that. He looked different. He even would change his appearance, the types of clothes he wore. He'd become a cowboy in a big black cowboy hat, black cowboy boots, put Marlboro in his rolled-up sleeve—he really did become macho man. And his conversation was different. Lindsay was a shy and sensitive person, really very moral. He never swore, and all of a sudden I'm hearing language beyond what I even know. And grabbing broads that went by, and conversation with other guys that was really so far away from who Lindsay was that it didn't make any sense.

I literally threw everybody out. In fact, I took the mattress, and I threw it and everything else out the window. I don't know how I had the strength. I was that angry with what was going on in my house. I took a group of these broads that were using all my clothes, I took their suitcases and dumped all their stuff in the horse shit out back. I was screaming "How can you people come in here when you can see there is a baby here, there's a wife here, how can you do this?"

That was just the beginning. Lindsay just could not understand why I was upset. He took off. When he would get so high, he couldn't sit still. He would drive for miles, he would go to another state. When he was high, he would go in search of a ranch to buy, which is not what he wanted to do. He couldn't maintain a ranch, he knew that and I knew that. He was wheeling and dealing, business deals, meeting people on the highway, picking up everybody he met. Men and women. They would all flock around him because he would spend a lot of money, give away a lot of things. The people he would attract at those times were dangerous people. They were big drinkers, and abusive.

At that time, when I talked to people who knew Lindsay, they said I must have done something wrong. Twenty-five years ago, it was assumed to be the wife's fault. I was told over and

over that if I would just calm down and stop being so hysterical
that it would be all right. And I believed that. I believed that,
although it just about destroyed me. They'd say things like "If
you wouldn't be so hysterical, Susie, if *you* calm down, he'll calm
down. Take a Valium, don't get him so upset. Guys just do this.
You know, guys are allowed a little fun, don't rain on his
parade."

I tried to tell them "Look, this is beyond that. This is dangerous." He didn't have any idea of the connection between his
behavior and the repercussions of what he was doing. If he had
held Chip, he could have just as easily dropped him somewhere
and forgotten about him.

By the time I realized this was happening on an annual basis,
we had our second son, Kevin. I took them and ran [home] to
Alaska to protect them, and to protect myself. I went to an Army
port outside Fairbanks and talked to a psychiatrist. I wanted to
find out what was wrong with me, how I could cause such horrible things to happen. What had I done? I'm destroying my marriage—look what I've done to my husband. Sounds funny today,
but boy, back then that's just exactly the way it was. But the
psychiatrist looked at me and said, "Mrs. Crosby, I don't think
there's anything wrong with you, other than you're trying to live
with a manic-depressive."

That was the first time I had heard that phrase. My mother
and I went to the library [but found only] a few clinical state-
ments in passing, not information, not what it looks like, not
what you do about it, not what the family does about it, not what
the treatment is, not who you go to see.

We just suffered along for about four or five years after that,
riding out the highs. I would take the kids and go to Alaska until
he came down. I could deal with the depression more easily,
because I didn't have to handle all the physical stuff, or all the
other people around.

At this time, when Lindsay was in his late twenties, the
downs were not so devastating. I was a really good codependent.
I would straighten everything out and try to handle all the
money matters and get rid of the people and sell off the horses

he'd bought so he didn't have to face it. I was petrified of him committing suicide at that point, on those downs, because he was so embarrassed and so humiliated at what he'd done.

I also was afraid when he was on the highs. He would drive cars right to the edge of a cliff, tempting fate to see if he got killed. He would call me and say he had just about driven off a cliff, and he'd made it right to the edge and slammed on the brakes. He would get injured jumping in and out of fast-moving cars. He'd get on horses he knew nothing about to try to break them. One time I watched him out in the back. Had both his shoulders dislocated, and two guys standing next to him just popped them back in. He didn't even bat an eye. He didn't feel a thing. He was on the high.

Another time he was working on a movie in Miami, and he picked a knife fight that he couldn't possibly have won with a kid on the street. Thank God there were friends of his around. He would challenge everybody. That wasn't what he was normally like. He was a very gentle person, very calm person, very quiet, very bright, well read.

After I got the diagnosis in Alaska, I came back and just tried to live with it as best I could. Until I really fell apart. A friend came by one day and said, "Susie, you're going with me. We're going to see a psychologist." God bless that woman, an incredible friend. Rather than just watch me flail out there trying to handle this, she got me some help. I still didn't understand mental illness. I still thought it was my fault, no matter what they said. I thought if you understand, or you take care of it a certain way, it can be handled. I had no idea that it's not about emotional support, this was a chemical disorder, and it needs to be treated chemically.

When I first started seeing the doctor, I cried continually. I started doing major work with the therapist under the guise of "How do I help Lindsay?" But really the point was to help Susan to figure out what she needed to do. And finally after one incident, I got Lindsay to come in to therapy, too.

That time, I'd obviously seen the mania coming on, because the kids were in Palm Springs with my mother. I was alone in the house with him and he was really flying, becoming more and more violent. It didn't take long for him to get up that high. He'd say every disgusting thing, that he was going to tell my father who I really was, that I was a whore, every bad thing that you ever hear when somebody is really being degrading to women.

He had a gun and I thought he was going to hurt me. He backed me into the bedroom. I'd try to come out and he'd holler. I can't tell you how frightening this person was. Lindsay would turn the stereo up as loud as possible when he'd get on these highs and turn all the heat off. And he'd lock me in the bedroom. I became so cold, and I hate to be cold, I hate it. That probably got me more than the music, more than everything else. It had been more than twenty-four hours. I was so cold in that room that I tried to sneak out down the hall, and he saw me, and he chased me back in. And I had just had it. I knew it was going to be him or me. So I grabbed a lamp and somehow I broke the cord in half. I swung the lamp at him and I cut open his stomach.

He stood there, and he looked at me, and he looked at his belly, and he looked back at me, and then he left the room. I was shaking so badly I couldn't stop, because I knew I would have killed him. To know that you are capable of doing something that bad is tremendous, and very scary.

He came back in the bedroom a few minutes later, bleeding, with a vacuum cleaner in his hand. Without saying a word, he plugged it in, and he started vacuuming up the glass. He looked at me and he said, "You look upset, Suze, what's wrong? Here, let me fix you a bath." And he took my arm and he walked me into our bathroom, and filled the tub for me. And he was still bleeding. I was waiting for that other person to come back. He said, "Well, I'll leave you alone in here because you probably want some privacy."

I took a bath, and when I came out, I said, "Lindsay, we have to get help. If you don't get help, I'm going to get help, because I'll kill you, I know that now." I was more afraid of me killing him than of him killing me. And I did get help. Lindsay went, too. He tried harder than anyone. To me, he was one of the most courageous men I know, but he couldn't control this disease. It was much bigger than the two of us combined.

We'd work on it in therapy, but everybody wanted to say that his problems were because he was a Crosby, or because of Bing. That had nothing to do with it! It's not that easy to grow up having a celebrity parent, but you can do it. Lindsay was Bing's favorite, so he didn't get a bad deal. I was so tired of hearing that. Had it not been for him having this chemical disorder, Lindsay would have been a fine guy.

People have asked me if it was worse or better because he was a Crosby. It was worse. Everybody wanted to be associated with Bing's son. If his name had been Jones they might not have put up with the behavior, and he could have gotten help sooner and gotten into a hospital sooner. All those people who thought they were protecting Bing's son did Lindsay a great disservice. People need to know that they're actually helping to kill the person they think they're protecting, by not letting them get the help they need, or getting them to a place where they can get help.

Once we knew what it was, Lindsay went to the hospital every year. I'd know when it was time to take him to the hospital, whether I put him in the hospital myself or he went voluntarily after he crashed. He'd let me know. The last time before he died, he stuck a bouquet of flowers on my car, and I knew that's what he meant. We went to the hospital at Calabasas, and he was doing real well there until his so-called friends came and took him out. That's the only time anyone else ever got him out of the hospital, and I think that helped contribute to his death.

When we first tried the lithium, we didn't see any major difference. The depression looked worse. Looking back, I think it looked worse because he was on other drugs that were compounding it. But Lindsay was saying "My God, if the medication is this bad, I can't live like this." The lithium made him sick, and he had tremors, so there went the golf game, and anything else he wanted to do. He couldn't even hold a pen. He would drool, and he would be very lethargic. That was really difficult at the beginning, because he still didn't have a real understanding of it, as much as he'd try. But at different times he would try the drugs again. At the end, he was on lithium. He'd been on lithium for six months when he died. And he had been going regularly to the therapist.

Lindsay was having regular lithium blood level checks during those six months, but when it slipped, they didn't notify us. I was trying at that point not to be so controlling. It was up to Lindsay to take care of Lindsay, which is what I learned in my therapy, to start letting him do it, as much as he could. But he had slipped so far. He did make the phone call to his therapist asking for help, but they couldn't hear him at that point. And they didn't call and say "You'd better come in, Lindsay. Your lithium level has slipped," which I do think is their responsibility.

Psychiatrists shouldn't agree to work with somebody with major depression where it's a life-and-death situation, or a bipolar personality, unless they're going to be there for that person. For some reason psychiatrists don't feel that kind of responsibility, and I am amazed at that. Maybe we as a society haven't demanded that.

The psychiatrist who came in when Lindsay was in the hospital told me, "Jeez, he's great, you know, and his cowboy stuff . . ." and I said, "You don't understand! He's not a fuckin' cowboy! He knows he's not a cowboy. You haven't met Lindsay yet." Obviously I had no confidence in that one.

I really believed something would come along, and if it doesn't, so help me God, I'm going to scream about this as much as I can so that more people talk about it, because it touches so many people in this country.

I don't think that lithium is the cure-all that they publicize. It helps, but [for Lindsay, it was] like a Band-Aid on a major incision. There are too many variables that can upset their systems.

You need the therapy, too, because of all the damage that gets done in the interim, and we can all use a little help that way, but if you don't have medication, you don't have anything. There's nothing even to work with. Lindsay could have been in therapy every day of his life talking about every traumatic thing that happened. Wouldn't have made a fucking difference.

I used to get so upset. People would say two things to me: "Well, he's in therapy, isn't he?" and "Well, he's on lithium, isn't he?" Hey, he was in major therapy and on major lithium and he took a gun and blew his brains out. I don't want another person to tell me that lithium is the answer, or therapy is the answer. Lithium is the beginning, and I'm glad there's something that will kind of help. But it doesn't do it. Usually the people [for whom it works well] have had real strong support around them, and that's contributed, probably as much as the lithium.

What if in Lindsay's case everybody in his family, and all of his friends, or the hangers-on that I do not consider friends, if they had been supportive about what Lindsay needed to do to save his life? If they had helped him, if he looked a little shaky, to get to the doctor, or called me to say "It looks like the lithium is slipping"? That would have helped him and probably saved his life.

We had started living separately before that because we did not want to lose each other. I didn't respond well to people saying "He's a jerk, so go away," or "He's mentally ill—why don't you leave?" They would not tell a woman whose husband had cancer to leave him. I couldn't believe what I was hearing all the time, that I'm supposed to leave because he's sick, because we don't have the answers. And I tried. I tried to start another life, for the good of the kids. I couldn't do it. I missed Lindsay too much and I appreciated his struggle, too. I could feel it in the air, if Lindsay was in trouble. He could feel it if I was. But we had two houses so we could live apart when he was high. I was afraid for the kids and afraid for me. And we didn't have the answers yet.

At the end, we had to get a divorce because of financial reasons. That was the only way to protect any money for the kids and me, and that's pretty sad. If we were married, I'd have to pay all the claims against Lindsay from when he was manic. A great deal was lost, because it wasn't done when it should have been. I got very upset when the attorneys wouldn't understand what I was dealing with.

Attorneys, doctors, police—even the people we turn to for help don't understand. Most of the manic-depressives are thrown in jail. That's how they're treated. I bailed Lindsay out of jail all the time.

One time it was funny. Sick funny, but funny. Lindsay called late one night to say he was coming out to the house to pick up our dog and told me to put it outside the door. It was an excuse. He didn't want to see me, but no woman needed to have this dog. He said he was on his way out and he was going to slit my throat. Now at this point—I can't believe it, it was really stupid —but I said something very blasé, like "Okay, Linds, come out and slit my throat." And I thought I'd better take a bath, this means hospital or jail, and I'd better get in gear for something. So I took a bath, and got ready for Lindsay to come out and slit my throat. Which he certainly could have done. But I also knew that he couldn't maintain anything, so I didn't think he'd make it. He was in North Hollywood, and Hidden Hills is a ways out, so I thought something would happen before he ever got there. It did.

He decided on his way out to slit my throat to stop off and buy a pizza, because he thought I might be hungry. This was how his thinking went; this is the insanity of this stuff. He drove up on the sidewalk and got out of his car, and the police picked him up for drunk walking and threw him in jail. He called me from jail, said he was just going to get me a pizza and the police arrested him. And he said he thought he would piss on everybody that's in the jail cell.

"Oh, good idea, Lindsay," I said, thinking "Let the rest of them see what's going on, so I don't have to deal with it."

"Will you come down and bail me out?" he asked.

Well, I didn't have any money, and I didn't have a car, and it was raining, but I knew if I didn't bail him out somebody else would and then he would be back at my doorstep and he *might* slit my throat, so I thought I'd better get down there. I called my sister-in-law, Barbara, to bring the cash, and I borrowed a friend's car, and drove to Van Nuys in the rain.

I took the money to the bailiff, and then the bailiff said, "Okay, I release him into your custody."

"No no no," I said, "You don't understand. I'm not taking him home. He's violent. I'm here to see that he isn't going anywhere. I'll pay his bail and you keep him here."

"No," he said. "He's released to you the minute that bail is paid."

I didn't know what to do. I just knew he couldn't be out on the street, because he'd hurt himself or me or whomever he came in contact with. So here I was in a battle with the bailiff trying to take my money and me saying "No no no no!" I called the psychologist that we were working with, and I said, "How do I get him in the hospital?" In California, you can't commit someone against their will.

The psychologist said, "Let me see if I can find two ambulance drivers who will come get him."

I knew Lindsay would respect their authority, and if I said, "This is the way it's going to be," and if I looked as though I had people backing me up, he'd go along and commit himself. Because he really didn't want to be out there flailing. He really didn't.

When I knew the ambulance drivers were in the back, I finally paid the bailiff the money. He let Lindsay out and the gurney was right there, and the drivers just told Lindsay to lie down and he did. And he put his big cowboy hat over his chest, and they wheeled him into the ambulance.

I climbed in the ambulance in the front, sweating bullets. I didn't know what I was going to do with him if he wouldn't go in. And the ambulance driver looked over at me and said, "So, tell me, Mrs. Crosby, how long has your husband been a rodeo rider?"

"You see, that's kind of a part of the problem," I said. "He isn't."

When we got out at Brockman, he started screaming "Patricia Susan Marlin!"—he always called me by my maiden name when he was like that—"Patricia Susan Marlin, we don't even have insurance! I can't sign in!"

I was saying "Don't pay any attention to him, he doesn't know what he's saying." We didn't, you know, but they believed me, thank God, not him.

There was no family insurance or anything and to have to pay for it out of our pocket did make a difference when he needed treatment. It limited us greatly. We had to decide "Do the kids get this or do we pay this hospital bill; it's becoming large?" Many of the hospital bills and things like that my parents paid. It was a big drain on all of us, and that was a major problem. Actually Bing had offered to help, and I was too proud to ask him. I hadn't been brought up that way. He always said, "What can I do?" As with anybody else dealing with this disease, I didn't know how to tell someone to help me, because I didn't know how to fix this.

I have cluster headaches, which have been one of the reasons at the end, with Lindsay, that I wasn't there. Sometimes I think God came up and put a rock on me and said, "You will not move, Susan. This is going to play out the way it's going to play out."

I was in bed for about three years. I didn't leave this upstairs room. Almost three years. I would get up maybe one or two days out of the week. Lindsay started having strokes toward the end, too, so when he was down, he was real down. He was slipping and his heels would collapse—real tough stuff.

I could hear him shuffling around and barely making it, but I couldn't take care of him. It was horrible. Finally I told Lindsay, "One of us isn't going to make it." This is too hard to say, even now. . . . "The kids need a strong parent. So you're going to have to go back to the condo. I can't take care of you. I've got to get myself well before anything. I really feel like one of us is going to die. And, Lindsay, it won't be me. It can't be me. I've got to take care of the kids."

So I made him go back out to Calabasas, to the condo, and

live with those creeps he was around. I hated being forced into that choice, but I knew I had to save me.

I had moved him back in right before he died. I was stronger, I'd gotten better. But I still hear me making that decision.

He was on lithium when he died, he was working hard with his therapist, but he was really beat up from this happening so many times. He was fifty years old and he had the body of a seventy-five-year-old man. I had just come back from Alaska and Lindsay had picked me up at the airport. He had just found out that his trust fund income was going to be cut in half. Lindsay was so in debt from the last high, he was very nervous about our finances anyway. He kept saying "I can't believe what I've done to you." He kept ruminating on the money he'd spent, and the other broads and all the stuff he'd done. I said, "Lindsay, there's something physically wrong with you. Look at me. I'm not upset. We will make it. I can see a way out of this. Look, we'll sell my house. We'll manage. We might have to change the way we live, but so what? It's fun to start all over, you know? This is great. You're doing well on your medicine, we have another chance here." That's how I saw it.

He only saw it as the end of the world, that he could never pay back the money, and all the terrible people that had been around him were going to come in and hurt the kids and me. He didn't want me to sell everything I had. He was just so devastated, he said, "I can't do this to you, Susie. I just can't do this."

It doesn't take much when you're taking lithium to get thrown off an even keel. He kept going down and down until he was almost catatonic. Sunday night, I had him call the doctor rather than me calling, because I wanted him to hear Lindsay's voice. It took Lindsay five minutes to dial the phone. When they answered, he could barely talk. He kept saying, so slowly "Help, I need . . . help. I really . . . need . . . help."

Whoever he got on the other end of the phone said, "Well, the psychiatrist isn't here. I don't know what you can do. Maybe you could make an appointment next Tuesday." Well, Lindsay was dead Monday.

If we had known the level was low and it had been brought up, he would have been alive. We could have handled everything, because I could see the difference in the lows. Everybody needs to be more educated about this. Lindsay's biggest problem in fighting this disease, more so than mine, was everybody else saying to him he could straighten up if he wanted to, that if he didn't want this to happen, he could pull himself together. And because he came out of that generation, he believed it, too. And that was the killer, that's the killer to anybody that's dealing with it. It's a chemical imbalance, so it's going to be chemicals that will work in the end.

Although for many people lithium is the answer, since Lindsay's death new medications, and combinations of medications, have come on the market that also are successful in treating bipolar disorder.

9
Suicide

I couldn't sleep. I couldn't sit still to watch TV. There was nothing in the world I cared to read. I looked in on the children again and again. I roamed the house. I thought of escape—go get drunk? Drive off into the night? But to where? I found myself in the kitchen, opening cupboards—looking for what?

On a top shelf, safely out of reach of the children, was a blue and red and white can of drain cleaner. In a cartoon, or a dream sequence, a beam of light would have shone upon it. I put out my hand, remembering hearing of one who had died this way, thinking it must have been awfully painful, though. At that moment, the pain of burning out your insides seemed small. But the import of what I was contemplating was enormous.

I walked in to where Bill sat in his easy chair, watching something pleasant on TV, and said, "Bill. I'm in trouble."

I never really tried to kill myself, although many times it seemed the only solution, the only way out of the pain. When I was younger, I thought how much better off I would be; as a wife and mother, I thought how much better off my family would be. Both were delusions born of the illness, for hopelessness is as much a part of depression as fever is a part of the flu. And in my saner moments, I knew that the psychic burden of losing their mother to suicide would scar them far more than would dealing honestly with my illness.

Jules Feiffer

In the year or two after my first marriage broke up, the guilt was so enormous that I used to think that the easiest thing would be to die, and if I hadn't had a seven-year-old. . . . One of the things that got me through was I never believed that parents have the option of suicide. It's one thing to do it to yourself, it's another thing to do it to your family. You can't do it. You simply aren't allowed to, because you're taking them with you. But there would be these moments where the guilt and the rage and the self-destructiveness would be so strong that while not trying to kill myself, I would do my best to arrange accidents.

I was living in the Upper West Side of Manhattan before it was fashionable. I would come home in those days so drunk I could hardly stand up. One morning I found that I'd left the keys outside in the door all night, where anybody could have gotten in. That seemed to me a kind of prayer: "Come and take my life, please. I can't do it, but Mr. Outside, Mr. Burglar, Mugger, Killer, come and do it." That so stunned and shocked me that it made me more cautious, because it put me on the edge and I came back from the edge.

Mary Jones

I can remember carrying around, for a long time, a Gillette razor blade in a blue plastic case with the date of my twenty-first birthday written on it. It was my vow that if I had not figured out a good reason for living by the time I was twenty-one, I would do away with myself. By the time I got to be twenty-one, I actually still hadn't figured out a good reason for living, but I thought I should give it more time. And now I think the reason you shouldn't kill yourself is because it's just so interesting to see how it all turns out. It's like being hooked on a soap opera: "Good grief, what will happen next?"

I do know the kinds of thoughts I have when I'm depressed. One is thinking that if someone were to say to me that I had incurable cancer, my first reaction would be a sense of profound relief. "Thank God I don't have to struggle with this shit any more."

I keep thinking the easiest way if you were going to kill yourself would be to get in a warm tub and slit your wrists. But it would be such a mess for the people who found you. It would be so thoughtless of you. People always shit when they die. I was a police reporter for a long time; corpses are really unattractive. You think, "God, what an awful thing to do to whoever comes across you."

I'm trying to remember what I said to my friend who tried to kill herself. I think it was "Well, shit, baby, I love you."

Jim Jensen

Everybody gets the blues from time to time; that's normal. The blues are like a hangnail. Depression is a paralyzing shotgun wound. You lose all desire to participate in life. They use a Greek term in this business, anhedonia, the absence of joy.* You can intellectually tell yourself, and your friends and loved ones can tell you, "You have intelligence, you have talent, you have physical health, you have money . . ." It doesn't amount to a hill of beans, because you can't enjoy it. It is impossible to enjoy it. Because you can't feel alive. Can you possibly imagine what it's like not to feel alive? Where you don't enjoy the sunshine, or a movie, or a book? You can't concentrate. Food has no appeal. The spark is buried, you feel like you're walking dead. So if you're walking dead, why not go all the way? You are thoroughly

* Literally, the absence of pleasure in acts that are normally pleasurable.

negative, and the only thing that you believe will relieve you of the pain and not-feeling of life is death.

In twelve-step programs—I am in one of them—some people say that there are no coincidences, that coincidences are just God's way of remaining anonymous. When I was in the hospital in Minnesota being treated for depression, three times I set out to do it. I never mentioned suicide within the confines of the hospital, because then I would have been locked up and I wouldn't have the freedom to go outside and take a walk. So I kept those thoughts to myself. I wasn't stupid. Because if I wanted to kill myself, I had to get out of the hospital, right? I walked to the bridge, there wasn't a car on it, nothing, just me. It was very cold, and it was very dark, and I looked down and wondered what it would be like. As I put my foot up on the railing, all of a sudden a car appeared. A man got out of the car and said, "Are you all right?"

Embarrassed, I responded, "Yeah, I'm okay," put my foot down, and I continued walking to the other side of the bridge.

Another time I was sitting in the little coffeeshop near the hospital thinking about going down to the bridge. A young man walked in who was the son of a lady I knew in New York, who was going to school out in Minnesota. I'd met him once in my life. He walked into this out-of-the-way coffeeshop, saw me, intuitively knew that I was in trouble, and sat down. What do you think the odds are of that happening? Millions and millions to one. So that stopped me.

Then I figured out a new way. I thought I could go to the airport and rent a car, then drive as far into the woods as I possibly could. I even thought about camouflaging the car. And an old Swede whom I had met at a meeting in the hospital came walking into the hospital as I was walking out. He was coming to see me. So we sat down, and I told him what I was going to do, and he said, "Too many people want you to live."

I said, "I don't want to live."

He said, "We don't really care what you think."

A. John Rush, M.D.

Probably everybody, somewhere in their life, has at least had a fleeting thought of "Well, gee, one more thing like this and I'll kill myself." Not everybody sits around and ponders suicide multiple hours per day, multiple days per week. That is just not normal. That is a person with a very serious problem. With a very severe stress like a terminal illness or a bankruptcy, sure, some people can think about suicide for multiple days. If you put suicidal thinking together with no eating or no sleeping, they can't concentrate, can't make decisions, now you're talking major depression. Clearly bankruptcy, childbirth, death of a loved one, another medical illness, substance abuse, or genes can all precipitate it, but it's precipitating an illness. It's not just precipitating a reaction.

Judith Belushi Pisano

It seems totally foreign to me now. It was totally foreign to me before that time. I could never understand how anyone could kill themselves, but my life was just extremely unhappy, I guess. I really couldn't find anything that was interesting me. You know, when George Sand killed herself, her note said something like "I'm bored." It wasn't like I was bored, exactly, but it was almost that blasé. I just didn't want to do it any more. But I thought, "I'll try, I'll go on for a while, because everyone says it's going to change." And I did remember that I used to enjoy things and have things I wanted to do, and I still had people I loved, a lot of people, and I knew they loved me. That feeling of not wanting to hurt them made me say "Well, I'll hang on, I'll hang in there."

About a year and a half after John died, I started saving my sleeping pills. I thought I would just get another prescription and keep it around so that I'd have it if I wanted to. That was an action, a plan. I recognized when I thought of it that there was something serious about that, and I chose not to tell that to my psychiatrist because I didn't want him to know how serious I was.

I thought, "If I want to do this, I don't want to give signals to someone who could try to stop me." Maybe I really wasn't as serious as it seemed, but at that point I thought I was serious, and I wanted to have a free hand to do it if I were going to do it.

One day I read something in the paper that made me very sad. It was one of those articles that you read that is just meaningless and senseless and sad. It was about an eighty-year-old lady who had gone out to the mailbox, and her neighbor's dogs had attacked her. Her husband came out and tried to fight the dogs off, and he was injured, and she was killed. It really made me hysterical. It just seemed so stupid, these two old people, the man's fighting to save his wife, and the dogs kill her.

That was one of the times I was really thinking about suicide. Life was just too negative, it made me too sad, I couldn't handle it. A friend of mine came over, and I said something to her about understanding why people would kill themselves. She got very upset and started talking about how that wasn't right and people shouldn't kill themselves and there's a bigger reason for things, even if we couldn't understand them, and you just had to hang in —the whole pep talk. She was very upset, because she knew that I was not talking in the abstract, but that I was talking about myself. I sensed that; I sensed her concern, and I sensed how upset she was. She was almost crying, and that feeling of someone caring so much seemed to shake it away from me. Had I not spoken with her, I don't know if. . . . Sometimes it may be that simple, reaching out and someone reacting.

Susan Crosby

[When Lindsay's brother Dennis killed himself seventeen months after Lindsay's death] it hit Kevin really hard. Now there are two adults who are giving permission to suicide, and that's real scary. Even though they were numb when their dad died, all of a sudden their Uncle Dennis dies, and it just . . .

[Dennis's wife] Arlene had been screaming "Please help Dennis!" and I was screaming "Please help Lindsay!" and nobody heard us. Maybe now with two men dead, people will listen. And to make sure that we do, we're going to have annual family gatherings so that all the kids and the cousins know there's a [safe] place where somebody can speak up.

Linda Freeman, M.D.

If the child is talking about suicide, she or he is at some significant degree of risk, and the parent should try to find a professional to help. Sometimes that is very difficult for the parent to hear. Very commonly, I'll hear a parent say "Oh, they just want attention." Then I'll say "But what do they want it for? And if they need it, then let's give it, at least at this point."

The suicide rate in children under twelve is quite low. There have been maybe two to three cases in a long period of time in the United States of children under twelve actually committing suicide. Nonetheless, when a child is talking about it, he or she may be in real distress, and suicide truly may be the intention. If anything, the low rate may have more to do with their lack of cognitive ability necessary to organize an effective plan that will complete the suicide. A major risk factor for completion, of course, is the child having access to the tools that can help them, like firearms in particular.*

---

* In a study published in the *New England Journal of Medicine,* the presence of one or more firearms in the home was associated with close to a five times higher risk of suicide.

Jan Fawcett, M.D.

Between 93 and 95 percent of suicides are suffering a psychiatric illness, most commonly depression, substance abuse associated with depression, or schizophrenia. (And in science, if it were 100 percent, I'd be suspicious.)

Is there such thing as rational suicide, as Dr. Kevorkian would have us believe? Possibly in certain instances, but my concern with that movement is that there may be a lack of sophistication about assessing for the presence of depression underlying that decision. People in clinical depression may have a "reason" for killing themselves that they or others come up with; cast in philosophical garb, their decision sounds rational. They may or may not have a terminal illness, but that does not mean the depression won't respond to treatment. Often people will justify depression because something bad happened. If that were enough of a reason to justify it, we'd all be depressed.

[I'm not comfortable with] the implication that a person should commit suicide if his or her illness is too much of a burden on others. I wonder whose decision is it really? Where does this lead to? A major issue today is life quality and a person's right to decide on his or her own life. Many assert this right, but for many, when the depression is treated, they no longer want to die.

It depends on how severely ill the patient is. Some people can ask for help and some can't. They're distrustful or feel it's not acceptable to ask for help. Some people have better coping skills, although even they can be overwhelmed.

My own work suggests that many people who kill themselves develop tremendous anxiety and panic attacks prior to suicide. They are in severe psychic pain; the pain of going on is too excruciating to tolerate, it's never going to stop, there is no relief. Suicide seems like a logical thing to do.

There is not a lot of [evidence] yet, but it appears that only 7 to 10 percent of attempters die by suicide. That's pretty low. It appears that attempters and completers are two distinct groups that overlap.

One difference between the two groups is that the completers have a higher rate of substance abuse. Alcohol plus other substances like marijuana or coke increases the risk by ten times. It has been shown that depressives' risk is thirty to ninety times higher than the general population, times ten with double abuse! (With just alcohol abuse, the increased risk is not as great.)

An abrupt improvement in symptoms often increases risk. Not all symptoms improve at the same rate. [The problem is when] energy and the ability to make decisions improves, but hopefulness doesn't improve as fast.

Sometimes suicide attempts are an effort to communicate, an attempt to live. Less commonly, they are a rehearsal, trying to get up the nerve. Self-cutting or burning is often called a suicide attempt, but is not so much an attempt to die as an attempt to relieve pain and is usually seen more in severe personality disorder associated with depression.

Seven to 10 percent of those who attempt suicide end up killing themselves, and 60 to 70 percent of those who talk about it to relatives or friends do it within six months. *A suicide attempt should never be blown off.* Either consider it an attempt to die or a negotiation for more help. If one of my patients makes an attempt, I take it as a message that I'm not doing enough, that they need more.

Depression is treatable if someone recognizes it. If you suspect someone is suicidal, and he rejects your help, it's hard to prevent. You can't force someone over time to accept treatment. You can hope they get better enough so they don't want to die. You cannot leave them alone; people rarely commit suicide in front of other people.

If the worst happens, I would say to the family "Predicting suicide is like finding a needle in haystack, even for professionals. We did our best, but like cancer or any other illness, you fight the battle as best you can, but sometimes you lose."

The point is that suicide may not be 100 percent preventable, but we should not take the position that it's inevitable. If we can get people into treatment, many can be saved.

Rod Steiger

The thing I remember about suicide in particular that bothered me was not the idea of killing myself, but that I would leave a mess for my loved ones to see. That shows you how far gone I was. "He's not worried about killing himself, but he shouldn't leave a mess." I didn't discuss these thoughts with my wife. These are the deep dark secrets of being mentally disturbed. But the love of my wife, her presence, so attentive, would give me a little reason not to.

Once I started looking for a rowboat, to row out to sea. I couldn't find a rowboat around here. Then I stopped myself. I had a millimeter of control left someplace. If I had been just a little sicker, I probably would have done it. I still was healthy enough to know that it would hurt whoever I left behind tremendously, and I couldn't do that to my daughter, and I couldn't do that to my wife. The initial impulse was very strong. But you get an impulse and then you fight it with whatever physical health you have and whatever mental health you have left. In a depression, you're way out of balance. Anything is possible on a given second. Life can change one second to another. You can go from heaven to hell in less than a second. But you have more chance if you're healthy, to do something about where you're going.

Rona Barrett

I never quite understood how I could be sitting here so happy and suddenly—whap!! This huge dark cloud would descend and envelop me like somebody was putting me in some kind of gauze sheet. I could see, I could breathe, but I was being suffocated.

And sometimes as quickly as this cloud descended, it would lift and disappear. For the longest time they treated it as normal depression. "Why do you feel this way? What's happening in your life that makes you have these feelings of hopelessness and helplessness?"

I could always come up with a lot of reasons. I realized that a lot of it was really attached to who I was and what I was, which were often in conflict with one another. The image that I had created for myself in my career in no way matched the person that I was as an individual. I would hear all kinds of things about the perception of others toward me. One was tremendous awe. One was fear. One was loathing. One was great admiration. One was love, but how do you loathe somebody and love somebody? What is it that these two separate people or groups of people were seeing? Why was it that somebody could look at me and see only hatred and disgust, and another group could look at me and see only love and honesty? It was producing for me, from the outside, the same feelings that I was producing on the inside. There were moments when I hated the work that I was doing even though I was enormously good at it.

Yes, what I had wanted all my life was success, recognition, fame, doing something that I thought would be good and positive and valuable. After I got there, a series of circumstances occurred that resulted in me hating myself so much that I just wanted to lay down and die. I thought I'd go to sleep for the weekend and when I would wake up, I would be different. But I nearly died.

Several things were occurring at the same time in my life. One, I had received a great deal of recognition for being one of the most powerful new voices in Hollywood. The other was my assault on the beginning of what I saw as a dangerous drug movement in this country. Lots of people were dabbling, and more than dabbling. I knew; they knew I knew. Several of my friends, very successful young men both in the entertainment industry and on the periphery of the industry, died from major drug overdoses—cocaine. So I began doing lots of editorials, and my film reviews of pictures were now stating things about the drug culture. I was always giving little warnings: This is a dangerous film because it glorifies drug use. It wasn't just the glorification of it, but they just were not disseminating accurate information. At several parties that I went to with some of the most prominent people in this community, many way older than myself, many my age at the time, I literally heard people say "Shh! Shh! Dummy up, here comes Rona. Get the stuff away! Hide it!"

It was a cross-section of this society and this community and I've always maintained that if it's happening here, it's happening elsewhere, too. This place is the research center of social behavior in this society. If you want to test an idea, you test it here in Hollywood. Hollywood tests it via its films or via its television shows. If there is public acceptance of those ideas, then you can see them permeating throughout the entire society. It's very scary. Therefore, I've always felt I had an enormous responsibility regarding my profession. When I treated the drug situation very seriously here, there were many in this community who considered me a pariah. On one hand, I had a great deal of respect for the position I was taking. On the other, the external pressures made me feel like a monster! I would hear people say, "Get her away. We don't want her. Why does she have to do this? Why can't she be like one of us?"

I began endlessly asking myself "Am I doing right? Am I doing wrong? Who am I? I'm not God! Why does my job make me feel that I have to do this?"

I began causing myself a lot of internal grief. I was involved in a very unsatisfying relationship with a young man that had gone off and on for ten or eleven years. We were two people who couldn't live with each other or live without each other.

One day I was sued for the first time in my career. I knew my story was right, but management didn't support me. After about a year of talking every day to lawyers, the management of the broadcasting entity for whom I worked said, "Let's just settle this thing, let's just get it out of our hair, it's ridiculous."

I kept saying "But I'm not guilty of something. Why should I settle something when I know I'm right? I know I'm right." They told me not to worry; let's just get it out of our hair, and

blah, blah, blah . . . so forth and so on. So they made a settle-
ment, and then the company turned around and sued me for the
money that they settled for.

I didn't have that kind of money. It was quite a large sum.
With the help of a very, very prominent person in this community who took me to the bank, and got me a loan, I was able to
pay off my employer the money that he swore I would not have
to pay anybody. It taught me a great big lesson. I kept saying to
myself "How does one get punished for being right? What is
this really all about? What lesson am I to learn? I just don't
understand. If I were wrong—fine! But I'm not wrong. Why am
I being punished like this?"

During this whole period, while all of these other things
were going on, I lost eighteen friends in twenty months, the
majority of whom were thirty-five and under. They all died. A
lot of them of drugs, and a lot of them from strange diseases that
hit them. It was just the weirdest period. I developed a cough
during this period, and I couldn't sleep. For three, four months,
I was just a walking nightmare, trying to get through a broadcast,
coughing my way, begging could I pretape because I was too
embarrassed to continue to choke on the air.

My gentleman friend promised to do something with me one
night. It was a big charity event, and I went to get my hair done,
despite the fact that I was sick. I didn't know how sick I was at
the time. When I got back from the hairdresser, there was a
message on the answering service that he wasn't going to go with
me that night. And coupled with all this pressure, and all of this
unbelievable, for me, grief that I didn't understand—I was just so
tired. What I didn't know is that for three and a half months, I
had had walking pneumonia. During this period, in order for me
to sleep, because my eyes were getting blacker and blacker underneath, the doctor gave me sleeping pills, which I had never
taken before. I looked at the bottle of sleeping pills and said, "If
this is the career that I wanted, if this is what life is all about, if
. . . if . . . if . . . if, I want out. I don't ever want to be in this
life again. Not this way." I took the whole bottle of pills thinking
I would just go to sleep for the weekend. A friend called me, I

guess, as I was slipping off. She got panicked. She raced to my house, and it took the ambulance an hour and a half to find my house. They pronounced me dead in the ambulance, and my doctor, whom she had called, said, "If you don't keep working on her, you guys will be dead."

When I woke up, I was sad. I was sad because I realized that I may have done something that was injurious, and sad because I knew that I was going to be facing a new world. But also a part of me was joyful, because I realized that I had to find a new path for myself, something that would make me feel proud. It was time to learn that there was no way that I should allow outside forces to play havoc with my mental being. All I had been doing was catering to the victim side of Rona, the crippled side of Rona. And I wasn't going to do that any more.

Barbara Parry, M.D.

Women are more likely to attempt suicide, but men are more likely to complete suicides. Men also tend to use more violent means, like gunshot wounds right to the head. Their suicides are more aggressive. Women are more likely to take an overdose and then that often can be salvaged, more like the cry for help. And they tend to do this earlier in the treatment, whereas men would wait till the very end, until they feel like there's no hope and no way out. They won't acknowledge it; it's more denial on their part. But each should be evaluated on an individual basis.

Joan Rivers

Everything went wrong. Edgar had killed himself, I was fired from Fox, Melissa was in college in the East, I was stuck alone in a big house, and the career was nowhere. I had nobody. I have no real family, just a sister I'm not close to.

I was alone upstairs. I opened a drawer and there was a gun. I took the gun and sat down in my dressing room, with the gun in my lap, and I thought, "It would be so easy. I want to be out of all this pain. I just want to be out of it." It's not even so much pain, but the aching weariness of the whole thing; I just wanted to be out of it all. Oh, I was so down, I thought, "I can't fight any more. I can't go on any more. I'm so weary, God, what's the point?" But when my dog came in and sat in my lap, I thought, "Who's going to take care of Spike?"

I know it sounds very corny, but for the sake of my daughter, I couldn't let myself go under. I thought, "My husband did it, all right, but if I did it, my daughter doesn't have a chance." I said to myself, "Edgar's gone under; I cannot be the second." For most people, suicide is just a thought, it's just a concept. Then after it becomes reality in your family, it's a definite way out. That's why suicides' children have such a high rate of suicide, because it's a very viable option: "Yeah, well, I can either go to church or I can kill myself. Mom did this and Dad did that." I said to myself, "I cannot let her see this."

I'm always slightly depressed. People ask, "Is the cup half full or half empty?" And I'm always the one to say it's half empty. I'm always the one who sees the down side of everything.

One of the two times in our marriage when I was in a bad depression was after my play *Fun City* closed. I was terribly low. I couldn't believe that this play that I'd worked so hard on was not going to run. The second time was after I was fired from Fox. My husband, who was battling his own depression, couldn't support me, which is one of the reasons it was so hard for me to crawl out of my depression. We weren't there for each other, and that made it very difficult for both of us. Instead of reaching out to help each other, we both were going down at the same time.

Edgar had had a heart attack and bypass surgery, and that means you'll never be the same again. Then he had felt publicly humiliated when he had been fired as producer of the show I hosted for Fox. He went into a major depression and never came out of it. At the same time, when I was fired, I went into a depression myself, which is one of the reasons my husband killed himself. We couldn't help each other. It was a house of two people for whom the sun just wasn't shining.

A week before he killed himself, we took a trip. Everything was wonderful about England, wonderful about Ireland, but we were both so down, we couldn't enjoy it. He stayed in bed in the hotel room and stared at the ceiling. And I just got out and walked and walked and walked and walked and walked all over. But I couldn't help him and he couldn't help me.

He stopped reading. This was a man who read—you have no idea! The bedroom was full of books, it was like a joke. We got the *New York Times* Sunday Book Review first, and then we would go to the bookstore, no matter what. That was our big thing. There was always something that we had to have, and we always came back with shopping bags full. But he stopped even going to the bookstore. He wouldn't even go in to look. He stopped wanting to see people, I understood that. He stopped wanting to go out, okay. Especially in California. You don't want to go to Spago where everybody says with a leer, "Look who just walked in." Then he stopped caring about the business. Okay. That's all part of it. But he stopped reading, and that was when I knew we were in very big trouble.

When he finally went for therapy right before he committed suicide, he wouldn't talk about his problems. They talked about South Africa, where Edgar was from. Imagine, South Africa! And when he committed suicide, the psychiatrist said, "I had no idea." He said, "What a charming man. We would talk about all the problems in South Africa, and your husband's viewpoints, and blah blah blah . . . I had no idea." Edgar was able to hide it very, very well. Except in the house.

Looking back, it was all over the place. Looking back, he had checked with the lawyers on the will, and looking back, he had straightened up his desk, and looking back, when he went to Philadelphia, he took all the important papers with him, he met with his business partner. Looking back you see all the red flags, but at the time, I wasn't seeing any flags. I couldn't even see myself. I felt like "Leave me alone. Leave me alone. I'm the one this has happened to, not you." But when you look back, you see of course it was all there.

It's so different from any other bereavement, because of the guilt. I work very hard for suicide prevention now. No matter how many times you say "It's not your fault, it's their fault, right, right, right, I got it," you still say "I should have made the one more phone call. I should have been there with my hand out at one more point."

How do you recover? I don't know if you ever really recover. I think the anger pulls you through. You get through the guilt by saying to yourself, which I truly believe, that you can't take a splinter out in depression; a person has got to cure themselves. You can't do it for them, there's no way. If a friend has cancer, you can't take the cancer out of them. It's the same thing. If they're lucky, they're going to come out of it.

Sometimes when the burden was just too much, when I was really depressed, I'd turn the depression to anger. At one point, I was sitting at my husband's desk, and I was so angry that I took the desk, which he had loved, and emptied every drawer and threw it all away. Turned all that emotion into energy. It was like getting back at something, beating somebody up for making you feel the way you feel. And that was very helpful.

One of things in the house that was absolutely my husband's was a medicine chest that he kept all his stuff in. I went in and, like a child, I emptied everything and threw it all away, whap! whap!, in the trash, yelling "Son of a bitch!"

I get very physical and that will pull me out of a depression, kind of like sports, or running or anything. The body finds a way. When you're that low, or unlucky enough, nature takes over and says "Okay, we've got to do something now. She's had it." And turns it into rage or turns it into activity, so those little endorphines start jumping around.

In her acceptance speech for the daytime Emmy, Joan Rivers said that Edgar was the one who always told her to hang in there, that things would turn around, but that he forgot that advice for just one moment in that Philadelphia hotel room. One moment is all it takes—one moment of hopelessness and lack of belief in available support, one moment in which the dramatic cry for help accidentally slips over the edge into death, one moment that can lead to a lifetime of agony for those left

*behind. Maybe if we pay attention to the behavior of our loved ones, if
we listen to the pain and take it seriously, if we seek out competent
professional help and aren't embarrassed to risk being wrong, we can
prevent some of these deaths. Some, but not all. And if we are left
behind in the wake of a suicide, we must absolve ourselves with the sure
knowledge that, ultimately, we could not have prevented it. As Susan
Crosby and, in the next chapter, Leslie Garis tell us, even when the
worst happens, we do survive; life goes on.*

10
Leslie Garis

On a bleak winter day during the Christmas holiday, I drove up from my parents' Manhattan home to interview Leslie Garis in Connecticut. Rose Styron, a neighbor of Garis and her husband, playwright Arthur Kopit, had introduced us by phone, although I was familiar already with Garis's work for the New York Times Magazine. *We curled up on the sofa in her wood-paneled study, sipping tea and chatting like old friends. Maybe it was the atmosphere, or the camaraderie, maybe it was our children playing together in the next room that elicited a strong feeling of empathy. Writers, mothers, inheritors of fame, we have a lot in common; even the quality and symptoms of her despair were familiar. Yet as her tale unfolded, I realized how much worse the experience of depression can be, and how lucky I really am.*

I was touched most deeply by the reactions of her children, listening outside the heavy wood doors, listening perhaps for clues to their mother's behavior, and by how shaken she was to discover them there. Although Garis and I differ on how much children can and should know about a parent's illness, she has an acute awareness of what some of their worries may be; she, too, grew up in a house of sadness.

When I was about twelve, my father had his first hallucination. I thought some terrible curse, some horrendous evil thing had settled upon this sweet man and was going to destroy him. It was his battle to the death, and who was going to win? I saw him as victimized both by his mother, whose depression and fearfulness had crippled him, and by this illness which we couldn't put a name to. For a while they were calling it schizophrenia, and I felt good about that because there was a name to it. But I don't think it was. I think it was depression.

Looking back on my family history, I see that my paternal grandmother, also, was very depressed, very anxious and fearful. Yet she was extraordinary. She was a suffragette, the first newspaper woman in New Jersey, and she wrote the original Bobbsey Twins books under the name Laura Lee Hope. My grandfather was an alcoholic, but a very functioning alcoholic, whose disease only got bad when he saw his son crumbling before his eyes. He wrote hundreds of books including Tom Swift, under the name Victor Appleton, and Uncle Wiggly, under his own name. He was very well known and well loved, followed by packs of children when he went downtown, and here was my father trying to write serious fiction. I used to attribute my father's depression to that. But now that I've gone through my own depression, and I look back, I think that my grandmother was clinically depressed, and I think my father, too, had the disease.

My childhood was fraught with my trying to save him from killing himself, trying to give him hope, trying to keep the despair away. All my childhood, he was in and out of hospitals, all over the whole circuit of private mental hospitals. I tried to understand the pain. I thought if I burrowed deep enough inside of him that through understanding love, I could find it and root it out and help him. Of course, I couldn't, and he ended up killing himself.

At one point, when I was a sophomore in college, I said to myself, "I will survive. He's going to go down, and I will survive." Then I had a nervous breakdown.

I come from a crusty New England background. My mother

is quite English, of English extraction, so we grew up in a very puritanical kind of situation, and I've always been somewhat stoic. But throughout my teen years, I remember a sense of crushing loneliness. And then the episode in college.

I started drinking heavily. I got very, very thin. I started feeling almost as though I had a double personality, the good and the bad. If I let the blackness, the bad part, have its way, it would destroy me. For a while, I even allowed that personality to take its lead. I would say "Okay, I will go with you. I will become the dark soul." I remember sitting in class and having the dark person welling up inside me, and wondering why everybody didn't see. And feeling just about as separated as if I were in another universe, as if I were a complete alien.

Then, when I woke up one Saturday, I went into a horrible bar in town and had two double bourbons at ten-thirty in the morning. All I remember when I went back to school is walking into the dormitory, looking around and suddenly screaming and crying in hysterics. The next thing I knew, my parents had come and they were taking me home. I was on the Taconic Parkway, thinking that we'd crash any moment, shaking and crying.

I didn't drink any more after that, but I did smoke grass a lot when my children were young. I felt that if I didn't do something to change my consciousness around four or five in the afternoon that I would just explode. Then I stopped smoking grass. Then I started drinking, and then I stopped drinking. My doctor says I've never been an alcoholic. I don't experience it that way, because whatever it was I was doing, I felt that I had to.

When I was twenty-three, I wrote in my journal that I felt that I had to deal with what I called "the Thing" that would come to me, like an enemy entering me, and how finally I had come to recognize it like a friend. I would know it was going to come, and the only thing that I could do would be to let it do its work. I couldn't get rid of it before it had made me feel helpless, and hopeless, and depressed. But if I worked, if I practiced the piano, if I tried to write something, then I could at least feel as if I was surviving during its visit.

[One psychiatrist suggested that] a young person who is saying "I will fight it" is not depressed. But the fact is I was dealing
with it, and dealing with it, and dealing with it all my life. I used
to have periods of terrible blackness, but I would feel them start
to lift after about six weeks. When I turned forty, [these periods]
started getting longer, and longer, and longer.

It started hardly ever lifting. By the time I was around forty,
it just settled in. My life got smaller, and smaller, and smaller. I
stopped writing for the *New York Times*. I told them I was working on a novel. In fact, I was just so sick. I stopped seeing friends.
A lot of people got mad at me, thinking that I was a bad friend,
not understanding.

Every time I would approach the house, I would imagine that
it was in flames. As soon as I came around the corner and saw
that the house was there, I would say "Okay, that's all right,
that's all right." The only real hallucination I had that I remember was of a huge black spider. I was in bed, and a gigantic black
spider was climbing on the quilt up toward my face. I leapt out
of bed and crouched in the corner like a real crazy person, and
said, "It's there, it's there!" Arthur woke up and said, "What is
the matter with you?" I said, "There is a huge spider on the bed!
Get it! Get it!" I couldn't breathe. It was very terrible.

Finally, all I was really able to do is take care of my children.
This is where I think it's different for women, because there was
no possibility of my being taken care of, really, because I had
young children. There was always the laundry to do. There was
always the marketing to do. There were always the meals to
make. When I'd go to the market, I wouldn't know anybody's
name. I wouldn't know what I was supposed to be doing there. I
would forget where I was. I would be holding my list and looking
at the things that I had to get. And I'd somehow do it, and I'd
come back. The meals got simpler, and simpler. But somehow
my children were a connection to life. It was the one thing I
could do.

I don't think the children really noticed. I was able to mask
it. If I went to bed when they did, which I did for many years,

and got up when they did, and just lived their lives, and only that, I could do it. It was like knowing that you're going to get up and go to war, every single morning. I have two sons with learning disabilities, and they needed so much extra care. Coming from a situation where I was almost destroyed and my two brothers were almost destroyed by a parent's illness, I knew I had to keep up a front. You look at those lovely little faces, and if you can't keep up, they're going to be distraught.

I was so afraid that I was going mad. As it got worse, and worse, and worse, it turned into a prolific, generalized panic. Every time the phone rang, I was afraid it would be something I couldn't handle. In the end, I couldn't answer the phone. I was afraid of the mail. I was afraid of going out. Every time I had to go to a school event, I was afraid that I would be seen as the crazy freak I really was. And then, my son, who is seventeen now, said to me, "Mom, you know, you have such a wonderful life, and you're so unhappy. You hope that you will have a minute of happiness during your day, and most people are afraid they might have a minute of unhappiness during their day. Something is terribly wrong with you."

I said, "No, no, I can handle it, I can handle it, I know what it is."

But I decided I would go see a real psychiatrist. I knew I was sick. After our first meeting, I called Arthur from a phone booth on Park Avenue and said, "I have good news and bad news. I have clinical depression, so I suppose that's good news, but it scares me. And he wants me to take medicine."

Arthur said, "Well, I think you should."

But I said, "Well, I think I can handle it without doing that. I think I'm feeling better already." Of course, I wasn't. It was getting worse and worse.

Then Arthur had to go away for three months to make a movie in Paris, and I was alone with the children. I got so much worse. I kept thinking that I couldn't breathe. It was like being in a psychedelic nightmare all the time. The dread, the dread, and the anguish of that dread, was like a physical illness. It hurt so much, like being in a fire. It hurt all the time. It was unbelievable.

I called the doctor back and said, "Look, I just can't go on another day."

This time he wrote a prescription for Prozac. He said, "Sometimes it can cause an increase in anxiety. It may be very, very bad."

I said, "If it causes an increase in anxiety, I'm dead! I have no room for that. What happens if it does?"

He said, "Well then, it probably isn't the drug for you," which actually is not correct.

I started to take it. My anxiety level got so bad that I could hardly move, or dress, or walk or think or breathe. It was really like nothing I've ever experienced in my life.

I thought "If this drug doesn't work, then as soon as the children don't need me, I will kill myself."

I understood for the first time about my father's suicide. He couldn't endure it. For me, it seemed the only place where there would be any peace. I thought maybe for my children, I might be able to endure it for a few more years, but I wasn't sure.

Meanwhile, I had to bring my twelve-year-old, Ben, who is on medication for attention deficit disorder and hyperactivity, into town to see his doctor at Columbia-Presbyterian.

I don't know how I even drove. As a child, I had to cope through finding my father in comas, driving him to the hospital when I was fifteen. The loss of our money. My grandfather's alcoholism. The children of alcoholics and drug dependents and depressives are used to coping way beyond themselves at a very young age. Somehow I drove Ben to Dr. Greenhill.

I asked to speak to Greenhill myself. "I'm taking Prozac," I said, "and I'm so sick."

He told me I was taking twice the dose I needed. He cut my medication back and became my doctor. He really held my hand through that, and knowing that I had a doctor I could speak to at least once a day when I was getting on Prozac was so important to me. For me, it was a very hard drug to get onto. He was there to say "You can have these extreme reactions, and it can, eventually, be the right thing for you. You have to wait for six or eight weeks, and then if it still doesn't work, we'll see." That was so important to know.

Then I was to go to Paris to be with Arthur, while my mother cared for the children. I remember thinking "There is no way I can do this." But the Prozac started taking away some of the anxiety, so that by the time I was on that plane to Paris I wasn't afraid. I didn't care if I lived or died. I hardly knew who I was. I hardly knew what was going on, but at least I wasn't afraid. I wasn't yet alive, but at least I was no longer in danger. And a month later when I came back, I went onto [a larger dose].

I remember waking up about a week later and feeling actual happiness, a kind of feeling that I hadn't felt since I was a child. Suddenly I had this feeling of hope. It was like some kind of miracle. I went to the market, and I remembered people's names, and I remembered their children's names. I could say "How is Timothy?" I remembered their dogs' names. It was phenomenal. As that month went on, I began to see color. I looked around me, and I realized that my whole wardrobe was black and brown, that all the colors in the house were pale, pale, pale pastel. Suddenly I wanted color. I wanted rich reds, and deep greens, and I wanted to read books again.

I felt so humbled, so happy to be alive. All I wanted to do was be a mother, just to be an elemental women. None of the real higher functioning returned, at first. It took me a year of rediscovering life before I began to get back on track with working, and wrote my first piece again for the *New York Times*.

I had been so separated from myself. Now I began to find that I could do seven or eight things during a day and not just three or four. I hired someone to do all our accounts for us, even though it isn't something we could easily afford, because I realized in the light of day that money matters would always make me upset.

I still have a ways to go. My friends would not know what I'm talking about because I seem self-assured, but I feel I have to learn to be partners with people instead of supplicants with people. I have to learn a new way to live, because I've lived so much of my life as a depressive. Now, three years later, I've finally been able to start a work of serious fiction, and I can say "I've survived."

11
Ya Gotta Have Heart

*The heart. Our very essence. What happens when the heart is threat-
ened? Heart patients often slip into depression after their first heart
attack—"heart event" is the current term—or heart surgery. Dr.
Hersh suggests that the chemical changes that occur when a patient is
on a heart-lung machine may be a factor in postoperative depression, as
may be the frightening operating room conversations that the partially
anesthetized brain may record. But even without surgery, one psychological component affects all heart patients.*

Stephen P. Hersh, M.D., F.A.P.A.

All of us carry around inside the way we felt when we were sixteen or seventeen. We knew about mortality, but it was meaningless to us. That's why teenagers are the best soldiers, because
death wasn't anything that applied to us. So, when you have a
cardiac event, suddenly you are confronting the issue of loss of
control and then, secondarily, your own mortality. It's your bad

dream [come true]. And there has got to be some depression in that context. For some people, depression is transient and mastered fairly quickly, often not recognized by them or anybody else, and excused with "They're recovering and their energy is kind of low." Other people take months or years to snap out of depression if they don't get appropriate intervention.

Ann Buchwald

The depression came while I was still in the hospital. I started to cry a lot. They sent someone to talk to me, but even the doctor said, "We know we don't take care of the whole person." Hospitals are just not equipped to take care of the emotional and mental side. When they wake you up at six A.M. for blood, they don't ask you if you slept well. They don't care.

Depression is not moaning and groaning and crying. It's just not caring. Not caring what they do to you because you have no say about it. You're too weak.

When I came home, I didn't want to see anyone. Who does when they're sick? Art would say "So-and-so wants to come see you; when can they come?" and I said, "Never!"

[Public television commentator and author] Jim Lehrer was the first person to take me to lunch as soon as I could get out. I've always thought of him as my idol as far as what happens after heart surgery. He cheered me up by saying he's never felt better or done so many new things. He's written four books since then.

I think all major surgery leads to major depression (except maybe cosmetic surgery—they must be the only happy surgical patients). You get depressed about how tired you feel even long after the surgery. You can't walk up steps, you can't breathe. Maybe if you could still do the same things afterward, there would be no depression.

Eventually you come around to thinking about death, regardless of how high-spirited you are. But if anyone has any sense, that's normal after fifty or sixty anyway. It just hastens it and deepens it. These macabre things they take out of your leg and put in your heart, you don't know how long they're going to last and you don't want to know. It's not a phobia, but you become aware that you're not a good risk, say, for a face lift—I'm not going to amortize it!

I saw a shrink for a while afterward. I wanted to see a woman. There's something about having your chest carved up that I thought a woman could understand better. The doctors have to carve their way through breasts and they must get awfully nervous because my scar is all jagged—they still remember their mothers, right? They're somebody's son.

My moments of depression are due to two things now: the things I can't do, like run, and the things I have to do, like rehab. When we were playing softball Labor Day, I said, "I don't think I can do that," but Art said, "Look, you hit the ball and I'll run." Oddly enough, I did hit the ball and Art ran to first base for me.

You're always aware that your heart is damaged; it's not the same one you were born with. And you always wonder if it will happen again.

Joan Rivers

After his heart surgery, Edgar was very angry all the time. He was very angry. He would go upstairs and lie down and just stare at the ceiling—a very classic sign of depression. He would retreat. We would go out for dinner and he wouldn't talk.

I was warned that after open heart surgery and bypasses, that the patients had a personality change. Standing outside of the intensive care unit, a woman said to me, "Wait till you see how your husband's personality is going to change."

I said, "Oh, thank you! Nice to hear this, thank you." You're warned but you're never warned enough. Even I, as his wife, at one point about four months later just couldn't deal with it any more. "Just, come on," I'd say. "We've got to go to a business meeting, and I'm depressed, too, you know. I don't want to hear any more, you've got to move on." He never went for help, which I think was a major mistake, too prideful. Our doctor put him on medication, but he wouldn't go to a psychiatrist.

John Kelsoe, M.D.

Frequently, people don't appreciate the course of recovery from a heart attack and the impact on your life that it is going to have. They have different expectations; they think, "Well, I am going to get out of here and go right back to work." And that may not be possible for them. Some of that is simply denial. [Heart patients] would like to believe that it is over with, it never happened, pretend it wasn't real.

Now, there is some evidence to suggest that some kinds of brain damage may predispose people to depression. It is not impossible that during a heart attack, blood fails to reach your brain and you may have very subtle damage to the brain. In other words, a microscopic stroke as a result of a heart attack. This can potentially result in a depression later on. But I would consider that far and away the exception rather that the rule in what makes one depressed after a heart attack.

Lewis Judd, M.D.

There are two components to the depression that follows heart attack and heart surgery. These people, who might or might not have a genetic vulnerability to depression, are in very difficult, stressful circumstances, so if they have that vulnerability, then the circumstances will exacerbate it. Suddenly people are going from able-bodied to invalid, and people tend to get really depressed.

It has been reported that anywhere from 10 to 25 percent and even more has depression, after a heart attack. If you have an enlightened physician who is aware of this issue and sensitive to it, that will be part of his clinical practice in management of his patients. Otherwise I would suspect that you would have more surgeons saying "It's not my problem."

Denton A. Cooley, M.D.

I don't follow patients, I just don't have the facilities for doing it. I'm busy taking care of surgical problems, you know, so I can't do it. So we'll turn them back to their doctor. Patients have to leave the hospital within a week after surgery, and the psychiatric therapy may take months.

Psychiatrists clutter up the floor here. They like to keep their patients sick. I just never had the need for one.

James Farmer

I had a very mild heart attack after I finished my book while I was making a speech at a Martin Luther King birthday celebration. I continued the speech for an hour and twenty minutes and then I asked them to get me to a hospital. So they kept me there for ten days in intensive care. But I had no depression after that. I was just glad to get out. And I quit smoking by the way. I was a chain smoker, three packs a day. And I quit cold turkey.

I always knew that life was fragile. I knew that it was fragile throughout the civil rights movement. I knew that my death might lurk around every corner. I didn't have to learn that lesson from the heart attack. Especially a heart attack that did not lay me low. No, I experienced no depression after the heart attack. In fact, it was nice to lie there in my bed and read the telegrams that came in.

Rod Steiger

Whether one wants to admit it or not, every human being put on this earth in their heart of hearts are convinced that they have a secret bond with whatever gods that may be, that everybody will die except them. You've got to have that to get up in the morning. Well, when they're rolling you down the cream-colored halls of the hospital on a gurney, and into a bright shiny stainless steel operating room to give you a bypass, you are told in no uncertain terms by whatever fates may exist "Sorry, schmuck. Nobody's immortal, including you."

You have to have some kind of ego, you have to be some kind of masochist to perform in front of the world. If you'd ever stood backstage opening night on Broadway and your name is up in the lights, knowing that if you blow the performance a lot of people are out of work, ten seconds before the cue for your entrance on Broadway, all you want to do is run away. One voice is saying "It's too late now, too late now." The other voice is saying "Mama, mama." Something makes you stay. Well, I was so shocked that I, the great one, had to have a heart operation. I didn't have a heart attack. That's very important. My heart's very strong, thank God. The veins were clogging up. And they said, "You may go into depression."

Well now, I'm convinced the greater amount of narcissism you have, the greater will be your depression. I believe there's a balance in nature. If you've got a huge powerful ego and then all of a sudden it is proven that you're nobody but another human being, you can slide down a long way because you're way up there. And sure enough, after the bypass I slid into a depression. It got deeper and deeper.

Don't forget, when you are told there's something wrong with your head, your heart, or your genitals, you get a bit upset, like terrified. My depression, as far as I know, was born because I was convinced in my silent subconscious, like everybody is, that I'm gonna live forever. Everybody else is going to die. Why are you gonna live forever? Oh, because my name's Rod Steiger.

Trey Sunderland, M.D.

The depression following heart surgery is not so different from any postsurgery depression or from the depression that follows the mourning of loss of spouse. Any major life event, and certainly cardiac surgery would classify as a major life event, can trigger a depression if a person is prone to depression. I would look more for the symptoms rather than the precipitants. We don't say "Oh, this person had a heart attack, they're definitely going to get a major depression." Instead, we have to be well educated about what the symptoms of depression are and sensitive to the early warning signs, no matter what the precipitant is.

As long as mankind has had language, poets have explored the depths of the broken heart. Now cardiologists and surgeons dissect and reconnect our vital organs, while wondering still at the anguish of the human spirit. Post–heart event depression may be one's first experience with the black dog, adding psychic pain to physical discomfort. The good news is that because it is so common, many patients are warned to expect it, and many doctors are equipped to deal with it.

12
Living with Loss

One of the mysteries of depression is why people succumb when they do, why a blow that cripples one person is taken in stride by another and why a person who has survived great adversity is laid low by one of life's predictable stumbling blocks.

James Farmer, an early leader of the civil rights movement and founder of the Congress of Racial Equality, or CORE, was devoted to his ailing wife Lula. I was particularly struck that a man of such personal strength, a man who had seen so much pain and suffering, who had fought courageous battles himself, would be knocked down by a death he had been expecting for thirty years. But that was only the first of his devastating losses. Within a few years he lost his sight, and once again had to face and conquer his despair.

Judith Pisano's first husband, comedic actor John Belushi, died young, and unexpectedly. The insights she gained as she fought her way out of her subsequent depression helped her cope later with her father's demise.

Judith Belushi Pisano

My father passed away a month ago. And I've certainly been sad about it, but it's not taking over my life, and it's not with me every minute, in the way it was when I was depressed. That was a very physical heaviness. And although I've always had that sense of the spiritual, at the time when John died I had no idea what I thought or believed. For me, that added to the confusion of what happens when someone dies and all those questions which I couldn't deal with at first. I felt overwhelmed, defeated. I just wanted to stay home. It wasn't only negativity, because grieving is not necessarily negative. But the intensity of it, the sadness, was something that I suddenly felt as though I really wanted to wrap myself in. It was all I had.

Everyone has his or her own time for mourning. Because I was writing a book on it, I delved into it in a way I might not have. I began to wonder if the book was hurting me in terms of healing and getting out of it. I wanted to observe it, so I sort of made myself into an experiment. Where the mourning left and became depression, I couldn't say. At the same time, I think I came out of it very well. I was able to get through the anger, and the sadness, and the pain, and move it along. Who's to say that it was too long a period, or just a perfect period? It was my experience, and I'm in a good place now.

The really negative time lasted close to two years. The second year seemed a lot better than the first year, but when I got into a third year, I realized how bad the second year was. It was almost as though I was in a very smoky room and suddenly I opened the door. I hadn't realized that opening the door would clear out the room, and it was such a relief. But two days later when I went somewhere else and came back, I found the room was still smoky.

I don't think I was the depressive type, but I think I was a candidate for depression by virtue of living in a state of denial about certain pain from my life. I think that's probably something that's true of people with depression.

I think there are physical, emotional, and spiritual reasons that you have these problems. I think you can focus everything into those categories, in terms of any illness, it's physical, spiritual, or emotional illness. I ultimately feel like the spiritual one is the key.

Fred Wright, Ed.D.

If you look at normal bereavement, for example, the death of a loved one, you'll find the bereaved might want to spend certain amounts of time withdrawn from other people, but usually it's the time when people cling to each other. When they are depressed, people can get to the point where they withdraw from friends. They just won't get out of bed. They want to not eat, or to constantly eat. They stop going to work.

One of the characteristics that clearly makes a distinction between depression and normal sadness, or bereavement, is that depressed people sink into what we call a depression triad, as far as the way they think. That is, they have persistent, chronic negative thoughts about themselves and their current situations, and they make negative predictions about the future. When people lose a loved one, they might think "I really miss the person and I feel really down about it. This is terrible and awful." The depressed person will start having such thoughts as "I can't live without this person. The future is hopeless. My world is crumbling down around me. There is absolutely nothing I can enjoy any more. And on top of it, I am a terrible person."

Linda Freeman, M.D.

They used to say for adults "A grief response is six weeks. After that, they're in pathological grief." No one has ever said that for

children, thank goodness, and even for adults I don't think that's
fair to have a cutoff like that. But obviously, if someone has had a
loss and has been dysfunctional for two, three, four months, he
or she may be suffering a depression even though it may have
been precipitated by the loss. I don't know that you need to
make a distinction. Probably a majority of people who lose
somebody close to them are going to have depressed mood
states. A large number will, on a temporary basis, have the full
depressive syndrome. We don't tend to treat it unless it has become so severe that the person feels incapacitated and/or is suicidal. In that case, I don't know that they'd be managed a whole
lot differently than people with other kinds of depression.

James Farmer

Lula's illness was with her almost as long as I knew her. She was
suffering from Hodgkin's disease, which was a killer in those
years. Now Hodgkin's is 95 percent curable if caught in time,
but back then it was considered incurable and inevitably fatal.
They started out saying she had eighteen months, and it ended
up thirty years. But it got to the point where the surgery, the
X-ray treatments, and the chemotherapy were ineffective, with
all kinds of side effects. She was skin and bones. At five feet five,
she was down to eighty-three pounds and spent the last six
months in the hospital. It was a pretty horrible experience for
her, and bad for me, too. She was dying and knew it and I knew
that she was dying. It was something that we had waited for, but
the living had not been pleasant for her, though we had worked
out a life and she showed great courage, great courage.

She had handled my paperwork at home. I had an office and
a secretary, of course. Through the CORE years, she was active
in CORE, where she was a volunteer comptroller. And she handled my personal finances. She was trained in accounting, Price-
Waterhouse. She was a Phi Beta Kappa from Northwestern in
economics and econometrics. She kept all of my financial work
and opened all of my mail coming into the house; I wouldn't

have to bother with it at all. She would dictate a reply and let me read it and sign it or if she could send a reply over her signature then she would do that. When she died, I was unable to cope with that mounting mail on my desk in my little study. That was her. That desk became her tomb as far as I was concerned. I hired people to come in just to go over weeks of back mail, to try to put it into some order and get some replies out. If I would walk through the study, I would imagine that I saw her sitting there. If I had to walk through, I would look in another direction rather than at the desk. The desk was Lula. Every night I was dreaming about her, not dreaming of a lost loved one, but dreaming of a part of me that was gone. I could not cope with it.

I was never able to ask for help. No, no. Me? Too much pride. I was in trouble, all right, but I had no friends that close. Even to my best friend, I was only able to say "Look, what I can do is take a big suitcase and rake all of that mail off the desk into that suitcase, close it and take it to my office. Will you come there, and go over that mail and separate them into disaster piles? Decide what can wait and what has to be done now. And if I am not able to do it, you do it." And he did some of that. But I was not able to tell him "Get help for me, not the mail." There is some of that mail that has never been opened. Some of it is still in a cubbyhole at my present house in Spotsylvania County here, just outside of Fredericksburg, never opened. When my papers went down to Austin to the Barker Center at the University of Texas, the ladies who went through it and catalogued my papers sent me back some mail that had not been opened, including some checks, from five years ago. Checks that I could have used at the time very much. Checks I still haven't done anything with because I'm sure they are worthless now. I wouldn't know how to handle them. No, I needed help, but I had nobody I could go to. It was ego, I guess. "You mean you're not able to deal with that? What is wrong with you? Just grit your teeth and open it."

I think one needs friends and I had none, no real friends. I was on stage all the time. Now people think that there was only King. That was not true then. There was King. There was

Farmer. There was Wilkins, there was Reuther.* I was an image. And it was hard to develop personal friendships that were really personal friendships. People became friends for what they thought I could do for them. Or for what they thought they could get out of being friends with me, a phone call I could make, or a letter that I could write, or what others would think of them being seen with me: That is not friendship. Few of those "friendships" have survived, two or three. Others "ooh" and "ahh," but no personal friendships. There was nobody that I could sit down and talk with.

I don't think it ever was just a normal grief at the loss of a spouse and helpmate, because I know that people dream of lost ones as though they are still alive. But every night? And all during the day? And to the extent that I was not able to open a letter on my desk? Not able even to look at it? Insurance on the house was canceled for lack of payment, for I had never seen the bills. It is a wonder that I wasn't foreclosed for the mortgage. One car was totaled and I woke up to the fact that I had no insurance because I had not paid it. Can you imagine? An otherwise intelligent guy? This was not normal. This was not normal grief; this was psychotic. She died in '77 and the depression lasted into the early '80s. Not at the same intensity, of course.

Getting rid of the house and moving to new surroundings here and starting on my memoirs was kind of like starting a new life. The book, the book—I put my whole being into that book.

I was in the process of doing my autobiography when I started losing sight in my one good eye. I had lost sight in my right eye in 1979, and lost most of the sight in my left eye in 1982. Then in about 1988 or 1989, I started going downhill fast. After three and a half months in the National Eye Hospital, I had very, very little vision. I could see lights and shadows, occasionally some color. For three months I just sat there trying to make peace with my virtual loss of sight. I had a very strong feeling that total blindness was my destiny, since the disease that

* Roy Wilkins, Leader of the National Association for the Advancement of Colored People, and Walter Reuther, United Automobile Workers president from 1946 to 1970.

had destroyed the right eye was what laid the left eye low. So, for three months I simply sat there, unable to write, unable to do anything, unable to come to terms with my own disability.

First, I went through the stage of denial, denying that it happened. "It is not true, this is some horrible nightmare. It's a dream." When it was clear that it was not a dream and that it was a reality, then [I thought] "It's a temporary reality. And I will wake up." Lo and behold, the reality of yesterday would disappear during the night and I would be able to see. But when I came to terms with the fact that that was not going to happen, then I had to try to learn to cope with the limited vision that I had.

Usually diabetes produces eye problems, but in my case it was a combination of glaucoma, which I had had for years, and something called retinal vascular occlusion, which translated means blockage or stoppage inside the blood vessels in the retina. They do not know what causes it. It is a fairly rare eye disease. It is possible that it is also hereditary. My theory is that it's the result of the prolonged absorption of tear gas, which I experienced in a place called Plaquemine, Louisiana, during the civil rights movement for three-and-a-half to four hours in a closed house. To go out meant to die. The mob was looking for me, the lynch mob made up of state police, with name plates and badge numbers taped over. I had to stay in. Others who were with me dashed out into the backyard to breathe air. And then they were gassed back into the house and then back into the yard. I stayed in all the while, absorbing more and more tear gas. Well, I felt and still feel that that was the source of my retinal problems. But my ophthalmologists were quick to point out that there is no "evidence in the literature." Of course, they don't have many people to study. Who has absorbed tear gas for four hours in an enclosed area without going out?

One of the things that produced the terrible depression this time was the fact that the book appeared to be stymied. I almost exploded with the inability to get out what was building up inside me. I thought that I would never be able to write it. So, when I found a way to do what I had to do and was able to conclude that which was difficult and arduous, I was able to cope with the blindness. The depression lifted itself.

The incident which helped me come out of the depression is cliché. I was crossing an intersection in Washington, D.C.—cars were honking at this crazy old coot who was walking across the street against the light. They were in a hurry to get across the street, with no place to go. Honk, honk, honk! "Get your blankety-blank off the street!" I was mad at them, practically cussing back, waving at them and gesturing. As soon as I got across to the other sidewalk, a little old voice said, "Mister, would you please help me across the street? I am blind." I said, "Oh, yes, darling, of course I would." And I put my arm around her, this little old lady, and helped her across the street. These big monsters of steel that are coming at me, I stopped them. They put on their brakes. SKREEEE! And I got her across. I don't know how she knew I was there. She must have heard my footsteps. And how she knew I was a mister, except the pacing of the feet. "Mister, would you please help me across the street, I'm blind!" So, after I had helped her across the street, I said, "Okay, I can do it. Enough of this feeling sorry for myself." I thought of the man who was bemoaning the fact that he had no shoes until he saw somebody that had no feet.

I am fortunate never to have suffered the death of a very close relative or friend, but I have discovered through my own therapy that for many people given to depression, any loss can be as dramatic as bereavement. Trading in a car, leaving a job, being graduated from school are all events that may need to be mourned and the feelings of loss worked through, supported by friends. In particular, the loss of a pet, as trivial as that may seem to many people, can be devastating. That warm feline body sleeping on your chest, that dog resting his head on your knee, waiting patiently for a walk, may represent the only unconditional love you feel you have.

Some of my most difficult and lonely years were spent in Los Angeles. But I had a dog, as sweet and loyal a mongrel as ever lived. She accompanied me everywhere, lying under my desk at work, waiting patiently in the car at the supermarket, even attending acting class. She was my alter ego.

During the time that I was writing my first book, On the Edge of the Spotlight: Celebrities' Children Speak Out About Their Lives, *she was killed by a car in front of the house, plunging me into one of the deepest and longest-lasting depressions I ever experienced. Did the stress of trying to finish the book combine with the accident to produce one of my worst episodes? I don't know. I know I couldn't work and avoided answering the telephone for fear my editor was calling. As I sank deeper, I was unable to answer the phone at all, to talk to anyone. I remember lying on the couch for what seems like weeks looking up at the ceiling or staring at late-night television.*

I pulled out of it slowly, with the help of friends. My best friend would come pick me up in her car, even though she lived only blocks away, so I wouldn't have to walk past where the accident had taken place. She would take me to her house, a change of scene, and I'd lie in the sun by the pool. Gradually she lured me into the water, where the cool, quiet environment restored me. Eventually I went back to work.

I was most fortunate to have family and friends who were as deeply attached to their pets as I had been to mine, who never ridiculed or suggested it was time for me just to get over it. Instead, they wept with me, kept me company, and when it was time, dragged me back into life.

Now I am a cat person. Never again have I been able to love a dog that much.

13

Being Woman,
Hard Beset

Women suffer from unipolar depression twice as often as men, at least in industrialized nations. (The few cross-cultural studies that have been done in underdeveloped nations are not held in high esteem by the professionals whom I asked.) But is this a physiological phenomenon or a psychosocial one? Until puberty and in old age, rates of depression are nearly the same. Does this imply that reproductive hormones are involved, or that we treat women differently during the years that they are most in competition with and threatening to men? Bipolar depression (cycling between depressions and manias), which effects men and women nearly equally, has a stronger genetic basis than most unipolar depressions. Does that suggest a greater cultural basis for unipolar? Even the data yield no answers—as you will see, the same studies are interpreted differently by different mental health researchers, supporting the notion of medicine, and especially psychiatry, as an art as well as a science.

Mary Jones

If we assume that serious depression is an illness caused by some
as-yet unknown chemical imbalance in the brain or some sort of
minor disarrangement, then the gender difference is a real puzzle. If you assume that part of the puzzle of depression is societal
factors and/or psychological factors that are a result of the society, then I don't think it's at all difficult to understand. Women
in this society still have an incredible amount to contend with. I
don't like to appear to be the kind of feminist who whines "The
only reason I have problems is because I'm a girl," but in fact,
it's very real. And there's nothing terribly mysterious about it.
Women don't get paid as much, and they suffer from poverty
and violence in this country to an extraordinary extent. The only
real feminist issues are poverty and violence. And I will tell you,
they will give you a very serious case of depression.

Jules Feiffer

One of the things that has always provoked my interest is that all
the women I've known have this problem of low self-esteem,
which men don't have nearly as much, if at all. Some of the most
poorly equipped men I know have never had a moment's doubt
in regard to their abilities, while some of the most talented
women I've known will recoil if you praise them and will deny
that they're good. It's something that I've never really understood.

I'm not sure how connected to depression this is, although it
may well be. It's a field that deserves a lot more study than it's
been given. Most of the women I know are smart, intelligent,
and in many cases a hell of a lot more interesting to be with than
the men I know. And none of them are as certain of themselves
in what they do as the men, even when they are infinitely more
talented and brighter.

Kitty Dukakis

When women drink, society says to their husbands "How can you stay with her? How come you are so tolerant and loving and patient?" When men drink, the expectation is that their wives are going to stick by them. Women have a particularly difficult road with both depression and chemical dependency, because they're not supposed to get sick.

Physiologically and societally women are supposed to be perfect nurturers, taking care of everybody else's problems and emotional well-being, and it's difficult for them to deal with their own failings and to admit them. Certainly in my generation and older, men have more satisfaction in life professionally. They're permitted to do what they've wanted to do and women are not. Women my age and older have had a very difficult struggle deciding whether or not to work and to pursue a career. But I don't think we recognize the amount of depression in men, because we think it's not a manly disease. I think there are many men who suffer from this disease and who can't possibly admit it.

Pat Love, Ed.D.

I do believe there is an answer but I don't think we have it yet. It could be hormone-related. What is the purpose of how we feel during menopause? It's nature's way of saying a woman is not of any use because she can't bear children, but we know that has got to change. We are pioneers, with biological dinosaurs for bodies and new-age brains.

I have been in perimenopause* for ten years. It's a new phenomenon because women are living longer. We're the first generation that is looking at menopause in a sophisticated way. And

* Perimenopause refers to the years preceding cessation of menses, often marked by early signs of menopause such as changes in menstrual flow, mood swings, loss of bone mass, changes in skin texture, interrupted sleep, vaginal dryness, hot flashes, and thinning hair.

of course, estrogen relates to serotonin and other neurotransmitters. I have a feeling that if I were on the right hormones, I wouldn't have to be on Prozac.

The book I'm working on is about solving the desire discrepancy in couples. Estrogen can affect your libido, and when your estrogen goes down, then sometimes you can be depressed, which also causes your libido to go down, not to mention [the effect of] vaginal dryness and all these other symptoms that go with that. Now, there's a reason why we haven't figured this out. First of all, there aren't enough female doctors, and they aren't old enough yet.

I went on testosterone for a short while because I wanted to see what the male experience was like. I was so irritable, sensitive, and overreactive, I wanted to fight the paper on the wall. I told two of the guys that I worked with "God, I feel so mean and irritable. No wonder you guys don't talk, because if I talked all I'd be doing is bitching." And they said, "All right!" The truth of it is, I think they feel as much, maybe even more than we do. They don't express it like we do.

Because of menses, because of childbirth, women are able to endure physical and psychological pain more. We say that men can't complain, but I think when women do complain, we aren't taken seriously. I suffer a lot before I go and ask for help. Most women with my symptoms probably wouldn't even go to a doctor. You just suck it up. We complain to each other a little bit, but you know, it is [often] uncomfortable to be a woman, and we get jaded. With depression, because you can function and it only has to do with quality of life, a lot of us don't give ourselves permission to feel [better].

Leslie Garis

If a man who is out in the world with a reputation as being a strong person says "I have depression," then you look at the man, and you see all of the things he has done in his life and continues to do and will do, and you say "He has a disease." But if a woman who is known for her attributes rather than her accomplishments says "I have depression," then you immediately apply that to the roster of attributes you [associate with] her. You don't see it as an outside disease. You see it as an integral part of her character and strength or weakness. That's why I don't like to talk about my illness. I don't want to walk into a room of people and have them say "Oh yes, you know Leslie, she's depressed." Whereas if someone like Bill Styron walks into the room, they say "Oh, you know Bill Styron, he's a writer. I gather he has depression." I don't mind if people know that I'm depressed. I just don't want to be explained away as someone who is depressed. It's only incidental to who I am. It's not who I am. I see depression as a force that comes and twists and distorts the essence of a person. It doesn't tell you anything about a person to say that he has depression. It may tell you something about how it's been coped with, the strengths that have been brought to bear, or all the hiding or pretending that's needed to be done, but that's all. That may be the main difference between why men and women have difficulties.

I imagine that the chief investment banker of Morgan Stanley, if she's a woman, wouldn't have quite as much trouble saying she has depression as someone like me who has a small career because I've been raising children and because I've been sick. I don't know. That may be wrong. Maybe the person who's the chief investment banker at Morgan Stanley is afraid to show any weakness at all because the men are ready to eat her up.

Susan Crosby

In some cases it's a little easier for a female manic-depressive. In our society if it's the female out there spending all the money and screwing everybody in sight, society says "Hmm, we don't think that's right for a woman to be doing that." And she can get some help. But if a guy is out there like Lindsay was, everybody is saying "Look at that life Lindsay Crosby is leading. All the broads and the money and the partying. That's the way a guy should be." But meanwhile, it's not what Lindsay wanted. And if I had done that, they would have picked me up and put me in the hospital immediately.

Jane Doe

Depression is more of a woman's disease than a man's disease, and it is still misunderstood as a sign of weakness, of instability. More hormones, more complicated chemistry is part of the reason, but I also think that if the things in society that trigger depression could be eliminated and women could be equal people in this society, then there would be less depression in women. Women are constantly battling the glass ceiling, the self-esteem problem, the little putdowns, the little words here and there.

Not a day goes by that I don't fight on the basis of my gender in this town. Not a day.

Women suffer terribly. Women are lonely. Women are disappointed by men. Women can network together and get their nurturing, their lovingness, their caring, their advice, all the things that one needs, with other women. You don't get that from men mostly. Women are nesters; men are hunters. That is how it is. A few men are fighting their hunting instinct all the time, but for the most part, they don't like feelings. Women think that being friends is talking to each other about books, movies, anything, looking at each other's faces; men think that friendship is doing things together, going places. They did a study with children of the same gender, five-year-olds, ten-year-olds, and fifteen-year-olds. Outside the room, they gave them chairs. Then they went into an office place, not a hostile-looking empty room, and said, "Go ahead, take the chairs in and sit and talk to each other." In every case, the girls put the chairs facing each other, very close, and were leaning in, and looking in each other's eyes. The boys from five, ten, and fifteen went to the corner of the room, put the chairs side by side, and looked out.

Our society doesn't support softness in men and doesn't support toughness in women. And men need to be soft and women need to be tough. Women go to support groups, take Prozac, do whatever they need to do when they need help. When men can't stand it any more, they have heart attacks. Because men don't know how to cry, to ask for help, to say "I feel sad. I feel bad. I hurt." They don't have the words, the language; and the society doesn't permit them to do it.

Barbara Parry, M.D.

Before puberty, women really are healthier mentally and physically, with fewer neurologic problems. The sex differences in depression don't appear until after puberty.

One study by Jules Angst out of Zurich, Switzerland, looked at the incidence of depression and found that it was more equal in men and women. When people came in to register for the draft as everyone must, they would diagnose the depression by interview. And then they would follow these people up with questionnaires. And they found that men would forget they had been depressed by six months later. [Angst] suggested that the sex difference was really due to men forgetting they'd had a depression. Now, this has not been replicated, but it is just one exception.

The only other exception I know of is a study done in the Amish population. There's no alcoholism among the Amish, and that may be why you get more equal distribution by sex. We can't go in among the Amish and diagnose depression; we have to be dependent on what the elders tell us. And if a woman has a depression, it doesn't show up as much; she's still in the home, baking the bread, or expected to, whereas if a man gets depressed, he's not out there helping to build the barn. It would get back to the elders and they'd report it differently. But other than that, [the predominance of women with depression is] a very consistent finding.*

Over the course of a lifetime, if depression is not treated aggressively in its early stages, it tends to get worse, not better. You don't develop antibodies. Women are more prone to this phenomenon; they are more likely to become sensitized to depression and psychosis if they are left untouched. If they don't get their depressions treated, the depressions are longer in duration and ultimately more difficult to treat. On the other hand, women with recurrent depressive disorders are much more amenable to treatment, both pharmacologically and particularly psychotherapeutically, than are men, meaning that when they get treatment, they get better.

Now, is that because [women] are more compliant, more willing to be treated? We don't know, but once treatment is initiated, women do better. Even without drugs, women respond better to psychotherapy. I don't know if you want to call that dwelling on it, but let's say they're willing to deal with it and acknowledge it. Because men deny their depression, or forget about it, treatment is inhibited and the depression gets much worse. Then they lose work and have to be hospitalized and that kind of thing.

It's worth putting it into perspective to say that women may be more vulnerable to depression, but they're less likely to get such chronic illnesses as alcoholism. They don't have the same problem with violence or cardiovascular disease as men. Day to day, women tend to express their emotions more, they cry more easily, and being able to get it out like that may mean that they don't crash—big time—when they reach the age of fifty. They don't get heart attacks or something. So this fluctuation, whether

* Dr. A. John Rush also cites this study: "Although men and women looked to be equally affected, the argument against that is that men may have left that culture if they developed an alcohol problem, because you can't drink in the Amish culture. Men will tend to drink more than women will, so it could be that a subset of men who are heavy alcohol users—not to say all alcoholics, because it's a separate disease, but a subset—may, in fact, be self-medicating their depression, and when they do that in the Amish culture, they leave. Now the incidence of depression in men and in women could look equal when it's really not equal; it's just that there's an attrition from the culture. But that's all theory. Nobody knows for sure."

it's daily, or seasonal or menstrual, may be protective in some way in the long run.

Men have much more cardiovascular disease and they miss much more work because of that than women do because of depression. Women tend to go plodding on and try to continue doing the job. Also, depression is much more amenable to treatment than heart disease is.

Estrogen can induce rapid cycling, one of the most severe and traumatic forms of bipolar illness; ninety-two percent of the people who get this are women. And women who are on antidepressants are more vulnerable. Women tend to get more thyroid disease, and thyroid disease can predispose to this. With estrogen and thyroid, it's a matter of getting it in the right amounts. I think treating the depression is the most important thing; I think estrogen is a modulator.

Some people have theories that it's the testosterone in men [rather than the estrogen in women], making them beat up on women, and that's why women feel bad. Suggestive evidence that female hormones may be involved is that when you change the hormonal milieu, you can either alleviate or precipitate depression. When you put a woman on oral contraceptives, that can cause an atypical depression in some women. Even women without history of depression can get depressed on birth control pills. It may be because the estrogen effects pyridoxine, vitamin B_6, which is important in regulating hormones involved in mood, such as serotonin.

Menopause may be a vulnerable time period, and bipolar illness also may have an onset at this time. It's not been given a lot of attention in the literature. Some women may actually do much better at menopause. The kids are off and they've got a lot of freedom. But other women can get major depressions at menopause. The good news is that it's pretty treatable. If a woman is starting to feel depressed, she shouldn't ignore this.

It's an interaction. From what we know biochemically, estrogen is needed to regulate serotonin receptors, so antidepressants aren't going to work unless estrogen levels are okay. That's why it's important to get evaluated for hormone replacement first. There is a therapeutic window. You've got to have the right amount for your own system.

Norman Rosenthal, M.D.

Women in their reproductive years tend to have the most seasonal depressions. In the winter type, it is three or four to one, women to men. After menopause, the degree of seasonality among women tends to equalize with that of men. So, something about the cyclical secretion of reproductive hormones seems to sensitize the hypothalamus to the effects of light or the absence of light.

In children, often times the problem takes on a slightly different clinical character. Children often don't recognize that they are undergoing these seasonal changes. They project it onto the people around them. They think that the parents are being mean or strict. Or the teachers are being unfairly demanding. Their grades slip in the winter semester, or they stay the same but the kid has to work much harder to keep the grades constant. There is also a lot of irritability, frustration, temper tantrums among the kids. Going off to college is often the time that it really hits the kids.

Is Seasonal Affective Disorder (SAD) different from any other form of depression? On the one hand, those of us who work with it a lot, who have treated patients with lights, feel as do the patients that they are dealing with a rather specific entity. And then there are others who are more skeptical. They say maybe these are just depressed people who happen to get it worse at one time of the year than another. However, the patients with SAD show a different group of vegetative symptoms more typically, namely overeating, oversleeping, carbohydrate craving, weight gain, fatigue, and slowing down. Other forms of depression often have patients losing weight, eating less, sleeping less, and sometimes being quite agitated. However, even if you take that cluster of vegetative symptoms, it is not specific for SAD.

For example, patients with atypical depression will be more anxious or more reactive to rejections than the more "typical" depressive who sits there wringing his or her hands regardless of what is going on. So, some have said that maybe these seasonal affective disorder patients are just atypical patients with a little flourish on them.

What really makes the seasonal patient different is his or her reactivity to seasons, to different latitudes and the different amounts of ambient light. For example, somebody here in Maryland who might have had bad seasonal affective disorder might have been disabled when she went up to Toronto and might have felt much better the few years that she lived in Florida and might have been completely cured in Guam. That would be not only corroborating evidence that this person indeed has seasonal affective disorder, of the winter type, but it would also be of prognostic importance in terms of predicting how this person would be likely to respond to light treatment. The more reactivity this person has shown to environmental light in his or her own life, the more likely you are to see a positive effect of modifying the environmental light therapeutically.

While anecdotally there is a fair amount of evidence that these patients will respond to antidepressant medications, there are no controlled studies of commonly available antidepressants in this condition. If you were to ask me which medications are best, the medications that seem to intervene in the serotonin system have had particularly promising results, such a fluoxitine, which is Prozac, or trazadone, which is Desyrel. However, other kinds of antidepressants that don't specifically work on the serotonin system also seem helpful, such as Wellbutrin, which is thought to work on a dopamine system, and desipramine, which is predominantly a noradrenergic antidepressant.

What one often finds with these SAD patients is they are lethargic, they are tired, they are dragging in the winter. When the spring comes they frequently come out not just to an ordinary even keel, but they sort of overshoot. They are extra-energetic and extra-vital and vivacious. They don't need as much sleep as their friends and family. They are often the life and soul of the party at those times. Previously, this would have been enough to give you a diagnosis of "hypomania," but the current diagnostic schema says that in order to append such a label to somebody that person has to be dysfunctional during that high period, and they mostly aren't. These are mostly very productive times for these people. So currently most of them are given the diagnosis of unipolar, according to present diagnostic schemas, although in the spring and summer they are often more ebullient and more exuberant than the average person.

It was through the research that I really recognized that I was seasonal myself. I am sure that is what led me to it, because one is drawn to certain things sometimes because one has a special interest. While I have never been dysfunctional as a result of any seasonal problem, I have nonetheless recognized a rhythm in myself of energy, of enthusiasm, and of creativity that has led me to be interested in the area. I feel different, less creative, less enthusiastic, less full of joie de vivre. There is not a big story there, perhaps because I have myself used lights for many years. How I would be if I didn't have the assistance of lights and I had to conduct the hectic life that I lead, I don't really know. And I don't really want to find out. I think that what I would probably need to do would be to cut back substantially on my commitments, because what people find is that their capacity to process information is not as good in the winter as in the summer.

Most creative work in the arts and maybe even in the more basic sciences is somehow informed or inspired by one's intuitive feeling about the nature of the world and the nature of oneself. And so when I began to see these folks with these problems with their eating, and their sleeping, and their energy level, and their concentration, and I saw in them an extreme version of what I had experienced, it gave me a feeling that I was dealing with something rather interesting, somewhat important, not trivial, worth spending a lot of my time and energy on. I have spent the last ten-plus years working predominantly in the field of SAD and light. What has helped me to stick with it is not only the observation of people suffering and the light helping them and the fact that it is really a marvelous model to study the interactions between the environment and the susceptible individual, but also my own internal feeling that this is important. There is some basic truth that can be learned here.

Mary Jones

In the winter, I become far more solitary than usual. I can make a speech and be amusing and meet and greet and then go back home and watch television. It's very isolating. A general sign of depression with me is watching television, which I consider a waste of time. When you watch television, you don't think. It's another self-medication. Or I will spend all day reading if I don't have any outside commitments. I just never get out of bed. And then, of course, I get very angry at myself, and feel pissed off and depressed. Because I always have six thousand things I *should* be doing.

There is a wonderful expression, neurasthenia. In the nineteenth century, women who didn't have enough to do were much given to being neurasthenic. It was quite a fashionable disease. But the depression of shortening days, getting dark early, is a very real thing for me. In the winter, I tend to be extremely lethargic. I can even remember when I lived in the North, where it gets dark about four-thirty in the afternoon. I found it absolutely horrifying. Every time I go to New York and it's gray and cloudy and lowering, I just go "Ohh, I hate this, I hate this, I hate this." I suspect that one reason I prefer to live in the South is . . . there's more sunshine here.

I suspect a large part of my mood has to do with how I feel physically. I have a tendency to abuse myself in a lot of ways and feeling physically well, being terrifically healthy and fit and eating well and exercising, is a relatively rare experience.

I never thought that I would float through life merrily, enjoying every single minute and thinking life was divine. It just doesn't seem to work that way for me. And, in fact, I'm not sure I have the gift of being happy. It's unfortunate, but it's true. I can count literally on the fingers of one hand the times I have been genuinely happy and known it at the time. It seems to me that as you go through life you look back and say "That was a wonderful time. That was really a good period." But at the time you're so busy trying to do whatever it is you're trying to get done that you're not even aware of it.

And yet the only thing that makes me think that I'm not chronically depressed, although I suppose that like everybody else in life I've had some fairly grim moments, is that I can't remember not being able to laugh at the situation, no matter what disaster I've gotten myself into, for any longer than maybe twenty-four hours.

Barbara Parry, M.D.

One of the things that bright light does is suppress the hormone melatonin, which is secreted at night. We think it helps to regulate rhythms, and it seems to be the best measure we have now of the biological clock or the internal circadian rhythms.

What it does in animals is much better worked out. For example, if you're a hamster and you hibernate in the winter, you need to know when it's time to hibernate, so when the winter approaches and the light gets less, there's more melatonin to send the message. When there's more light in the spring, melatonin levels drop, sending a message for the animal to wake up and get moving and start reproducing.

All we've done in human beings is measure it and it seems to be lower in some groups of people who have depression, including women with premenstrual syndrome, and the elderly. Whether that's because the circadian clock isn't working as robustly as it should, or whether that's a form of premature aging, we don't know.

If you change hormones, you can precipitate depression that occurs with the menstrual cycle. By definition, with premenstrual syndrome you get mood changes and depression before the onset of menses which go away after menses, so a change in hormones is associated with the change in mood state. Women who have a history of depression are more likely to have PMS, and a majority of women who have PMS are more likely to have a history of major depression. If women who have PMS don't have any depression when they start, but their PMS goes untreated, they may later develop a depression. So I think there's a cross-vulnerability. Now, the symptoms tend to be more like that of what we call the atypical depressions or the [winter type,] seasonal depressions. They tend to be more lethargic, although some of them get more anxious and keyed up. And they get the same carbohydrate craving that women who get seasonal depressions complain of.

A lot of women who have PMS do crave chocolates and other things. Some of them crave starches. If you look at the studies of what causes PMS, low serotonin in the brain is one of the theories that seems to have stood the test of time. When you are eating chocolate, you're stimulating a biochemical process that may help to increase the serotonin in the brain, so it may be a way of self-medicating.

It may help in the acute stage, but then your insulin kicks in, your glucose drops, and you may get a hypoglycemia. Instead, have protein meals throughout the day in small feedings so you don't get the major change in your sugar concentration. But if you're feeling pretty bad, that's hard to do.

PMS often has its onset in the postpartum period, even if a woman hasn't had PMS previously. The time that a woman is least likely to get depressed during her lifetime is during pregnancy and the most likely time is postpartum. We don't know why. It suggests that these changes in hormones during pregnancies have a protective effect, and the precipitous drop-off afterward makes [a woman] much more vulnerable.

I like being pregnant. I am lucky enough to have relatively easy pregnancies, with little morning sickness. On top of an overall sense of wellbeing, a wonderful calm settles over me. When I was pregnant with our older boy, William, I had no idea that that calm was anything more than a nesting instinct. I believe now that it was as much as anything a relief from pervasive depression.

*When my husband and I decided to have a second child, I was
warned not to become pregnant while I was taking an antidepressant.
At that point, I was feeling confident and healthy so I stopped taking it.
Within a few weeks the black dog had returned, ferocious as ever. This
time Bill and I did some research of our own on what the reported side
effects were in pregnant test animals, and decided we were willing to
take the risk. We wanted this child, but we could not live with the full
force of my depression. I went ahead with the medication until I became
pregnant, then quit taking it. My psychiatrist even suggested that some
people found that their depression went into lasting remission after
pregnancy, but I was not very hopeful, since that had not happened
before. However, I felt fine throughout the pregnancy, Jack was born
whole and healthy, and the levels of hormones that continued while I
nursed him seemed to keep me on an even keel.*

*Although I feel that in my case, the black dog was held at bay by
maternal hormones, I still had my moments, about a week after birth,
of classic baby blues with inexplicable tears and emotional vulnerability.
When William was born, Bill hired a close friend of ours, chef Dennis
Starks, to come cook during the immediate postpartum period. I will
never forget the evening he set down before me one of his exquisitely
prepared and presented oeuvres, only for me to burst into wracking sobs.
And I'll never forget the utterly perplexed and hurt look on his face as I
tried to explain, wailing "Dennis, it's n-n-not th-the fo-o-od."*

*Six years later, when Jack was born, my parents flew to Austin to
be with us.*

*Mom and Dad stayed a week, keeping William happily occupied
while I mothered the little one, until finally their other commitments
pressed in and they prepared to leave. Over the years, I've become used
to the frequent comings and goings of my family, but this time I lay
curled up and crying on my bed when my mother came to say good-bye.
She sat beside me, murmuring sweet encouragements and patting my
back softly.*

*"Oh, Mom," I moaned, "I just wish you could stay right here by
my bed, just like you used to when I was little."*

*"Honey," she responded, "if you need me, I'll stay." Seldom have I
heard more loving words, or more welcome.*

She stayed, and within a few days, when the blues had passed, she flew on home.

Jack was born a lively fellow and, at twelve months, pushed me away and weaned himself, cold turkey. Although I tried to pretend I could keep the darkness away, after a few months I had crashed again and was back on medication. Once again, in my desire to proclaim myself well, I had fallen off the cliff. I climbed back up, thinking "Maybe this time I've learned my lesson."

14

Lifting the Fog

In the depth of winter, I finally learned that within me there lay an invincible summer.

—Albert Camus

I'll admit my own prejudice: I entered into this project with a strong belief in the chemical approach to treatment of depression.

It had been a miracle "cure" for me. After twenty years of visits to a dozen different therapists of many persuasions, taking the right drug was simply like flipping a switch to turn off the depression, the erratic behavior, and the low self-esteem.

For a few weeks, as I was gradually increasing the medication to a therapeutic dose, I slept deeply, very deeply. Although I had some concerns about whether I could hear and respond to my children in the night, my husband was there to help, and in fact, that sound sleep was a blessed relief. I was a little slower to come to full wakefulness in the morning, so I adjusted my schedule to allow a little more time to do so. And I was very thirsty. In a short while those symptoms abated, and I felt fully alive for the first time in months. I had been afraid of what changes the medication might induce; nothing I had feared would change did. Except my whole life. I was relieved of the daymares that had haunted me, I was able to pace myself at work and at home, I was available to my children, and I was sexually interested in my husband. I had a real life back.

For me, psychotherapy seemed a failure at treating my depression; medication, a success. But after hearing so many different kinds of success stories, and interviewing numerous mental health experts, shades of gray emerged. I saw my success story from a new angle. Perhaps I needed the twenty years of therapy to clear away cobwebs of childhood misunderstandings and unfulfillments. Perhaps I needed to work on the various tangled issues I believe we all have by adulthood. Perhaps I needed the love and concern and expertise of those dozen different men and women who had helped me work through so much. Without them, perhaps I would never have been able to flip that internal switch that illuminated my problems and allowed me to confront them. For many people, the medication is necessary to bring the disease under control before they are able to work consistently with a therapist. For me, much of that work was finished before medications were started.

Still, it is appalling to me that people like Rod Steiger and Mike Wallace, people who have all the social and financial resources anyone could have, people who are well educated and well connected, who presumably can pick up the phone and talk to medical experts nationwide, still have to drag from doctor to doctor being misdiagnosed and mistreated before they find the help they need. Sadder yet are those who have not found help in the medical or psychiatric community, who still believe there is no successful treatment for depression because they have found none.

For some patients, finding the right treatment is as easy as taking aspirin for a headache. For others, the search involves trial and error, sometimes over an extended period of time. Some are still looking. Some have given up. And more than a few are enraged at the medical community that they feel let them down.

Jim Jensen

Do you know how many man-hours are lost in this country because of common depression? And how much talent is wasted? How many broken homes? Suicides? Drug addiction, alcoholism? It's all connected to it. And they're not doing shit about it. Research for mental health is almost nonexistent.*

It infuriates me. I've been in the hospital. I've seen wonderful people, talented, brilliant souls, frozen under despair. And they give them this pill and that pill. But it's a crap shoot.

The state of the art lags so far behind everything else, because of this medieval attitude we have about mental health. If there's something wrong with someone, we better lock them up. We don't talk about it. And it's still their fault. "You snap out of it." If they could, they would. You think these people like to live like that? The people on the streets, the homeless people? Most of them are depressed. The state dumped them on the city because they couldn't afford them anymore. They were going to have halfway houses. They don't have any halfway houses. So they're out on the streets. They need medicine and can't get it.

You know what the deadliest drug of all is? Valium. The doctors don't tell you that it's the toughest drug in the world to kick.

I know because I went through it. It was prescribed for me for four years by a doctor with a very prestigious reputation. Depression screws up your sleep. And I wanted to sleep. So he gave me the Valium. I never was addicted to Valium because I only used it at night when I was told to. That was all.

Now, when I went to [the hospital] for the cocaine, they pulled me off everything. Cold turkey. The Valium withdrawal was hell on earth. You see, it has a half-life. If you take ten milli-

* According to the NDMDA, we spend more in three years on defense research than has been spent on medical research in ninety years. "For every hundred dollars of costs imposed by mental disorders, 30 cents was spent on research," says Congress's Office of Technology Assessment. "In comparison, for every hundred dollars of costs of cancer, $1.63 [was] spent."

grams tonight, your system absorbs five and uses it. It stores the other five in your fat tissue. Tomorrow night you take ten more. Five are used, five more put in storage. That gives you ten. And so on and so on. Over four years, I had Valium coming out of my ears. Now, when you start to heal, the nature of the body is to get rid of foreign substances, right? And the body's gonna heal itself no matter how much it may hurt you. I would go through four and five T-shirts a night with sweat. My daughter would put hot towels on my shoulders and my back for the pain. I used to take a baseball bat and pound my legs to get rid of the pain. And that went on for months, as the Valium was working out of my system.

It's a matter of physics. For every action, there's an equal and opposite reaction. If your anxieties are quelled, and all of a sudden that which quells anxieties is taken away, there's a rebound. But they rebound about ten times out of proportion to what actually happens. So when your system starts coming back alive you go WHAM! When you're going through Valium withdrawal and you wake up from a nap, your adrenal glands are so screwed up, it pours adrenaline to your system and then you have these wild panic attacks. You have to run, scream, shout, hammer your head up against the wall. I've got taped recordings of me going through Valium withdrawal, and you can hear me moaning and screaming and wondering why, and praying to God I wanted to die.

They tried Prozac and almost killed me. The reaction was terrible. I kept saying "Don't give me this shit. I can't handle it." I was cold. I was hot. I was suicidal. When Prozac first came out, they were selling it like it was the end-all and be-all. It was the Holy Grail. Well, it ain't. Because there again they just give you the Prozac, not when do you take it, how much do you take it, what time of the day, after a meal, before a meal, what? Nothing. They treated everybody the same. Well, we're not the same.

Then I ran into an organization called ACI. It has a Spanish name and I can't recall what it is. They had a doctor there from England who is a psychopharmacologist. Not a psychologist.

Not a psychiatrist. Not an orthopedist. This is his specialty. Drugs. When to give them, how to give them, etc.

He said, "The people who pulled you off Valium the way they did should be shot," just for openers. He said, "These people have no sense." He was outraged. [Now] I don't take anything unless he puts me on it. Nothing.

Harry Wilmer, M.D.

If I see somebody who is depressed or is having alarming symptoms, I want to see what they're like for a while before I give them medication. You never know, sometimes if you don't jump to the drugs you hear the cause of the depression. Or you give them a healing message, "I'm not so scared of what you're going through, and I'm going to be able to tolerate it." One patient came to me with a dream she had had. [She said,] "I dreamt there was a dam breaking up ahead and I was rushing down the valley trying to get out before the flood—" and of course these patients are conscious of their fear of being engulfed by that, which is why they come to see me. "And then I came to you sitting in the middle of this valley, on a camp stool, just sitting there calmly, and I thought, 'Well, maybe I don't have to rush so much.'" You see, it bolsters the patients' confidence that this thing they're afraid is going to kill 'em is not going to do it. They have to have some kind of confidence and patience and somebody sitting there not panicking.

Leslie Garis

I was in Jungian therapy for twenty years. Then, after I was diagnosed, I sat down and read all those kinds of little inspirational books with titles like *Maybe You're Depressed.* I would read the signs, and I would say to myself "Yes, yes, yes, I've got every one of those signs." And I had gone through all those years thinking "Just a little more therapy. . . ."

I had decided that in order to save myself, I would have to cut loose emotionally from my family and try to have a happy life. I thought that the reason that I collapsed in college all had to do with the tremendous strains of my childhood, which was a red herring, because really, it turns out, I have clinical depression and need medication.

Stephen P. Hersh, M.D.

I absolutely do not tolerate from any of my staff in my clinic open-ended treatments. One has to have specific goals and a reasonable guess of a time line for reaching those goals that the patient has to be aware of and be a participant in. I'm absolutely and ferociously against patients being passive compliants.

If the major element of a depression is early trauma, and you don't pull it out, fish it out, and lay it on the person's mental table so they can look at it and put it back in a place where it fits better, then they don't do well long term. Most people are only interested in quick fixes. It's easy to do a quick fix, and we do them all the time. My bias is in the direction of making people long-distance runners. Some people don't have the time, money, and interest to invest in effective therapy. There's a lot there to help them; I know that the quick fix will also make them feel better and function better. If that's all they want, that is fine with me.

Once you've made a responsible evaluation of this person—and it's important periodically to reevaluate them—and you're sure of your evaluation, patient/doctor collaboration is the way to get the best results. You present: "This is what I think should be done, this is the kind of result you can get. Do you want to go along with this? Do you only want part of the program?" Sometimes people are only able to deal with getting rid of symptoms at point A, and at point B, which is going to be months to two years later, they may say, "Well, I want something more than that."

I think of medications as adjuncts, just like medications for hypertension are adjuncts. There are many ways of treating labile hypertension, and medication is among them. In a lot of people you can change the hypertension toward normal tension with such things as diet and exercise, changing of work lifestyle, and training in self-regulating skills using biofeedback.

So, when to use medication is a judgment call which is based partly on the severity of the person's distress and dysfunction. A person who has a long history of depression even back into childhood, of having felt different from other people in play and work situations, and a history of one or more aunts, uncles, or parents who were diagnosed as having depression, then probably that person has a significant biological component to depression. I would do my best to educate the patient to the idea of medication as essential, and to make it something that I use very soon, depending upon the individual. If I got a good response on medication, then I would try to educate the patient to stay on medication, to think of oneself as an insulin-dependent diabetic, needing medication at some level as long as they live.

On the other hand, some patients may have had no such history, and the depression seems like a result of life experience, whether repressed abuse in childhood or other life experience. If they were dysfunctional and uncomfortable, I would combine psychotherapy and medication, simply to reduce their symptoms and make them more available to psychotherapy as they began to feel better. But then I would start gradually, after about three months, to withdraw them from the medication and see if they could maintain a normal mood state on their own.

I think with molecular biology we'll eventually prove that there are certain healing interactions which actually make physiological changes, that in psychotherapy or individual or good group therapy, there are changes occurring in the balances of neurotransmitters, et cetera.

When a mother gives birth in a way that she's awake and alert, and the baby is put to her breast, that feeling, in the context of all the pain that she's gone through, is an extraordinary experience for her. If you were able to measure her neurotransmitters, there would be a change. Or people who are on a vacation and sitting and watching a beautiful sunset, their neurotransmitters are going to be very different than if you're measuring them in their office when they're behind in their work. That sunset, that vacation, that birth, holding that baby, smelling it, can make biological changes without medicine.

[As far as so-called alternative treatments,] some interesting new research data indicates that massage can alter mood states in positive ways. Neurolinguistic programming does many of the same things as cognitive therapy, but it is not as well developed. I would put yoga in the same ballpark as meditation and exercise as helpful for chronic low-grade depression, among a mosaic of treatment that would help a person move toward health but *not* as primary treatment. Alternative treatment techniques are not for those with more severe depression because they're too ill to engage meaningfully in those activities.

A lot of people with depression feel out of control and hopeless. Things like yoga, exercise, and meditation help give a person sense of control. They can see cause and effect when they get a positive response. Also, exercise and so forth can help channel aggression in those who have aggression turned inward (as part of long-term depression based on childhood experiences they haven't worked through). Exercise is not a cure, but a helpful adjunct to primary treatment like medication and psychotherapy.

My main interest is in groups and the healing power of groups and how it effects changes in biology. There already is the suggestion that we can change biological processes by changing mindsets and mood states. That's not fantasy, we can do it. We do it all the time. How we can master that skill is the challenge.

Jules Feiffer

In the first year or so of my psychotherapy, in the '50s, the stunning information came to me that I, who saw myself as a pussycat, was really an enraged person. I had no idea. I thought I was Jimmy Stewart. I thought I was this Mr. Nice Guy that the world was dumping on. But inside I was Model Boy Runs Amok, and had an Uzi and was killing everybody in sight. It all seems so obvious today and has become such boilerplate shrinkage material. That I could really be the aggressor, that I could set up these situations, that all these bad relationships that I was getting into with women weren't because I happened to meet the wrong women who did bad things to me, that I could promote and provoke a lot of this. I found that staggering information. . . .

At the same time that I was shocked by how little I really knew about myself, I also thought it was hilarious that somebody who professionally was in the business of pointing out what we didn't know didn't know about himself at all. Once I discover these things about myself, once I find what a trick I played on myself, I find this hilarious. I guess it's what makes me a satirist.

During the worst times, after my divorce, I could do the cartoons because I had to pay the rent, but any other work I was doing I couldn't do at all, and that represented most of my week. I knew I was not going to get back to work until I handled this creatively some way. So I wrote the play *Grown-ups*, which was about my family and my first marriage, and the most autobiographical work I've allowed myself to do, or wanted to do, ever. And that brought me out of it.

Once I had taken a situation that was out of control, that had thrown me for a loop, and placed it back into control by making a story out of it, making a play about it, making characters, some of whom were based on real people but who had sides to them that were completely my invention, once I had fictionalized the truth and thereby restrained it, then I was in charge again. Then I was okay. Then I could go out and face the world.

There are almost as many forms of treatment as there are people in this book, but the most successfully studied are a combination of medication and the short-term cognitive, behavioral, or interpersonal therapies. Rarely does talk therapy for depression involve years of lying on a couch relating last night's dream. More often, a therapist and patient will work together for a few months to find solutions and techniques to cope with the problems being faced.

For example, cognitive therapy, one of the most helpful therapies for depression, uses the examination and conscious changing of thoughts to effect emotional changes. To me, it sounds dangerously close to telling people that they can overcome depression with will. And I know with a certainty that when I was flat out, staring at the ceiling, I would have said to myself, "Well, my shrink says to examine—Ah, to hell with it." I would get that far and no farther, because a powerful part of the disease is an apathy insurmountable through willpower alone. To me, cognitive therapy sounded like nonsense. Statistics proved me wrong.

John Kelsoe, M.D.

Denial is a key component in the bootstrap lecture. "It is not really there." "It is not real." "It is all in your head." Whatever in the world that means. Of course it is in your head. Meaning that if it is in your head it is not real? All of that gives the message to the patient that you are faking it. It is not real. You are weak. All of the wrong, incorrect, negative messages to communicate.

The idea with cognitive behavior therapy is that if you change your thoughts your emotions will follow. But the bent on it is that this is real, that you do have some control, some power in overcoming this. The fact is that it works. The data indicate that those who get psychotherapy, like cognitive behavior therapy, and medication do the best—better than those who get the medication or the psychotherapy alone.

Every thought we think alters the biology of our brain. Every mood we have must represent some kind of chemical difference in our brain. So, behavior and brain changes mirror each other very closely. Under certain circumstances you can measure the changes in the brain chemistry that result from a change in thought or attitude or action. So why should it be surprising that changing your thoughts can affect the chemistry of your brain? They are intimately connected with each other, or they're different ways of looking at the same thing. It shouldn't be surprising that the two kinds of treatment together is really the most effective approach.

Some people may need to be on this medication for the rest of their lives, almost like insulin. But I think in many other cases, especially with bipolar disorder, you may treat them for a while and then if they do okay you may take them off of it. And it may be fine for many years.

Fred Wright, Ed.D.

In depression, the person tends to view his or her current situation in a distorted fashion. People who have depression slip into this depressive style of thinking and have negative thoughts about themselves, about their current situation or environment, and then they make negative predictions about the future. And this is something that is across the board, regardless of the origin of their depression or the particular type of depression that a person might have. It's like when you have the flu, you might end up with a fever. The fever, though, does not *cause* the flu. This negative thinking does not cause the depression, but it maintains the depression.

You break that cycle the same way you would break the cycle if the person has the flu. That is, you start off treating the symptom. If the person has a fever, you would try to get the fever down. In cognitive therapy we work, shall we say, from what's on the surface down. And what's on the surface is a style of thinking, and the fact that these people have slipped into poor problem-solving. When people are depressed, they have a terrible time solving day-to-day problems. One way to help them out of the depression is first of all to help them identify the kinds of errors in their thinking that they are making, and then to help them to better problem-solve.

If someone were to ask me what's the most important thing we do in cognitive therapy, I would say we teach people to monitor or pay attention to their thinking. Second of all, we have them examine or test out what they're saying to themselves, because with a depressed patient, usually there's a cognitive error there. And third, we get them to respond to this error.

We have to attack the sense of hopelessness that they have about their situations. When they're lying in bed, they really do believe that they can't get out of bed, or that they really can't go out and enjoy themselves. And all we ask them to do is ask themselves: "Is there a possibility that I could be wrong in what I'm saying to myself?" We might add, "Have you ever said something to yourself that was incorrect?" And most people will acknowledge, even depressed people, "Yes, I've done that." Then we say to them, "Well, if you have done that in the past, and my hypothesis is that you are depressed right now, and that you are saying many things to yourself that are incorrect, wouldn't it be to your advantage to test out some of these things that you're saying?" You get them to collaborate with you. You don't tell them "You will be able to do it." You say "Let's test it out. Let's find out what happens."

I would not argue with anyone who says there are some very, very good antidepressant medications out there. Curing depression is not the big problem. The big problem is what we call relapse prevention. That is, trying to build into the system some way where there is less likelihood of the person having a recurrence of the depression. And one of the things that we know from cognitive therapy is that you could give a person an antidepressant and they'll pull right out of the depression, and they'll go along smoothly. But sometimes you have to taper someone off the antidepressant medication. Then what happens? What you find happening many times is that a year or two down the road, the person has another depressant episode. With cognitive therapy, there is less likelihood of relapse.

Kitty Dukakis

For me, [as far as talk therapy goes] cognitive therapy is what it's all about—looking at a faulty belief system, dealing with the here and now, and the changes you can make to make your life happier. In traditional therapy, I've talked to death about my overpowering dogmatic mother and what happened when I was a child. I don't want to do it anymore. I've done it enough, and it's not terribly helpful.

For almost eight years, I went to a therapist when I was depressed and left when I felt okay. It wasn't going to help me when I was feeling good because I was feeling good, and it sure wasn't helping me when I was depressed. I would sit there for forty-five minutes looking at my watch. Because none of those therapies, behavioral, cognitive, or psychoanalytic, work when you're in that kind of state. They just don't. Medication is the answer at that point.

Traditional mental illness help has come in such a draconian kind of way. When I was at the Deaconess Hospital, many women who had been in that program had gone through electric shock. For me, it would have compounded the shame. Yet, as I'm sitting here talking to you now, I don't think there would be any [treatment] that I would say no to, in order to get well again if that had happened.

I'm on lithium, and I hate it because of the weight I've gained. But if that's the only negative aspect, it's a pretty okay trade-off.

It's very important for me to be physically active and in the sunshine, especially at this time of year. This morning I walked for about an hour in the bright sunshine. This is the second year that I've been without depression, but there's still a tiny piece of me that worries about whether or not it's going to come back. I guess that's normal. I guess it's always going to be there, but I'm taking responsibility now with the help of a psychopharmacologist, and medication. I've got a wonderful group therapy that I go to where I can talk about things like that. People who have not suffered with the kind of depression that I've experienced don't understand. They've just not been there. Michael is wonderfully supportive and helpful, but he can't possibly relate to the pain that I went through. And I don't expect him to.

Each individual's experience with the black dog is unique. In William Styron's case, the medications that were prescribed for him offered not relief but additional horror, and in his book Darkness Visible, *he offers the bleak point of view that ". . . serious depression is not readily treatable." I took exception to that, and believe he did a disservice to sufferers who would read his autobiographical work. The statistics are that eight out of ten people with depression who seek help are successfully treated. He responded to my concerns as follows.*

William Styron

Medicine is still largely unable to cope with this illness on a methodically practical level, but I think many depressives get well of their own accord. I stand by what I say. I still believe that medicine is inadequate, not because [the medical community is] not trying, but because many depressions are beyond medicine.

You see, I'm not categorically against medical intervention. I think that the hospital is a perfect example of my belief that there are aspects of medical intervention which are very, very good.

It was a last resort, of course. I didn't want to go to the hospital. I would have preferred not to have gone. But I had to go because it was the only place I could conceive of preserving my life. I was here in this house. I was ready to go off in the woods and kill myself. The hospital was the place I ultimately realized was the necessary way-station.

The fact that I went to the hospital was an act of desperation. Because I didn't think it would pass. The only way I could save, at least temporarily, my life, myself, from my own self-destructive impulses was to go where I wouldn't be allowed to act on them. As soon as I got to the hospital, I just began to feel better. I was still very, very depressed. But part of that was from getting off of Halcion. Understand, I would have gotten this depression despite the tranquilizers. I'm not trying to implicate them 100 percent, but they contributed heavily to my depression.

While I was in the hospital, I was taking Nardil, which I'm convinced is a dreadful pharmaceutical, in that I don't think it contributed to my recovery. I don't believe the medication was really as effective as the idea of finding an area of silence, and solitude, and refuge, asylum from which I could then emerge as I did, in the full belief that this illness is, and even the professionals use this word, self-limiting. Eventually it goes away. The antidepressants seem to work for some people. Psychiatry seems to work for some people. But there are vast numbers of people who are helped by neither.

Jane Doe

I had a very lucky thing happen to me. I was at a party in New York and I met this sort of crazy, frantic guy who is a psychopharmacologist, an absolute genius. He treats all kinds of famous people. He sees you for half an hour; he chews Nicorettes and then he sneaks a cigarette from the bottom drawer. He is young. His wife is a radiologist. He has a town house. So I was having these panic attacks and I called him up long distance and he called me right back. I said, "I'm really freaking out. I have to come to New York to see you. I really don't trust anybody here. I have had three bad experiences with psychiatrists here."

So, I went to New York. And he said, "We'll have lunch." We went to the Sign of the Dove. He gave me a prescription for Tofranil for the panic attacks and he told me for the next week to call him twice a day. "How are you? Did you sleep? What did it feel like?" Total hands-on. We adjusted how much and this panic attack stopped.

I now know that [my condition] has a name: dysthymia, low-grade depression, biochemical, and every couple of years I get a six-month clinical depression. So when that would happen, he would raise the Tofranil and lower it and so on. I had a few more panic attack episodes and he gave me Xanax, which I almost never took. I would take half of a half, because I am so drug sensitive. I would literally crush it and I would take a few crumbs with a wet fingertip.

When I read about Prozac, I called up my doctor and said, "Jesse, I want to try Prozac. If it doesn't work for me, it doesn't work. But Tofranil blurs my eyes and I am constipated and so on, let me try it."

He said, "Okay, but I don't think that it will help with your panic attacks."

Three or four days later, I stopped the Tofranil.

I am an educated consumer. I demand. I read. And I tell the doctor what I want; I wanted Prozac. And I was absolutely right. I will still get a little moment of paranoia, but I have never been tempted to go off the Prozac. As long as I feel fine, if it ain't broke, don't fix it. For me, it adjusts my brain chemistry and I am sure that I am going to be on it for the rest of my life. I take the minimum dose and except for the expense, I don't see any reason to try to get off it.

Rod Steiger

You've got to find a doctor that your spirits are simpatico with and the cure that works for you. But unfortunately in the beginning, they've got to experiment. They don't know. They've just got to give you this and "Oh, that doesn't work, let's try this one." That's why my wife got very angry, because she said, "Oh, these people, all they do is shove you different pills, and nobody's telling you what's wrong."

I had to go through what millions of people had to go through, going from one psychologist, one psychiatrist, one different medicine after another to fill my chemical equation. Each one of us is like a chemical electrical machine that's absolutely different from the other and is changing every moment we exist.

Every second that goes by, we're changing physically and mentally, getting older, getting nearer death, or what have you. You have to shop around for the right doctor, the right medicines.

Part of it's chemical, part of it's psychological. I have a chemical imbalance, that's why I have to take my medicines every night, whether I like it or not. The minute for some reason or another my system changes a little, and the medicine drops down, I have to increase it a little bit. I underline little bit because I don't want people to think you become like a dope addict.

When the doctor told me I should stop drinking I got very upset. I said, "I've been drunk maybe three times in my life, my mother was an alcoholic, you can't talk to me like that." It made me very angry, you know.

And then he explained, "No, it's that you cannot drink and have your medicines at the same time. You will get more depressed." It's like people I know who got hooked on tranquilizers and alcohol, or cocaine and alcohol, stuff like that. It just rips you, kills you.

Pat Love, Ed.D.

I went through Avatar.* It's not for everyone. It's an expensive way to convince you that you create your reality. I'm really glad I did it, and I really liked it. In eight to ten hours a day, you learn to take your experience down to the barest experience. You learn to become a rock. I know that sounds weird, but what it does is it gets you intensely in touch with yourself. I went through that a few months ago. It was wonderful, it was really wonderful. It helped me to perfect my thinking processes about positive thinking.

---

* A personal growth experience designed to heighten your awareness of your own reality.

Rona Barrett

Right after the attempted suicide, I was anxious to get help, but I didn't trust a lot of doctors. I went to two or three before I found one who was just wonderful. He had a philosophy. He said, "If I can't put you on your feet in twenty-four months or less, then I'm no good for you, and I believe that of all my patients." He used a combination of a lot of things. He used Freud and Jung and all the more modern techniques and teachings. He was a person who talked to you. It wasn't that you just talked and talked and got no feedback. He always asked questions, and you gave him answers, and then he'd say "By the way, did you ever think about this, this, and that?" All my life I've always been an analytical kind of a person. So the minute he would say something, if it was wrong and I didn't feel it, I would just say "I don't know. I don't think it's so." And then we'd work together to figure it out. I think people need therapists to give feedback. You have to listen a couple of times to the feedback that you might get from a doctor, and if you feel that either they're yessing you to death, or they don't give you the right feedback, move on.

I think for the most part psychiatrists, psychologists have gotten a bad rap. On some levels, I would say, rightly so. I think that to be a great or good psychiatrist and psychologist, it's an inborn trait. It's like being born a musician. You either have real musical talent or you don't. There is no teacher in the world that is ever going to teach you to have rhythm. They can teach you how to play a chord, but music, the music that we're talking about comes from the soul. It comes from the pit of the stomach. It comes from the bottom of your toes. [And when people hear it,] they know. They can feel it because it's a heart string that's just been touched. That's the same way I feel about medicine, and it's the same way I feel about psychiatrists or the field of psychiatry and psychology.

If you go to buy a car, you test drive it for the most part. You discover that there are a lot of things about this particular model that you like or don't like. You weigh the pros and cons. More pros, you buy. Buying without trying is usually a foolish thing to do. I think that's the same process you should use in finding a psychiatrist or a psychologist. Test and buy.

You have to realize that there are people out there who can help you. Also, today there are so many help groups that you can go to as well. Whatever course you choose, you will discover, much to your chagrin, that we are all cut from a very similar cloth. Most people feel that their problems only belong to them, that it never happens to anybody else. It's a great relief to realize that many people share your problem. At the same time it's a little ego-deflating to realize that you're not alone, not quite as unique as you think you are! I see no problem whatsoever in seeking psychiatric or medical help for the mind.

John Kelsoe, M.D.

Just because something is a biological brain disorder does not mean that behavioral treatments are not useful. Family therapy, and individual psychotherapy and different kinds of cognitive behavior treatment are extremely useful for what may clearly be brain disorders. So just to say that it is biological doesn't mean medications only.

Lewis Judd, M.D.

What inhibits people from getting help? Lack of awareness, some lack of training among the clinical community, and lack of essential availability of the services, because people with disorders like these are being kept out of the health care system. But primarily, a lack of the knowledge that what one is experiencing is a true disease.

It often will come on gradually. People will fall into a depression and be very, very dysfunctional and feel that somehow it's their fault that they can't pull themselves out of this. When one is experiencing two weeks or more of dysphoria, and all the other symptoms that we know go with major depression, there's a tendency to feel that that is not a disease, that it's just a state that you're in now, that you ought to get yourself out of. There is an intense lack of knowledge among all people that when you're in that state, you are having a depression, and therefore you must get treatment.

More often, people try to medicate themselves. They may drink alcohol; unsuccessfully, they may try to do all kinds of things to pull themselves out of this. The average depressive episode lasts about ten to twelve months, and then it will often spontaneously remit. But if you're in the midst of that, you are not going to get yourself out of it. You can't get yourself out of it.

If you try one therapy or medication and after several weeks still are miserable, it doesn't mean that you or the treatment has failed. It means it wasn't the answer for you, and you must try again. If a certain treatment helps after a reasonable time, keep with it. If it doesn't help, ask your doctor about changing the frequency, the intensity, or the dose, adding other regimens, or trying something new. Or consult with a different doctor. Eighty to 90 percent of people who get treatment are treated successfully, but that doesn't mean that you're going to find successful treatment in your first try. Keep fighting because there is *an answer.*

The medication I take is not the cure for all of life's problems. I still have a normal share of neuroses—I get angry occasionally at my husband for something someone else did to me years ago; sometimes I take out my frustrations at work on my kids. I still have bad days, even blue days, but rarely unrelenting misery, day after day. I called a friend recently to rant and to whine about my job and the day's stumbling blocks. "But, Kathy," she said, "I thought your pills were supposed to make you feel good all the time." It is a common misconception. In fact, life is not any smoother for me than it is for the average person, but when there are bumps, I don't fall apart. Medication does not cast a golden net over life and take away all normal human suffering, but it does take away the extranormal suffering.

Although many people take medication for only a short period of time, recent guidelines suggest that depression may recur without follow-up treatment (medication, talk therapy, or both) for at least six months. Patients with multiple recurrences may require maintenance medication for several years. Some people may take a drug only when needed, some may take it for a time then stop, some may need to take it without interruption for an extended period. As I write, I have been on medication continuously for three years. Occasionally I fool myself that I am cured, I cut back on my medication, and the depression returns, in full force. That is my failure; the drug is a success.

Eighty to 90 percent of people treated for depression have success stories like mine. But what do we say to the 10 to 20 percent who do not?

First, try again. Another doctor, another medication or a different dosage, a combination of medications, or shock therapy may succeed where other attempts have failed. Second, keep trying.

I was saddened by an exchange I heard on a notably ignorant nationally syndicated radio talk show when a right-to-die bill was being considered in the Congress. A woman called in to report on her experience with the so-called suicide machine doctor. In spite of his legal difficulties, he continued to accept patients who wanted to die using his self-administered overdose machine. The woman called him, but he refused to "treat" someone who wanted to die because of depression rather than a terminal illness. She said, "It is an illness. It's just as serious an illness. I don't see why it's any different." The host's response was to cut her off, then play the apocalyptic Doors song "The End."

I wanted to call, though I knew the single-minded host wouldn't put me on the air, to tell her one very good reason that depression is different from a terminal illness. We can't say it often enough. Eighty to 90 percent of people who get appropriate help are treated successfully.

Even if you are one of the 10 to 20 percent for whom we don't have treatment, keep trying, because tomorrow, or next week, or the next week, or next year, we might have a treatment. Isn't it worth it to stick around and find out?

If you feel discouraged reading these accounts of failed therapy and futile searches for help, they are here to illustrate the importance of perseverance, of asking questions, of arming yourself with all the information you can so these things won't happen to you.

You will read about many different experiences throughout this book, some encouraging, some not. Remember that what is only flotsam to one can be a life raft for another. The experiences of these people may provide questions for you to ask your own doctor, to help you be an educated mental health consumer. In chapter 24 read the conclusions of these stories and the ultimately successful outcomes.

15

Beauty and the Beast

Whether I am trying to write, to express myself musically, or to act, the downward spiral into depression inspires and inhibits creativity at different points along the way. As the melancholy begins, there is a heightened, though self-absorbed, kind of passion that allows the upwelling of those romantically bleak feelings that inspired Emily Dickinson or Gerard Manley Hopkins. Here is where I write poetry, where I can identify with the sadness or anger in a theatrical part, where I walk through the night, singing in full voice old hymns or folk blues. Here I feel most in touch with the deepest corners of my soul, and when I have a creative outlet, the junction of poetry and pain feels if not good at least satisfying.

But as the spiral continues down, I feel so inept, so incapable, so hopeless that there is no point in attempting to create. Anything I fashioned would be dross. Soon any effort at all becomes pointless, activity slows, then stops, and numbness sets in.

Why does it seem almost a given that creativity and madness go

hand in hand? Why are we less surprised by the suicidal death of a poet
than that of a doctor? From Van Gogh to Jean Seberg, some of human-
kind's most gifted artists have lost their battles with their inner de-
mons. As tragic as these losses are, still we ask ourselves, is it their
madness that imbues their creativity with genius? If they were well,
would their art still move us as profoundly?

Do we as a society have a stake in keeping our artists ill? As we
move closer to prenatal gene manipulation, will parents have to choose
between a well child and a potentially brilliant artist? Dr. John Kelsoe
poses the question: "If you eliminated bipolar genes from the popula-
tion, who knows what other beneficial effects you might be losing, even
beyond creativity?"

John Kelsoe, M.D.

There is certainly a link between the two—not to say that most
people who are creative have an affective disorder, but it certainly occurs at a higher rate, among poets most notably. I think
that is partly because when people with bipolar disorder go
through the stage of mania called hypomania where they are ac-
tivated and energized, their brains are going faster than usual.
They are not ill to the degree where they are impaired yet, but
they probably think better, faster, more creatively than the rest
of us. And are frequently very successful in our society. It is only
when they go on beyond that into full mania that they are impaired. Many of these very creative writers and musicians have
been creative as a result of or during their depressive episodes as
well.

Leslie Garis

I have one son with dyslexia, another son with dyslexia, attention
deficit disorder, and hyperactivity. All three of my children are
incredibly artistic, and they're tremendously gifted, especially the

one who is in a way the most afflicted. I have come to see with my family and with my children that the affliction comes with an artistic territory, but it's no gift. For their higher functioning, the price they have paid is a very complicated personality that short circuits.

Betty Sue Flowers, Ph.D.

I think great artists produce in spite of depression, not because of it. The artists I know are more willing than most people to feel the feelings they have. So the depression is more pronounced. Not that they value depression per se, but they value intense feeling.

If you're a materialist, you can look back on a lot of the descriptions of the ecstatic vision of saints, like St. Theresa, and say "Oh, well, yes, she was undergoing a schizophrenic attack," or "[El Greco] must have had a strange condition that made him paint elongated figures." That doesn't lessen his art, nor does it lessen the artists' visions if they were chemically induced, either through an imbalance or through something ingested.

I know many artists who suffer from clinical depression. What they create is not in itself a product of depression, even though it may reflect their struggle with depression as content. The difference between a mere expression of depression and a work of art that is *informed* by depression is that the first comes out of depression and stays in depression, as opposed to a work of art that takes me to the depths of darkness, to a dimension that is part of the human condition.

Have you ever seen the Rothko Chapel in Houston? To me that's a very moving, spiritual place. [Mark] Rothko was a severely depressed person. You could go into the chapel and if you didn't really *see* those paintings you might say "Yuck, what is this? Just brown dark paintings—how depressing. . . ." But if you're in there and *look*, you see the light *and* the darkness. You see behind and through those paintings. You see the tremendous power and sheer depth. It's a moving experience that lifts you

out of yourself. You end up being transformed rather than depressed. To me, the Rothko Chapel is a place of hope—or perhaps of faith in hope.

Mary Jones

There's the romantic notion of all these wonderful nineteenth-
century geeks who wrote romantic poetry and had interesting
lives like Byron and Shelley and Baudelaire, and screwed up everything around them. And I keep thinking that it is possible to
be sane and also do great creative art. Surely, it's possible.*

I think that in many ways the Romantic tradition is a great
trick that's played on people, the idea that to be creative, to be a
poet, to be a great writer, to be an artist, to be interesting, you
had to be outrageous, to live on the edge, to push things as far as
possible. Actually it's a bunch of crap.

I suspect we'd all be far more creative if we went to bed every
night at ten o'clock and got up at eight and ate granola. . . .
But it's so boring.

Jules Feiffer

I think artists are more sensitive toward their work, not necessarily toward anything else in life. Some of the most insensitive
people I know are artists.

I don't know that it's a given that artists are more susceptible
to this illness. I think what they are more susceptible to, just
because of the nature of free-lance work, is the ups and downs of
acceptance and rejection. If you're working in an office job, it's

---

* Dr. Flowers also mentioned this myth. "During the Renaissance, depression itself used to
be a romanticized state—melancholia, it was called. Hamlet is the archetypal case of the
depressed young man. During the early nineteenth century, in Goethe's *Sorrows of Young
Werther*, the depressed young man commits suicide for love.

"The Renaissance suddenly saw human beings as alone. The world was
demythologized for the first time, so the natural reaction was depression over the death of
God. Then when someone articulates that, that expresses the age."

likely that you can have a period of years without being tested all the time. While a writer or a painter or a playwright is tested every time out. The notion that this is not a statement on your worth as a human being, as opposed to your last work, doesn't carry very far. In the end you think "This is a statement on me. They don't like me." And in fact that's true, because if your art is representative of who and what you are, it is a statement on your worth.

John Kenneth Galbraith

I have a very strong feeling just from talking with other people about this, that there's a strong relationship between somebody who writes or is in some literary public role and depression.

There's a certain introspective tendency. You look at your work and say to yourself "Well, Galbraith, ah, this isn't so good, this is pretty bad." And if you're working with your hands or repairing buildings or something of that sort, you're not subject to bad reviews.

You hold yourself to a higher standard than most people. Hemingway had some of the same problems. You're depressed when you feel that the intellectual structure you have built somehow isn't up to form. Hemingway took an escape that I've never pursued by getting drunk. It's why so many literary people have resorted to alcohol.

Harry Wilmer, M.D.

There is almost a cliché in Jungian psychology that you welcome the depression as a necessary journey into the unconscious. Most people I know who are creative go through some pretty tough times, and I think some of the best things are done when people are in this mire, and they're trying to find some way out. [But] if a gifted writer, playwright, or artist comes to see me and they're terribly depressed, I don't say "Oh, that's nice, welcome it." I may feel compelled to work with their depression or give them medication until they can be stabilized, and then deal with the creative side.

I don't intrude in the creative process. When I find a creative person dreaming of a guide, I don't immediately say "Oh, that's me," I say "That's you, even if it's projected on me." It's important for the psychiatrist dealing with creative people who are depressed to help them see that their guide is in them, their inner analyst, their wise old man, their wise old woman. When any patient tells me a dream, I take that as a supreme creative act.

Judith Belushi Pisano

There are a lot of comedians who believe that if they don't have that tortured side they won't know what's funny. I think that it's true that there are a lot of people who are reacting to being unhappy or to negative things in their life by being funny. But I don't think one has to exist to have the other. Now, in my life, I have a new husband, and I have a baby. We have a nice life, it's very comfortable, it's peaceful. So the question is, do you lose your instinct to continue creating if you become too comfortable? I don't think so. I think you create because it's in you. It's almost Zen, opening yourself up for humor, to be funny. You put yourself there.

I've known some comedians who can't turn it off, and it's not something I would call a good quality about them. I think they're blocking something. They're afraid if they turn it off, it won't come back. Likewise, I imagine, depression for some people could get to be so familiar that they're afraid to let go of it, too.

John was not always "on" by any means. He was just funny in general. Just his look and the way he could move or react. He was a funny person, but he wasn't verbally on and making jokes all the time. It was more his mind, the way he saw things, and the ability to use it in political satire or whatever it might be. I don't think that has anything to do with whether you're happy or unhappy or on drugs or not, or depressed or not.

A lot of John's comedy started as a young kid at home; his mother was a funny lady. At the same time, they had a complicated relationship, and there was pain in it, too, so it was multisided. Maybe that's what makes someone more specifically a user of comedy to block things versus someone who's just a funny person.

Once when John was at the height of a binge, he said to me he didn't think he could be funny without drugs. Later, when he was at a period when he had not been doing drugs for some time, he knew that wasn't true. He might have had fears that life was getting a little too comfortable, and wondered if life gets too cushy, are you going to lose your drive and just want to work in the garden all day? And the bottom line is that actually, that's not so bad.

The depressed writer, or actor, or painter asks, "Without the highs of mania or the lows of depression, would I still live a life of creative intensity?" The question also might be "Without the distraction of mania, would I be free to make the most of my gifts? Without the shackles of depression, would my work soar?"

Writing, painting, acting, singing may help you feel a little better, for a little while, by siphoning off some of the painfully urgent emotions of mania and depression. If the internal pressure can be channeled artistically, at the very least, those around you may be spared some of the emotional fallout from your anger or your pain. The result doesn't have to be "good" by any objective criteria; all it needs to be is a release. If it is also well wrought, ask yourself, "Is that because of or in spite of my illness?" and remember that it is the artist who created the work, not the depression.

My fear is that we will glorify depression as a means to an artistic end, that we will say "It's not illness, it's art." I believe it is an illusion that art must be much larger or more passionate than life. One of the finest poems I have read in the last few months alluded to the death of a friend, but described riding home on a bicycle and clothes hanging on the line—ordinary experiences, poignantly, sanely rendered through the spare words of an artist. I have written some poems out of pain that I am very proud of, but the ones I remember are those written out of love.

16
Existential Blues

I remember lying awake in the loneliness of late-night anguish, strug-gling to find that special relationship to God that some have found in the Bible-imposed structure of a born-again life. Although these notions did not connect to my sense of Truth, I longed for some measure of peace and passed the night moaning, thrashing, and ultimately weeping in the effort to achieve it through Christ.

This could have been a moment of spiritual desolation, but the quality of the experience was no different from dozens of other nights of depression, only the focus had changed. Instead of my relationship with my husband, or my parents, or my children, or myself, it was my relationship with God over which I agonized.

The health of my soul and my mental health have intersected again and again: in the poems of Gerard Manley Hopkins, which I carried with me for many years, and later those of Anne Sexton; in the comfort I found in nature and in the old hymns; even in the person of my first husband, a church youth leader. When he abruptly walked out, my religious life ceased as well.

It was many years before my staunch atheism weakened when con-

fronted with the miracle of William's birth. "God could not be every-where, so he invented mothers," wood-grain dime-store plaques read. "Mothers could not be everywhere, so they invented God," I said with a laugh, while in my heart admitting at last that there had to be a greater force of creative power beyond genetic chance. I needed a belief in something larger than myself that would help me protect this most precious of beings. (Even my politics were commuted: As I nursed my baby before war footage on the evening news, I saw for the first time with horror that the dying soldier was somebody's son.)

Not many years later, I shared a tiny office with my first producer, a young woman of evangelical bent. I had learned through my experiences with my first husband not to trust born-agains and, like many people, was put off by street preachers and flower-wielding airport evangelists. But I respected Andrea. She held deep and sincere beliefs, and although they imbued much of her conversation, it was not an attempt to convert, but simply who she was. She introduced me to an example of piety that was noninvasive but a constant presence.

One day, when a member of my family was gravely ill, she hugged me, as friends will, adding "Would you like me to pray with you?"

"I wouldn't know how," I answered.

I don't remember the words of her prayer, but I remember the comfort of them. Utterly simple, utterly loving, utterly faithful, they touched my heart.

The next time I was at the depth of despair and depression, parked outside the radio station, paralyzed, unable to face the day, screaming out my pain in the privacy of my car, I found my voice crying "God, I don't even know if you exist, but if you do, please help me!"

No bolt from the blue split the sky with revelation but, simply by asking, a part of me admitted the possibility of Hope.

I don't know how much longer it was before I did find God, before I found a spiritual home in a congregation that had more seekers than pat answers, but after I'd been there about a year, a women's retreat was organized in the beautiful Texas Hill country.

The key speaker was a woman who was very Bible based, very Christ based, which I was not. On the final afternoon, we joined her for a guided imagery meditation.

She led us to envision Jesus in whatever style we found accessible—

traditionally white-robed, blue-jeaned, or in a three-piece suit. I found I could easily relate to Jesus not as the condemning, judgmental author- ity figure that is promoted by some but as a supportive friend and comforter, the Jesus of my childhood.

"Now I want you to go back to a time in your life," she intoned, "that was hurtful or difficult. Use all your senses to re-create that scene. What did the air feel like? What were you wearing? Who stood where? Be there in that moment and replay the entire incident but with Jesus at your side."

I went back to a time when I was picked on as a child and relived it, with Jesus at my side, with his hand in mine. I remember feeling reassured, less fearful, less hurt by the taunting of the older children, as though I had a big-brother savior to protect me. The sense of relief, of safety, was so affecting that I started to cry.

"Now that you know you have Jesus with you," she continued, "He can help you handle whatever adversities you are dealing with today and every day."

It was September. Although my depression had been diagnosed some months earlier, I had not yet achieved a therapeutic dose of medi- cation and was still very vulnerable. On hearing her hopeful message, I felt joy, and relief, and said to myself, "Yes, I see that, Jesus and I, hand in hand; we can lick it." I went home from the retreat, threw away my medication, and promptly fell off a cliff into a serious depres- sion.

This time around, the focus of my self-blame was religious. The interpretation I gave this episode was that obviously my faith wasn't strong enough.

I had reached a point where religion and psychology tangled, and I needed some special help sorting them out. I was very lucky that my therapist had a background in theology as well as psychology. When I had started seeing him, I was wary of his theological background—I had no idea that that would be exactly what I would need later on. To his credit, he had never introduced religion in our sessions, but now that I was deeply troubled by it, he had a perspective on the integration of body, mind, and spirit that was both psychologically and spiritually salutary.

Still, my religious construct—what I believed, how strongly and why—was shaken. Only now am I learning to see the benefit that has ensued this painful experience: the reevaluation of my spiritual life.

Lewis Judd, M.D.

Mood in general relates to one's spiritual well-being. That overlap may have confused this issue of mental disorders, because someone with depression in 1492 would have been considered to have an illness of the spirit. It would be seen as a religious issue, not as a health issue. Whereas we have evolved to a point at which we see it play out in those areas, but it truly is a health issue because it's a disease process, one that afflicts the way we perceive the world, the way we experience the world, and the way we operate in the world.

Harry Wilmer, M.D.

Belief in some divine order, belief in some something that may be called God is very important. It's something I don't analyze unless it becomes a neurosis.

Betty Sue Flowers, Ph.D.

I don't think you can have a spiritual dimension that doesn't affect the body. One reason we have so much trouble with this issue in society is that we have a mind-body split. If you think of the self as all one, then you would tackle the physical at the same time as the spiritual, knowing that it was all interrelated.

If you go in thinking there is just a spiritual problem, then that is a form of dualism, which, if you're speaking in Christian terms, disavows the Incarnation. Then it's a Manichean heresy, actually, not to go see a psychiatrist, because the tradition of Christianity said that the Body is real. If you see Jesus as meaning anything at all, it's an Incarnation in the flesh. If I were depressed, I would go to both a medical doctor and a spiritual counselor.

I think dealing directly with spirit is a more powerful form of psychology. But we do not have people as highly trained in that as we do in psychology. Psychologists are objective enough to listen, and many spiritual helpers are more interested in getting you to believe something, so they don't listen. That psychological language is very powerful language. It's just not as powerful as the language of spirit. The myths that you are permitted to make in psychology are limited; the myths you can make in the spirit are not. For example, you can have Jesus or the Buddha with you spiritually—you can't psychologically.

[What is happening to] someone who said they were having a spiritual crisis, a dark night of the soul, and someone who said "I'm an atheist, I'm just having a physiological depression" [is probably the same] electrochemically, but it would be *experienced* differently. In the dark night of the soul, although all hope is lost and you feel completely disconnected from God, you have a larger framework in which to put that; it's not like just being in a pit. You may cry "My God, my God, why hast Thou forsaken me?"* but there is the understanding of a story in which that has happened. In the old days people used to say "I'm being tested by God." Put in that context, it's a meaningful experience. If it's just depression, it's a meaningless experience, which adds to the depression, and then why bother existing?

Pain is just pain, but there is a lot of fear in it, too: fear you'll never get out of it, fear this is the way the world really is, instead of just pain. Even on a physiological level pain is much easier to

---

* "Even Jesus appears to have had a moment of disconnection," Flowers said, explaining different interpretations of this *cri de coeur*. "In esoteric literature, it's called the last battle, 'the battle of the angel of the presence with the dweller on the threshold.' The dweller on the threshold is the old self you thought you were and the angel of the presence is some reality to which you are going. The self you were, however resplendent, has to die before the presence. So one interpretation is the despair of the dark night of the soul. Another interpretation is that it is the last battle of the God-infused personality with the soul: Even something as beautiful and splendid as the personality of Jesus has to die for the spirit to emerge. A third one is that it is a direct quote from Psalm 22, which is a prophecy of everything that happens around the cross. He was saying, in effect, 'Now the Scriptures are fulfilled.' "

bear, if you're just in the pain, and not afraid of the pain, or resisting the pain.

Most psychological pain is unnecessary, in my experience. I think a lot of it is caused by expectations, which are based on old myths that we don't even know we hold. We expect things to be a certain way, and if they aren't, we suffer.

People have a lot of pain in marriage because they expect marriage to be a certain way, out of a myth they don't even know they hold. Considering how complex relations are, the myth of romantic love is too small for the reality of marriage.

Most of the people that I've talked to who have accomplished something in the world can look back at a time or an event in their lives and say "I thought that was the worst thing that ever happened to me at the time, but it turns out it was the best thing." How often have you heard that? There is a way in which that is literally true, but only for someone whose myth is large enough to make that transition, to contain the suffering. Most of our myths are not large enough to contain suffering.

If you think that the world is not a loving place, when something happens to you you're going to be defensive and respond as if you were being attacked. If you assume that the pattern is one of love, then there is a kind of peace with what happens in your life because you can trust that there is a larger design.

Judith Belushi Pisano

Depression is a void that is misunderstood. It is a lack of connection to the universe as one, or Jesus, or Buddha, or whatever you want to call it. It doesn't matter what your spiritual context is, but I think you need one. Even just love itself, loving your parents, loving someone, loving yourself, is enough because love is the essence of what spirituality is. Some people have a defined religion that doesn't seem to help them because they don't ultimately have a connection to it. And I think that's probably very depressing.

If depression is a spiritual problem, the problem in this culture is how do you direct someone to the solution and how do you find it? I think it begins with wanting to heal. Then you become open to finding something. In my case, in the beginning, I didn't want to heal. I was in pain and it seemed appropriate, so I don't think I was ready then.

John had problems like anyone, and I think the drugs were an attempt to mask them and block them out. I believe that his chemical makeup did act differently. But ultimately I think it was the spiritual void. He just didn't sense his own value. He sensed values about himself, and at times he could trust that, and not use drugs. You know, there was a happy sense of John, too, that he had about life. That's why people liked him, why they liked seeing him come down the road. But whatever the other side was that needed to be filled just, unfortunately, went that other direction.

I'm not a religious zealot or anything, but I really do think the spiritual level of it is the strongest. In the Bible, there are all sorts of accounts of Jesus telling people "You *are* okay." In essence, my interpretation is that we are okay, we just don't realize it. Perhaps there's something mystical or miraculous about why some people have amazing recoveries, and others try, and believe, and believe, and don't.

I was in Thailand, and Bali, and Jakarta, and the thing that impressed me was the sense that the people had a peace with them, and almost a light coming from them of radiated contentment. By our standards, we have so much more, and yet when you walk through New York City, or some little industrial town, or a western town, or any number of places, you don't often find that on the faces of people in this country.

Leslie Garis

I thought that inside I was blackness, and that that blackness was not only full of the most repulsive despair, the most horrible thing to see, but also that some part of it had to be evil, and that I was a force for evil.

I remember talking to my editor when I was writing a piece for *Vogue*, and I thought, "Poor Susie, she has to look at this monster who is talking to her." I saw myself as kind of like Medusa, a monstrous being. I excused myself and went into the bathroom and looked in the mirror. I looked in the mirror and sure enough, I was a monster.

I looked at my face, and I saw the blackness, the darkness, the despair, the destructiveness, the evil, like an open sore.

I had grown up in the Congregational church in Amherst, going to church every single Sunday and hearing all this stuff about the Good News. What is the Good News? What is the Good News? The Good News is that we are saved. I kept thinking, saved from what? What is the sin?

When I joined the church as a thirteen-year-old, having gone through the religious training, I didn't say the part about Jesus being the messiah because I wasn't sure. I wasn't sure He was the Son of God, but also I didn't want to think that we needed to be saved, that there was something inherently sinful in mankind, that God had to send His only begotten Son to be crucified so that our base natures could be lifted to something that would be acceptable to God and to a true Christian.

What is a true Christian? A true Christian is kind and good, and within his heart he does not have lust, envy, greed, all of these things we can banish. Whereas while I was growing up, as I would feel lust, envy, and greed, as every human being feels lust, envy and greed, I would be trying to say to myself that's part of the human condition, and that it is *not* necessarily inherently evil.

I see my whole journey through the depression as a kind of becoming whole, taking all of these parts, seeing that the depression is not evil but a blight, something that's suffered, not something I made, something that came from without and not from within.

These are things that I have always struggled with. I think that now, having come through this, if I can write fiction, I want to be able to write about things like lust without thinking that I'm doing a terrible thing.

William Styron

I'm a little puzzled by the word spiritual because I don't quite know what it means. If it means that the soul, whatever that is, is involved [in depression]—as in those cliché words "a trial to the soul," which it is, God knows—then there is a spiritual element. I'm not a religious person, so I don't know how close to religion you would be getting with using the word "soul." I do recall reading Job when I was able to concentrate, rather avidly reading Job. I realized that, as I had been told, this is very likely his expression of what it was like to be suffering from depression. And if he got through it, I could get through it. So to that extent there was . . . a sense that if I could get through this there must be some sort of redemption of myself involved.

Betty Sue Flowers, Ph.D.

It used to be that depression and other illnesses of the spirit were thought to be a form of possession by an evil spirit. But most cultures have not had the luxury to think about it. We have more time than others, and more interests and more tools to take the internal journey. I don't see it as an indulgence, but as a next step forward in our evolution in the West. We're exploring inner space.

Pat Love, Ed.D.

Given the state of the world, it would seem abnormal not to be depressed.

Jules Feiffer

After the Kennedy assassination, I did a cartoon where it ended with "You're no longer paranoid to feel paranoid." The American vision has changed radically in my lifetime, from a time of immigrant innocence when I was young. Even at the depth of the economic depression when I was a boy, one still felt idealism, Americanism. If you grew up more or less on the Left, as I did, you believed in the perfectibility of the world and the perfectibility of your social vision, that it was a struggle but by golly we would end poverty, we would end racism, we would solve the problems, and all it took was doggedness, organization, and refusing to quit.

The America I see around me today [1991] is an America that seems to have embraced the Reaganite philosophy that you can't throw money at problems, that in fact problems can't be solved, and there's no point in trying any longer. And that the poor will always be with us, and most of them are going to be black, so there's no point in caring about them anymore. They're not helping themselves and why should we? That education is a good idea but we really can't afford it. That it's bad to have such a sharp division between the rich and the poor, but it's not so bad that the rich will give up some of their money to stop it. That we're forming an increasingly separatist society, that the Balkanization of America is happening at a rate just as rapidly as it is in Eastern Europe and that the groups who are being Balkanized don't find anything wrong in this. That in the early years of this century, immigrants wanted to assimilate, but now the mood has swung in the other direction, and blacks are willingly self-segregating, as are most other groups.

The country is breaking down into a nation of fiefdoms, or as I've called it "Closet Americans." We have more loyalty to our own closet constituencies than we do to the Bill of Rights or any overarching government in Washington. Fewer and fewer people see themselves as having a national identity except at moments of

convenience like the Persian Gulf War. Generally, you're identified by whom you hang out with, by where your kids go to
school, by the clubs you belong to. And find isolation from all
other groups that aren't members of your club, that don't go to
your school. This is a peculiar and not a very good time.

The late sixties was another period when everything was going wrong in the society. There was rioting and demonstrations,
and the New Left, in which I had put a lot of my faith, had
turned into what we know it eventually became. I had gone
through a period of social depression, political depression. I just
didn't know what was happening in the country. What I had put
my hopes in clearly wasn't working, and I didn't know where we
were going. I spent months feeling very real gloom.

One day, driving up from Vineyard Haven, I picked up a
young woman hitchhiker, very pretty, and her little boy or little
girl, couldn't have been any more than a year and a half. She was
kind of a hippie or post-hippie. She said something that triggered off a series of responses in me where suddenly the connections I had been trying to make for months started popping into
place. I found myself talking to her, but really talking to myself,
and making these connections one after another about all the
things that I had been missing. I was grooving with it and getting
more and more excited and feeling better and better because
suddenly the cloud had lifted, and I understood what was going
on.

As I said before, when I don't understand I'm in bad trouble,
but however bad it is, once I understand I don't mind it as much.
By the time I let her out of the car, I was feeling euphoric. And
as she got out of the car, she looked at me sympathetically and
said, "Don't feel so bad, it's bound to get better," and left. I
drove off screaming with laughter, and I said out loud, "That's
my problem—what makes me happy makes them miserable."

It cheers me up to understand what makes a bad society bad
so you can start doing something about fixing it. What people
have misunderstood about me is they think that's a depressed
view of the world. If you look at a half-empty glass and say it's
half full, that doesn't make you an optimist. That makes you a

fool. An optimist is somebody who looks at a half-empty glass and says "It's half empty; what do we do now to fill it?"

That final quotation of Feiffer's resonated for me, and I have used it many times since our interiew: "It's half empty; what do we do now to fill it?" But I also know that when I'm depressed, *I look at the glass and say "Full, empty, who the hell cares?" I find it hard to remember that part of the disease of depression is a distorted and pessimistic view of the world, from which our relationships to Eternity are not exempt.*

17

The Black Dog at Home: Support of Family and Friends

Alcoholics say that for every one person who drinks to excess, ten people are affected. I imagine that would hold true for people affected by depression as well—from the friends and co-workers who are baffled by unexplained behavior, to teachers who are frustrated by periodic inattention or acting out, to siblings who see the "problem child" receive an inordinate share of parental consideration. These families and friends are in a position to provide invaluable support and aid to a depressed person, but often they simply don't know where to start. Sadly, not knowing how to help, what to do, they may turn away in helpless frustration, thus adding to the sufferers' fearsome isolation.

"What's wrong?" "Why don't you get out and do something?" "You'd feel better if you got up and took a shower." When I've started down that long black spiral into depression, such well-intentioned com-

ments are more hurtful than helpful. The first two simply have no answer, and all three require answers or action of which I'm incapable and thus feed my feeling of hopelessness. The words that are most welcome are "What can I do to help?" Sometimes I need a hug, or someone to do a specific task that I feel is overwhelming, or just a quiet presence in the room, someone not trying to "fix" the situation or supply answers or suggestions for improvement. Sometimes I just need someone to be there, so the dark isn't quite so big.

If you are in a relationship with someone in deep depression, a spouse, child, employee, accept that you may need to make adjustments to accommodate the person's illness, just as you would if s/he had had a heart attack, or pneumonia. Lower your expectations of what s/he is capable of, pick up the slack, take over some of the chores. If s/he is the usual cook, learn to cook spaghetti; eat simpler meals for a while. Let up on housekeeping standards. You'll find often you can stand anything if you know it's finite.

If you are helping a friend through a depression, remember that even if your depression was amenable to self-help, his or hers may not be. If self-help doesn't bring relief within a few weeks, seek professional advice. For both of you. Supportive therapy can be just as important for family and friends as it is for the depressed. If you feel it is somehow self-indulgent, remind yourself that you will need all the resources you can muster to see your family through a depression, for it affects the family as a whole, not just the individual. And sometimes the best way you can be available to help another is by strengthening yourself. If you wonder if you might need help, you probably do.

Know that depression can be a result of trauma—emotional or physical, especially after a head injury—and that early intervention may help deflect the worst of it. The relationship between substance abuse and depression may be chicken and egg: If someone you love is abusing, don't just assume s/he's an addict; depression may be an underlying problem, and may need treatment also. Remember that the depression is no more under his or her control than alcoholism is. Recognize it as both a real and a treatable problem. Encourage, support, befriend those afflicted, and take the time to help educate the uninformed.

Depression may masquerade as addiction, PMS, or workaholism.

But because depression takes such an enormous toll on the victims, their families, their productivity, and the nation, it behooves us to look carefully, and to offer suppport and help where we can. The encouragement and assistance of friends can go a long way toward helping a person through the miasma of depression.

And as Jennie Forehand, Susan Crosby, and Rose Styron show, those who care for people who are depressed can use a little extra care themselves.

William Styron

The single most aggravating thing that any member of the family could do would be to be anything but as sympathetic as you would be if your family member was suffering from cancer. The primary mistake would be to display lack of sympathy, to have the attitude of "Come on. You can pull out of this."

Art Buchwald called me almost every day, just to say "How are you doing?" Because he had been through this just a few months before. His support was very, very valuable. Rose's was, and Art's. It was a kind of insistence, of leaning on you and saying "Look, this is going to be okay. You're going to recover. Everybody recovers." In my case, the constant insistence that I was going to get well was so much more important than the medical intervention, even when I didn't believe it. There's a little residue of hope that hangs on. If I had [depression] again, the thing that would probably help me survive as much as anything would be my own recognition that I had been through this once, and I'm almost certain to get out of it again.

Dick Clark

My brother was five years older than I was. We had a wonderful relationship all of our lives. He was big and athletic and handsome and strapping and a much bigger guy than I. He was a football player, and so I always idolized him. I do to this day. He

said, "You have no idea how proud I am of you." He said,
"You've got more brains than I'll ever have. You are the most
interesting individual I've ever known." He zeroed in on my
head and what was inside it, because physically I was short and
skinny and couldn't do the things he could. He was in the service, so when he'd come home on leave he'd come into the room
and throw his arm around me and console me and say "It's
gonna be all right!"

[And with my mother's help] I began to realize that people
don't examine your physical countenance when they appraise
what kind of a person you are. And I began to become more
extroverted, more outgoing. Going into public speaking changed
my whole life. I'm still an introvert, but I became a professional
extrovert.

Anonymous

If you have the willingness to deal with your own discomfort of
being around somebody who tried to commit suicide, that in
itself is a great gift. Just be there. When I was in the hospital
[after my attempt to throw myself out a window], the only one
who really knew how to behave around me was my five-year-old.
He just ran in and jumped on me and wrestled with me, just like
always.

Jane Doe

Nobody ever said anything that was helpful. On the contrary, I
felt constantly frustrated by people trying to cheer me up and
not understanding me. I felt victimized and more paranoid. I
would have wanted somebody to say that you're an okay person,
that this is a disease, and there's help.

People are always saying "Well, go buy something, go to the
movies, go to a restaurant, go do something for yourself." Of
course, that is the worst thing you can say to somebody who is in

real depression, because nothing helps. Once, though, I called one of my closest friends in California that I used to stay with. I said, "I am a wreck and if I didn't have to edit this thing, I would just get on a plane and come out there. I am a complete basket case." He said the most loving thing to me that maybe anybody has ever said in a real moment of crisis, he said, "So, come. I'll pick you up in a basket." Very loving, very accepting; it doesn't matter what condition you are in, I'll be there.

For a year, Forehand commuted from the state legislature of Maryland to North Carolina where her eighty-year-old mother suffered severe depression.

Jennie Forehand

My cousin and I have laughed about this streak of stubbornness that runs in our family, and how if I hadn't been so stubborn, Mother might not be here today. My cousin is a clinical psychologist in the Navy, and she helped me through this. And I have a couple of good friends who are psychiatrists that I could call. I guess my whole thought was that if Mother died, I didn't want to have a guilt trip. All along I was thinking "Am I doing the best for her? Am I doing as much as I want my kids to do for me?" And I kept telling them "Look what I am doing for your grandmother, because you may have to do this for me someday."

Both my kids were in college the year my mother was ill. On the weekends that I couldn't get to Charlotte, one of my kids would go. It taught them so much. Trying to deal with somebody who is not rational taught them more than anything they had ever learned in school. Here my kids wanted to be helpful and Mother was slamming the phone down or wouldn't let them in. They were kind of afraid of her. They had known her at her best, and they saw her at her worst. I think that was a real opportunity for them. Now my daughter is dealing with her little kids. She said that at least if they misbehave you can send them to quiet time, but you can't do that to your grandmother.

Susan Crosby

If I hadn't had my parents and my family and the strength I had behind me, I would have been destroyed. I know I would have been a suicide, dead, long before Lindsay was. Because it's that horrendous, and you feel so guilty.

My mom was there all the way through. My father had grown up a lot like Lindsay's dad, that same kind of world, and they don't understand mental illnesses. Even so, my father was right there for me, and for Lindsay.

Joan Rivers

You can't just say "Okay, we're going to Disneyland" [to try to cheer up a depressed person]. There's nothing you can do; that's the horror of depression. The only thing I do with people, friends of mine that are in depression, is to let them know "I understand. I can't help you out of yours, but at least I can say, yes, I've been there, I'll probably be there again, I understand." And the other thing I say over and over is "Go get help. Get permission to be depressed." Getting permission gives you room to open the door to leave it behind.

Mary Jones

It seems to me there are people you're close to on different levels. There are political friends, there are people you do out-doors things with, there are people you enjoy other activities with, like going to the movies or the theater, and then there is a very small circle of good friends. I have a number of close friends and a few with whom I can talk about anything. But I must say, it's always been my tendency to wait until I was better and then say "Well, things are going relatively well now." Who wants to hear from somebody who's really a mess? I suppose there is some sense of presumption. I have friends I think I could call and say "Would you help me? I think I'm about to kill myself." But I have a hard time doing that.

A. John Rush, M.D.

Unless the person is completely disabled, that person has to show up and ask for treatment. Somebody has to diagnose them and then the diagnosis leads to treatment. The trick is how do you get the person with the illness to accept the fact that they're not normal—doesn't mean they're crazy, just not normal, they're ill—and get them to go in to see someone? The best way is to say to them "Look, I've known you a long time, and you are not yourself. Here's what I see. I talk to you, you break out in tears. You look like you haven't slept in a week. I ask you questions; your mind is not staying on track. I don't think you're doing this on purpose. I think you're ill. I think you have a depression or something is wrong, and you need, in my view, to go get a real expert opinion, not advice from the neighbor and the dog catcher and everybody else, and I'm willing to go with you. I'm willing to make an appointment for you. I don't want you to just sit on this thing."

And so you just tell them what you see, and often that person will say "Yeah, and I also don't eat very well, and I have no interest in sex anymore." If you know them well, they'll tell you almost all the symptoms, because they hurt, and it's often a relief to the person with depression if somebody close to them says "You look seriously ill, and this is what I see," and then they'll eventually go in for help.

Kitty Dukakis

I would ask families to stop blaming patients as though they have control over the disease, because they don't. There is nothing good or bad you can do to change that disease. You can't.

Norman Rosenthal, M.D.

Family members must understand that this is a real condition and not a character flaw. They must recognize the importance of the light and the other specific things that can be helpful and should encourage the individual to expose himself or herself to those things. They should help to alleviate the stresses and chores that make the problem worse, and just be there in a supportive way.

Things that they shouldn't do are to blame the individual and hold the individual responsible as though that person is willfully doing these things. That is all too common a problem. They should not feel that they have to fix everything; they can't. If they feel that they have to fix it, that can often lead to anger and frustration when the affected individual doesn't rapidly snap into place. Understand, encourage, support, don't blame, don't feel responsible for it.

Rose Styron

I'd say watch, look, and listen. And don't assume that everything that happens between you has to do with the interaction of your two personalities. Try to look at the totality of the person that you're living with and that you love, and be objective, more objective than I was, about where things might come from. Just be there to talk. Bill never wanted to talk, although I was always trying to talk, which is a very female-male thing, and so finally I stopped talking, too. You can't make your spouse talk, but you can still observe closely, or do a little more reading and exploring than I did. And just consider the possibility that somebody else may be in a different kind of pain than you recognize, because you've never been there.

Dick Clark

Be specific with the advice. Pick out the good things and highlight them for the person under stress and say "Remember, you've got this going for you."

Lewis Judd, M.D.

If you are an employer, you may be the first to discern the worker's depression. You may even want to approach them, very directly, in a kindly, warm fashion, as someone who is caring and concerned, and indicate "Look, I've read this about depression, and as I've looked at it, you seem to have all the symptoms of it. Has it occurred to you that you might be depressed and this may be affecting what you're doing? You know depression is a disease like any other disease, lots of people have it, it can be treated, you must get help." Not confrontive, but direct, affirmative, firm, straightforward, but out of motivation of concern.

It rarely requires the level of breakthrough of denial that is necessary in confronting people with substance abuse disorder. People are aware that they're feeling miserable. Sometimes an intervention is necessary, because it's not uncommon as a part of depression for someone to be pessimistic about treatment and to say "Yeah, I feel terrible, but that's just me. There's nothing you can do about it. No one can help me. Life is just terrible." Then one needs maybe to be more firm about seeking treatment; you may need to draw other people in and insist on it.

You might say "I know how terrible you feel. There's no

need for you to feel this bad. I know that you are feeling very hopeless about your situation and you feel it can't change, but that's really part of being depressed, rather than the way you really are, and so you must get help."

It's a desperate enough situation that people have to use as much pressure as they can to get someone in treatment, and to not give up, to not be discouraged, but to be very firm about it. But ultimately, you cannot force someone to be treated. If they're suicidal, a threat to themselves, then they certainly can be held for observation, and during that time we can often then initiate treatment.

Jennie Forehand

Don't ever just trust. Always get a second opinion or a third opinion or a fourth opinion. Don't be satisfied until you try some more things. People think that they are going to hurt the doctor's feelings. The doctors are on pedestals, but people put them there. The doctors don't put themselves there.

Another piece of advice that I would give people is that if this happens to your parents, don't hesitate to jump in. I just swooped in there and put something in front of her to sign and said, "I've got to have your power of attorney." Her lawyer was there and he agreed. I can't tell you how many times I have had to use her power of attorney. I changed the signatures on all the bank accounts. I got access to everything. I'm so glad I did that. It has been a pain for me to have to do that, but if I hadn't done that it would have been a disaster. I can't stress that enough.

So many people say "Well, she doesn't want me to have access to her money and everything." And the parents say "Oh, I can't trust my kids." Hey, if you can't trust your kids, it is too late. But she has always trusted me. I treated her like you treat your two-and-a-half-year old. I said, "Today we are going to do this. And we *are* going to do it." I just said, "You don't have any options. I don't have any options. We are running short on time."

I have worked through her friends. When she didn't want to do something, I would call her friend or her next-door neighbor and they would just happen by and say "Oh, I hope that you are going to do this." So I manipulated the process. That is kind of what you do with legislation. I call people from all over the state and say "Call so-and-so today and tell him that we need the such-and-such." And all of a sudden it looks like it is his idea, so he buys into it. And that is what I did with her.

Susan Crosby

Know that the family can be helped. You can survive it. My kids and I have survived, and we're okay, and we're going to be okay. Even when the worst happens, which is that they commit suicide, you do make it through, and you can go on.

There are other things the families can do. Number one, get support systems going and if you can afford it, therapy, absolutely. Films need to get made about it so that people recognize it in their neighbors or somebody in their family, and understand what they're going through, and have a little compassion for them. Then it doesn't get called all these other names that you end up defending or you can't deal with it, or it's embarrassing for the kids because they don't know how to handle it.

I wish someone had told me earlier that I didn't do anything wrong, that it wouldn't have mattered what I did. I wasn't responsible for it. Because I really thought I did something to cause this disease.

And the other thing is to find out what it is, because the term manic depression is used so loosely.

Rod Steiger

Be patient. Support. Support means to hold, not to grab. There's a big difference. To kind of sneak up and hold. Give the support to the spirit, give support to the shattered ego, without pity. Dear Lord, if you pity a sensitive person in an illness like this, you'll bury them.

The last thing I want somebody to say is "Oh, you look great today. You look wonderful." I guess I just want them to say everyday things. "Do you want your bagel or do you want your tea? Do you want the tea with milk or do you want a little sugar?" Maybe a hand on the shoulder. That's support.

Did you ever see a picture called *The Enchanted Cottage?* There are two people, the man was disfigured on one side of his face, and the girl was not, but she was ugly. But when they looked at each other, as they fell in love, they both became good-looking, until some idiot person said to the girl, "Oh, my darling, it doesn't matter if you're ugly or not." And she could never think of herself as attractive again. That's what I'm talking about.

"Oh, you poor baby, you're depressed, oh my sweetheart." Who needs a reminder? Try to keep everything as ordinary as possible, give little hints, like "I'm gonna go the store, you want to come with me?"

God help anybody who has any mental problems when there's no love within distance. Male, female, dog, or cat. Something trying to give back to you when you scream, because they love you. Something.

The friends I remember through the years as having been most supportive are those who were able to keep their own equilibrium in spite of my out-of-controlness, giving me something solid and predictable to bounce off. I hold in my heart with gratitude those who accepted me as I was, how I was—the college roommate who kept her sense of humor in the face of my despair and who didn't seem to mind if I sat in the closet for a few days; the not-quite boyfriend who any time of night or day offered safe harbor, a cup of café au lait, and a comforting and utterly undemanding bedmate; the nanny/best friend who would keep William happy, and occupied, and satisfied with simple and appropriate explanations, and who would cook and offer meals that I didn't have to think about planning or preparing, that I could eat or leave; and most of all, my husband, who at his best is able simply to hold me, without asking unanswerable questions, without impatience no matter how long I need his warmth, without expectations of that closeness solving my problems, and most of all, without judgment.

18

It Tolls for Thee

No marriage runs on a smooth and dry road all the time, but when the black dog of depression rides along, you're in for a roller-coaster ride of exhilaration and despair. Those of us whose marriages survive seem to agree that it is largely because we are married to extraordinary people —"angels" one says, "saints" says another. But is there an element of codependency in this saintliness? Of martyrdom, even?

How do they manage, burdened with their own fears, concerns, anger, and guilt as well as the daily pain of watching a loved one suffer? For many, the added vigilance, social isolation, and labor involved in caring for a severely depressed person becomes overwhelming. Others just take one day at a time.

Rose Styron is known as a very strong woman, but even her fortitude was tested by her husband's profound depression. She found ways to cope, and although few of us can escape to the Bahamas for a week, we can learn from her that giving ourselves permission to take care of ourselves, as well as our ill spouse, can be a vital prescription for our own mental health. We can take long walks, arrange for someone to care for the kids, go stay with family or friends, and learn to ask others for help.

Pat Love, Ed.D.

Family members don't know the difference between real anger and depression-induced reactivity. You can tell them, but they think you're not the best judge because it all *sounds* the same to them. My husband is still gun-shy around certain issues because of when I overreacted. And I say "That's past. I'm not that way anymore." It's probably going to take a long time of me telling him it's all right, and of me not overreacting. Now when I get angry it has a lot more impact on him. Before, it was more of the same, he shut me out. I guess he had to.

Leslie Garis

Arthur kind of drew into himself. Being a writer, he is able to draw into his own world, and it was okay. It just wasn't very good. A general unhappiness pervaded the household, but it didn't ever threaten our marriage. I loved him and needed him, even though I couldn't experience anything but me. But I knew intellectually.

I masked [the depression] so much, even from him. He saw heavy times, so he would just work all the time. He would go to his office out back of the house and work all day, we'd have dinner, we'd have little chats about the children, he'd go back out to his office and work after dinner. He'd come in, I'd be asleep. We'd get up and start the day again. So, I think that he just began to think "Well, this is maybe the way it is. Maybe life is not very much fun." He was just trying his best to accept the situation as it was. We didn't understand that what I had was depression.

Kitty Dukakis

Michael jokes about people like Rose Styron and himself being
saints, and I guess they are because they love people like us, and
they're willing to see this thing through. Rose and Michael are
two of the loveliest human beings. It takes a certain quality of
character to be able to live through that. It must be terrible. I've
never had to live with that. I'm married to a man, and Bill Styron
is married to a woman, who are always up. They are always
happy, always positive. I don't think Rose ever gets down.
They're steady, and I guess we marry people that are that way
because we're not.

Rose Styron

I am very attached to people. Maybe because I'm a poet, I've
always been able to put myself in other people's places and empathize with people that I'm interested in. Because I had experienced very, very low moods myself, especially when I was young,
I could make that leap of imagination from the little bit that I
had had to the enormous amount that Bill had. But without ever
really understanding that he could want to end his life, because I
have never entertained the idea of suicide for a second. He made
me understand it, by talking about it, by telling me about it. But
not until afterwards. We talked a great deal afterwards.

Nobody was really with him except me. In the country, we
lived a very solitary life. Sometimes I would invite people to dinner in order to try to get him out of himself, and everybody was
wonderful about coming. But I really felt that I was the only one
who knew him very well, since we've been married thirty years,
and he was very private.

He's always been known as a social eccentric; he always says
he won't have cocktails, and he often bows out of things that he
has said he would do. People knew him as a social curmudgeon,

if you will (although he is a terrific host and a terrific guest when he wants to be). That summer and that fall I sort of exaggerated [this eccentricity] and covered [the depression] that way. But his close friends knew exactly what was going on. I was prepared to be embarrassed, because I never knew what was going to happen next.

I was watching him and monitoring every change of mood or articulation that he made. I felt so ignorant. I didn't know what was happening, so in a way, I guess I was studying him. In case a doctor ever said to me "What's going on? What have you seen?" I started keeping a diary, making notes of all the various medicines he was taking. This was probably a month before he went into the hospital, when I couldn't keep track of the drugs. It turned out to be especially useful when his medicines got crossed up. He really had very, very bad reactions to having been given too much medicine of different kinds, and one drug not getting out of his system before the next got in.

I was scared of what was going to become of him, or us. It was getting worse and worse and I could not imagine how it would end. I felt very close to him; love is ever present at a time like that. You worry but you don't fall apart. You're just thinking of what to do next, and trying to learn more.

I stopped my work. The kids took care of me and us, so I had no obligations. I became their obligation, and they were absolutely wonderful to me and to him. They were an incredible support.

Once he went to the hospital and I knew he was safe, I just fell apart. I was still scared about what was going to happen to him, and about what the next weeks or months or years would bring, and whether they would have to give him electric shock, which I was very opposed to at the time. I really couldn't handle it. My kids suggested I go to the Caribbean for a week. Polly and her husband stayed with Bill, and Susanna and Tommy came with me and another friend, Bob Brustein. Suddenly I was completely physically debilitated. Bob kept saying "Well, let's play tennis." I like to play tennis better than anything in the world, and normally I play twice a day, [but] I got out on the court and

I just couldn't move. I still remember the feeling of having absolutely no strength, I couldn't even take a walk.

But it comes in on you when it's okay to come in on you, and after a week down there I felt much better, and I went back, and things got better.

Bill gives me a lot of credit for helping him, but I think I lost a lot of self-confidence. There have been many times since then when I have wondered whether I could deal with things or not. I'm sure it changed me in some real way. Things had always gone so smoothly for me, and I had always gone full tilt, feeling as you do when you're very young that life is forever and you can do just what you want to and everything is going to be fine. And when one of the pins is knocked over, it makes you much more tentative about other things.

While he was going through it, I took a lot of it personally. I had been disapproving of a lot of the way things were happening between us. And I'd been angry with him a great deal in the decade before this happened. I got to thinking "Maybe this wouldn't have happened if I'd been more understanding, the way I had been the first decade that we were married." I thought that a lot of what was happening to him was because I wasn't a good wife, and I hadn't been around, and I'd gone off and done my thing, and hadn't done what wives are supposed to do and always be at home. So I felt guilty about it, and I felt a lot of it was my fault.

After he went to the hospital and he began to get better, I had some time to think about it, and I thought, "How could I have been so stupid? This has been going on for twenty of the thirty years we've been married." There had been all these signposts, these very obvious symptoms, which in retrospect I could see. I always thought they had to do with me because we always fought on a very personal level. But it had to do with alcohol, incipient depression, with whatever he was going through in his head, and it really didn't have to do with me. Suddenly I had a whole new perspective on what he had been going through. And I was angry at myself for not understanding sooner.

I felt that I had had pretty bad judgment in not realizing all of this and not having gotten help for him sooner and not having gone to see a psychiatrist or psychologist myself. But I think we came out of it much closer and much more aware of what is happening. It certainly strengthened the marriage.

I don't think it strengthened me personally. There are still some nagging doubts there. Maybe it did. I think it gave me the insight to be more articulate and to have closer friendships with people. Maybe the fact that I can be more open with people and talk about things is a sign of acceptance or strength. It's certainly been a rewarding five years since then, in many ways, especially as far as friendships go. But there are a lot of hangups that I have that I wasn't really aware of before. Exploring anybody else's problems obviously makes you face your own.

Susan Crosby

I didn't have many close friends. It was very hard for me to have friends because I couldn't explain Lindsay's behavior; it was very embarrassing. Lindsay would hit on my girlfriends. Real close friends could slough it off. But I couldn't have somebody new around me.

I love acting, but because Lindsay's behavior was seasonal, there was only one time a year I could do that. Once, when I had an audition for *I Dream of Jeannie*, Lindsay called the producer and told him that I was a streetwalker and that kind of stuff. So I was told the studio doesn't need to deal with the hassle, of somebody calling in and causing a commotion. After that, I wasn't real eager to go out on auditions anymore.

I could not leave the kids. At one point, he took Chipper and I couldn't find Chipper for over twenty-four hours. He had taken him out to some people and left him there. Because it was Lindsay Crosby, these people decided to protect Lindsay Crosby's son and not let the mother know. That's horrible, things like that. That only had to happen once to me, and I never let the kids out of my sight again.

I felt so responsible for Lindsay's behavior, and then guilty because I stayed, guilty because I couldn't fix it, guilty because I thought I caused it.

Dick Clark

I don't know how you explain depression to people like my wife. I can't even approach the subject of anybody's emotional disorder. She can't even fathom why it would happen. Everybody says, "How do you live with this? Happy all the time!" Well, under normal circumstances, it's pretty easy on the receiver.

My wife has a chemical balance that works twenty-four hours a day, with very few ups and downs, and she has very little sympathy for anybody who has mood swings. Her reaction to the problem is "You'll be all right tomorrow. Don't even think about it." It's like Scarlet O'Hara, "I'll worry about that tomorrow." Those people are very fortunate. But they don't make very good counselors. If you are one of those people, in the company of somebody who's depressed, you've got to realize that your happy, cheerful, pat-them-on-the-back, it's-gonna-be-all-right attitude won't work.

Rod Steiger

If it wasn't for my wife, I wouldn't be alive today. She's thirty-four years younger than I am. She had to be young to put up with the behavior patterns. I'd come downstairs in the morning on the mornings that I made myself get out of bed—some days I didn't make it at all—and I'd say good morning. I'd sit and look at the ocean and about nine o'clock that night I would say good night and go back upstairs, or I'd go back and forth all day to the bedroom to the couch, to the bedroom to the couch.

There was about a year and a half during which I met Paula that I was in pretty good shape. That's twelve years ago. Then I went into a depression again. You're dealing with a girl who when I met her was twenty years old. I was fifty-four. And we've been together twelve years and we've been married five years, and this young "child" somehow hung in, and her being there saved me. One of the things that can save you is that through all the shadows that you peer through when you have a mental disease, every once in a while you see the passing face flick of somebody that you love or who has loved you, and that gives you a little strength for a split second. If I would have been alone in the house, I wouldn't have had to worry about embarrassing or hurting anybody if I knocked myself off. I would have worried about my daughter, but she wouldn't have been there.

My wife never once condemned me. You know? Someone you love is sitting there looking like somebody you've never seen before, deteriorating before your eyes, hardly breathing, not talking, smelling bad, looking bad. And because of the pain of it, you suddenly say, "What's wrong? For God's sake, I love you! Do something! Don't just sit there! You can't just sit there like that! What's the problem?" She never did.

You're not dead when you're depressed. You still pick things up. You may pick them up in a faster or slower manner, but you feel things. Feelings don't mean anything to you, but you still feel them. So she never condemned me with an outburst of being exhausted with not knowing what to do, which is one of the worst exhaustions in the world. She said, "I'm going to the Valley to play handball." That's when I knew she was fighting it. "I'll be back in an hour or so." And then she probably went to the Valley and beat the shit out of this ball. She took a healthy way out. She never lost her patience, although she was at the edge sometimes. She had years of silence. There were only two people in this big house on the beach. It's funny because—you want to hear an egotistical statement?—that kind of behavior from her taught me to say "Paula, you love me so much, I love you." I said that not meaning at all what it sounds like. If I heard it, I would say "Well, that's nice of you!" but there was a lot of truth in that. She loved me so much she taught me all about love.

Pat Love, Ed.D.

I think in many ways men feel more responsible for women than women do for men, even in this day and age. Depression taps into his inadequacy, "I'm not enough. I can't fix this woman." Then he feels hopeless. Because men are very action-oriented, they don't want to talk about it, they want to *do* something, and what can you do? He probably acts that out by working a lot, or extramarital affairs, or being depressed himself, or trying harder, or drug and alcohol self-medication, or sports-aholism, any way that he can dissociate from this because to look at it is too painful.

So, the advice to the husband is first, to know that this may not be about you, and second, not to take it personally. And it's so hard not to take it personally. And to the man who says "Get out of bed and fix my dinner," know that this is a physical ailment, that it's not just a mental ailment. You wouldn't say that to a person who had polio.

John Kelsoe, M.D.

The most important thing is that if you feel that your spouse's personality is changing and they are acting in a very aberrant fashion, try to get them to get help. Not only can it be a psychiatric disorder, but other neurological disorders can result in the same kinds of personality changes.

Depression is different from mania, because people feel miserable when they are depressed and they are willing to go get help for it. Although, typically it is ignorance that operates there. Mania is so different from the average person's experience that it is clearly identified as something that is abnormal, at least in the more extreme stages. Everybody identifies a little bit with depression. If nothing else, it is similar to the feelings of grief.

Many people for that reason don't identify it as an illness. But it can be treated. It can be helped.

Of the men with whom I have been deeply involved in my life, my husband Bill is the one who has stood by me through all the ups and downs, through the agonizing over treatment, through the joint therapy. Perhaps because he has faced down his own black dog, he has been exceptionally supportive. When I asked him about his perspective as the partner of a depressed person, I learned to my great discomfort how hard that had been at times.

Bill and I

There were several periods of time when I felt our marriage was threatened. Whether or not it was because of your behavior or because of my response to your behavior is a very difficult cause-and-effect analysis.

One time was not long after we were married. I was very frightened by your anger because I'd never seen anything like that before. I remember a lot of highly charged emotional confrontations between you and me, which I believe now were probably facilitated by depression episodes. But back then, it was ordinary. I accepted our behaviors as the way things were, feeling that there was nothing we could do about it but live with it.

We managed to deal with that in a way that was very efficient. We set up our lives, until shortly after William was born, so that we didn't cohabit. You traveled, I traveled, and we spent a long weekend together here and there and maybe once in a while a whole week at home together, but most of the time you'd be in Los Angeles or on location somewhere for six weeks, and I'd be in depositions in Chicago for three weeks, and we'd meet somewhere in between. That was a very romantic and exciting thing. We were always in a honeymoon mode. But it was not real life, so for the first two and a half or three years of our marriage, I missed observing what it was like living with you day-in and day-out as a normal married couple.

Our marriage was in greatest jeopardy of coming apart after I had had a major crisis and was in intense psychoanalysis myself. I became just healthy enough to start having interest in living and having a relatively normal life, and yet our life together was still severely crippled by my crisis and by your depression. It was very hard at that point. For about a year or longer, from time to time I had thoughts about the possibility of our marriage breaking apart.

The only other time I had any notions in that regard, though not nearly as strong, was actually late last winter or spring. I had come to realize that I desperately needed to identify and define my own needs and to start getting them met, and I wasn't sure that it was possible for that to occur in the context of our marriage. I am very confident that that's possible now, I just wasn't then. We have both grown since then. Through my own therapy, I'm learning to recognize my needs and to take responsibility for their fulfillment.

But at that time, you were in a depressive phase, and we were dealing with the whole issue of treatment of your depression and how much anger that elicited and how difficult it was to adjust my life and the boys' lives to dealing with your mood changes and behavioral changes when you were or were not on medication. There were episodes of low self-esteem on your part and mood swings from sad to angry to exhilarated. There were times when your personal hygiene was ignored, several days at a time with no change of clothes, no makeup, no bathing. There was a lack of ability to concentrate—on cooking, for example, or anything that followed a specific formula—forgetfulness, a greater than normal difficulty with punctuality, those kinds of things. I also saw a decreased interest in sex, a decreased interest in social intercourse and activities, just kind of a reduction in living.

And I remember being just absolutely exhausted from being if not obsessive, certainly overly concerned about making sure everything was okay with everyone except myself. When you're depressed that's a pretty big job, taking care of you and taking care of the children and taking care of my work.

I looked at myself in the mirror and said "You're running out of steam; you just don't have the strength to live this way any-more." That's when I first started seriously thinking about sepa-rating my therapy from ours and seeking my own therapeutic help again, which I'm now doing.

You ask me what reservoirs I tapped that enabled me to hang in there. I don't know the answer to that question. There is a part of me that believes it must be because I have some sort of extraordinary internal strength. Another side of me, though, be-lieves it is not some extraordinary inner strength, but that it is just my job.

I would be disingenuous and frankly foolish to ignore and to attempt to refute that there have been periods in our relationship and behavior within that relationship when I have been codependent and have been a martyr, but many times, being ex-traordinarily strong and creative and certainly loving has allowed me to succeed and prevail. So it's the yin and yang, mixture of both angelic, heroic behavior and malignant codependent behav-ior. I don't see why it can't be both.

Spouses can play a vital role in the management of this illness. Bill notices changes in my behavior that signal the beginning of an episode before I do. Informing me of his observations can be tricky, though—by then the low self-esteem and paranoia of my depression are starting and any helpful remark is likely to be heard as criticism. It takes bravery on his part and great trust on mine for him to tell me and for me to hear. My husband and I are still learning together to handle this illness as a team. During the time it has taken to write this book, we have climbed another few rungs on this ladder.

19
Families in the Dark

By observing and asking questions of their relatives, many people with depression are able to identify other afflicted family members. Some, like William Styron, missed the opportunity to share experiences with a depressed parent. Yet he was able to use his own experience to help encourage others who also suffered from depression. Likewise, if we can face our illnesses head on, we can use our knowledge to identify, educate, and support other depressed family members.

Dr. John Rush spoke earlier about the importance to your doctor of a family psychiatric and medical history. But getting a medical history out of my stoic, stiff-upper-lip family is about like getting military secrets out of the Pentagon. I remember one such conversation with my mother.

"Mom," I asked, form in hand, "has anyone in our family ever had . . . ?"

"No," she answered, before even hearing the noun.

"Did anyone ever die of heart failure?"

"Of course they did; if their heart kept beating, they'd still be alive."

"Well, has anyone ever suffered from arthritis?"

"I don't know. We didn't discuss it."

She wasn't stonewalling; she was telling the truth. They simply didn't discuss it.

Did any of my ancestors ever suffer from depression? I have no idea. But at least, starting now, my descendants will know and, I hope, will be able to learn and draw solace from each other.

Now there is greater recognition and treatment of the family as a system than there ever has been. One therapist described it as a mobile: Anything that influences one pendant changes the balance among them all. We ask ourselves, to what extent does depression run in my family? How does diagnosis and treatment of depression affect relationships among my family members? And what role do genetics play?

Susan Dime-Meenan

[My family's reaction] really hurt. Because of a genetic predisposition to the illness, there was a sense of attached blame—my mother felt responsible, even though I was twenty-seven, that she could have done this to me. I was angry at her because no matter how I tried to explain it to her, that it wasn't her fault, to this day I still can't convince her. She won't say it out loud, but when I'm having a rough time or a bad day, you can see it in her face.

It's not just my mother. Parents have been blamed for generations for what was wrong with their children. It's just dumb.

Pat Love, Ed.D.

The sad part came when I saw how everybody in my family had been endogenously depressed. When I looked at my father, when I looked at my grandparents, I had such new compassion for them.

John Kelsoe, M.D.

So many parents have suffered guilt needlessly. There are still those who advocate the idea [that a child's mental illness is the parent's fault], but for the most part, people don't accept that anymore. Part of the development of biological psychiatry has been telling them that it's not their fault. That is really what they want to hear. They benefit from that enormously.

Parents come to me all the time wanting to know "What's the risk to my kids? I'm worried about my child because he's having trouble in school." But I think that to label a child early on as being predisposed [to depression] may possibly have the bad effect of that parent treating them as more vulnerable and possibly causing problems for that child *because* they've been treated differently.

So little is known. I think that there's a spectrum [of causative factors], between environment and biology. People who have a strong genetic predisposition will get depressed for absolutely no reason, when their childhood has been as good as anybody's. And at the other end are people who have virtually no genetic predisposition (which is far and away the exception, I'll say, since almost everybody's family has somebody in it if you look far enough). These people may be subject to extraordinary stresses in their life or extraordinary abuse or neglect in their childhood and they may be depressed as a result of the environment.

Most people who suffer with depression are somewhere in the middle of that spectrum; they have some genetic history, and then they had something happen to them: a divorce, a loss of a job, or something like that. Or they may have had a developmental problem, such as abuse in the family or loss of a parent. In other words, it is a combination of all of these factors.

The bottom line is, the risk for children [of depressed parents] is probably around 15 to 20 percent of having any kind of problem with a mood disorder. It's going to be roughly similar for all first-degree relatives, meaning parents, children, or siblings. For second-degree relatives, like uncles and aunts, the risk becomes less. It depends on who else is affected on that side of the family.

I think it's important to emphasize that that 15 to 20 percent varies from somebody who may have one episode of depression during a lifetime and never have any other problems, to somebody who is virtually incapacitated with manic-depressive illness. There is a wide range of manifestation of this illness, and when you're looking at somebody who has one episode of depression in their whole life, well, you're looking at probably 10 percent of the population. This is something that's so common, it's more of a normal variant than an abnormal phenomenon. Do they have the gene? Well, I don't know. I think that it becomes very iffy to say that, because it's so common.

The real goal of my work would be to identify the specific genes that are involved and thereby have a 100 percent accurate test that would tell me whether someone in the family has the gene or not. Even so, if you inherit the gene, you probably only have somewhere between a 50 and a 70 percent chance of ever manifesting the illness in your whole life.

Denton Cooley, M.D.

[My daughter] Florence was chronically depressed. She became a classical case of depression with mood swings, valleys and peaks. The psychiatrist said it was typical psychosis, although we were not aware that it was that bad. You know, psychosis has such a bad connotation. It seems so much more serious than we thought Florence was. Nevertheless, she was in a depressed state and that's why she took her life.

She came to me and said she was very low, and I told her to talk with a psychiatrist. Then she started seeing him regularly, and he informed me that it was not just a simple neurosis, it was a major problem. She was even hospitalized for a period.

She had lived in Houston, about six blocks from where we live. She had lived at home off and on, but then she got married and that ended in a divorce, which is a real failure. It affected her.

You try to provide your children with a feeling of security. If parents stay together, I think that's an important thing. That makes the children feel secure, and my wife and I have stayed together and provided the family with one home, and one mother and father. You try to be as supportive as you can. Myself, I'm an extremely busy person. There's not a lot of free time to spend around the house and it's not easy to relate closely to any of my five daughters. I'm just too busy. That may have been a part of the reason why, but I'm not sure. It may also be that because I was an achiever myself, she felt like she was a disappointment to me that she had not achieved a good life pattern. I think that was a lot of it.

I'm sort of an internal psychiatrist to myself. I talk to myself and try to analyze situations and so forth, and I just keep trying to move ahead and try to overlook some of the disappointments of the past. I'm not one of those people who flagellate themselves over and over, trying to find reasons for this and why things didn't work and so on, worrying about it forever. That's not my plan of action.

William Styron

After my mother died, when I was fourteen, my father suffered a very severe depression. I didn't realize it at the time. He was in a hospital. But in those days they didn't treat people in quite the same way they do now. He was in a regular public hospital, not a psychiatric. To this day, I wish I knew more about it. I kept a diary at that time, in which for four or five weeks I talked about going to visit my father almost every day. I had buried all knowledge of it in my own memory, until I began to read this diary. Then it all came back. It's still vague to me what his real problem was, but I now know that he must have been suffering from severe depression. There was no sense of his having anything organic wrong with him—I would have known about that—and it was slightly secret. In those days still, to some degree, it was a deep, dark secret to suffer from what they usually called a nervous breakdown.

Soon after that he went to Puerto Rico for three or four weeks, where my mother's brother was a high-ranking Army officer. When he came back, he was totally recovered. He died about ten years ago, at the age of about ninety. Unfortunately, because I suffered my depression after his death, I never had any reason to ask him about it. If he had lived longer, kept his marbles, I would have loved to have known what his experience was. I only know that it must have been severe.

Susan Crosby

I'm sure that [Lindsay's brother] Dennis was unipolar and probably Phil, too. Gary works a lot with AA. I think Gary stopped drinking twenty-some years ago, but he didn't start working the program until ten years out. He just had his ten-year anniversary. Gary had that kind of fight and anger that helped him through. Dennis drank his life away. Dennis and his wife Arlene lived with Lindsay and me at the beginning, when we were young. Then [after they moved] to Palm Springs, Dennis lived with us for another year while he worked in town. And periodically, if he was drinking, he would come down and stay at Calabasas with Lindsay.

There was never a rise out of Dennis. Never. He would drink not to have to deal with anybody. I would come out in the morning and Dennis would be sitting wrapped in his blanket like an Indian with a teepee over him, watching the TV with a mug full of vodka. I never saw Dennis be excited and happy. He was just really sensitive, and really sweet.

But Dennis was in a major, major depression for a long long long long time. He wouldn't leave the room, he'd stay in front of the television. All of them, actually, sat in front of the TV. Lindsay's the only one who really had a life outside. Gary has more since he's been working in the program. Somebody had said to me they wanted to do a movie about the Crosbys and I said, "What is the story? You tell me how you photograph the brothers sitting in front of televisions for thirty years." And that's really what they did. They watched television. And to me, that's major depression.

Jane Doe

Both my parents were immigrants and they clearly both had very severe problems. My mother is manic-depressive. No question about it.

She is still alive, but I haven't seen her for twenty years. She brought out the monster in me. She devoured me. No matter how much therapy, how long I lived away, Europe, whatever, it was just irreconcilable.

My father, who was called the black sheep of his family, clearly had the same disease as I have, lifelong biochemical depression. He died. And he was terribly, terribly depressed his entire life, withdrawn and sad.

Now, my sister and brother, I don't see them either. The brother is eighteen months younger than me. And the father didn't like him, and the trauma of the family—he was practically catatonic. He would either read five or six books per day or he would sleep for twenty or thirty hours at a time. I took over the family of five and we lived in an apartment about the size of this room. A ten-year-old kid has to have lunch and breakfast and clean clothes, so I just took over. I ran the house. I did the laundry. I did the cooking. And I resented every second of it. So, I forced him to help me. I made him do the vacuuming. I could boss him around. And I am sure that I saved his life. I am sure that I saved him from really becoming psychotic. My brother and I, by the time we were grown up there was just nothing left. Nothing bad happened between us; there was just nothing. Whatever energy we had for a relationship was used up.

My sister is six and a half years older. She escaped as a child at the very earliest age listening to Texaco on the radio, the opera and Vivaldi, and reading. She got eight or ten scholarships and really got into the intellectual stuff. She detached, which saved her sanity. But I am convinced that she is also depressed. She's fifty-eight and she has a more than thirty-year marriage. I hear from a friend of hers that they recently separated. He found somebody else. And I am sure that she is depressed, but I am also sure that because she lives in her head, she is not doing anything about it.

Bill and I have now expanded our therapy to include our children as we continue to deal with the repercussions of this rocky road. It was our family therapist who gave us a definition that has become a touchstone of courage for us: We are a family that solves its problems. We are a family that confronts, airs, discusses, deals with, and solves our problems, together. And together we tackle the manifestations and the repercussions of depression.

Support groups have proved helpful for all manner of problems and ailments—a safe place where fears can be aired, hurt comforted, experiences compared. I can envision, in families that can discuss such things, a gathering of relatives—a cousin, a grandparent, a sibling, a spouse—reaching together across the generations of silence to find a shared hope.

20
Children of
Depressed Parents

Parents with depression suffer a triple burden of guilt—whatever in-
ternal torture our disease puts us through, the normal amount of self-
doubt that many parents feel, and the added worry of the effects of our
aberrant behavior on our children. Even now, with my disease in check,
I feel deep grief over the years I lost, that my children lost, when I was
unable to be responsive to their needs. I remember a moment one fall,
after my usual August/September low had passed, when I was leaning
over baby Jack on the changing table, cooing and chuckling. With a
great and sudden pain I thought, "How long has it been that I've been
just going through the motions, never smiling down into his face, never
making contact with his bright little eyes?" I wondered what effect it
has on a child to live some of its first months tended to by a grim-faced
automaton, with no warmth, no cuddling, no mothering.

Worse yet may have been the unpredictable emotional storms to
which my children were subjected. From the time my depression was
first diagnosed, we have tried to reassure the children by helping them

to understand that this was not something that they caused and that it was outside either their control or, to a certain extent, mine. We have not always been successful.

My older son wandered in to my home office one day when I was just a few months into this book, asking what I was going to be doing when the book was finished.

"You know what I was thinking?" I said. "I was thinking it would be really fun to write a book together."

"Yeah!" he responded enthusiastically.

"I was thinking we could write a book for kids whose parents are depressed."

His manner changed; he ducked his head and muttered, "No."

"I thought that might kind of be fun," I said, fishing for clues to his change in behavior.

"No," he said again. When I asked why, he answered, "Because I don't really like to think about it."

I realized that although my husband and I thought we had explained my depression thoroughly, a big gap existed between our explanations and his understanding that had left him with a sense of hopelessness. We had talked about the depression as something that is in my body that I've had all my life and that I'll probably have all my life, but we never had emphasized what we were doing about it and that it was going to get better. He explained his feelings by saying "Well, you've had it all these years. It's always going to be this way. It's never going to be any different." It was so sad, and so stupid of us. We thought we were telling him all the things he needed to know, but we had left out the most important part: that it was going to be okay.

Linda Freeman, M.D.

If you're depressed, you take to bed a lot. You don't have a lot of energy. You get irritable, you don't have the patience for them. If it's very bad, you feel as though you're barely holding on. That doesn't leave you with a whole lot to give to someone else who's at a stage of their life where, of course, they require a whole lot from you. So, often a parent will withdraw from their children, as self-protection and sometimes as a way of protecting the children, because the parent knows that she can become very irritable and lash out, and say things that she doesn't mean.

When your own self-esteem is suffering, one of the things that you tend to do is bring other people down around you. You feel better about yourself temporarily when you make someone else feel bad about themselves too.

Depressives are not able accurately to observe the effect that they have on their children. It's almost like walking around in a cloud, or feeling like the light is only halfway up. Or they may think that things are going okay, but they're really missing the nuance of experience for their children.

When the parent is not available for the child, the child experiences that as rejection, thinking that perhaps it has something to do with him, or the way that he's behaving or not behaving. He feels that he may be to blame for the parent's behavior. One of my colleagues who has done some research on this strongly believes that many of the difficulties that children run into when their parents are depressed are because the parents don't talk about it. Therefore, it leaves the child feeling confused, frightened, and guilty.

The first or second time a parent is depressed, the parent doesn't know what's going on with himself either, and he may not be available to do this kind of talking. But over time, and particularly after the diagnosis is made, it may be useful for the family to sit down together, either with a professional's help or without, and review those times when the parent was not feeling well, and see how various members of the family felt about it, and what they thought was happening. The parent can express appreciation for the little ways that the family was trying to help out that he couldn't appreciate when he wasn't feeling well. It's a very valuable experience for the children and spouse of a parent who is depressed to share their thoughts and feelings about it, even after the episode.

It may not be useful for the depressed parent to go into great detail, however. Certainly, it's not a situation where the parent confesses everything she did and apologizes. It's not appropriate for her to take on blame and express her guilt. But she can say "This is something that happens. It has happened to me periodically. Do you remember Christmas when it happened? Or, do you remember in the springtime? You may have thought that I was mad at you, and I just want to let you know now, I wasn't. I wasn't feeling well. I had a depression."

You can explain what a cranky mood is. You can explain crying: "Do you remember how I was crying? Yes? Do you remember how I was feeling sad? When I was feeling sad, I also was feeling mad. It wasn't because you did anything. It was just the feelings that I had because I had the depression." If it helps you to feel better when you cry, you can say so. If it doesn't, say that. A lot of people are very good at this instinctively. They hear the language that their child uses, and they can use that.

You can say "I'm tired because I'm not sleeping well. My temper is shorter because I am tired. Sometimes my temper is so short that even though you haven't done something that's very serious, I'm going to need to leave and go take a walk because I'm getting too angry, and I know it's too angry for the situation. This is part of what the depression does to me."

Explain to them in terms of the things that they remember. You can give them their own memory of it, which increases the child's sense of competence. You're saying to them "You can remember. You lived through it. I was there with you. Now you can understand it better, and if it happens again—which we hope it doesn't, because I get my treatment now—it won't last so long." And you can tell them "These are the kinds of things that you can do: You can remind me, 'Mommy, are you getting depressed?' or 'Daddy, are you getting depressed again?' or 'I'm trying to help, Mommy.'"

It's very important to tell the child that you can make it through. Remind her and yourself of the many times that you have made it and she has made it. You know, it looked like you weren't going to, but you did. All of that is a self-esteem boost and promotes a greater sense of competence. Because if you've handled something before, you're going to be able to handle it again. A lot faster, too.

The trauma comes when people feel as though there's nothing that they can do, and they don't understand what's going on. Helplessness is the worst feeling that any of us can experience. For a child to feel helpful in a crisis—and a depressive episode is a temporary crisis for the family—is going to be useful to her or him.

Tell her the kinds of things that she can do to help that are age-appropriate for her. If you know that your irritability is higher and you're going to be less available, then you may say to her "It would really help me if you keep your room clean. That's all I'm asking," or if she would keep her radio turned down, or whatever it is that would help you.

You may want to say "You can help me, and I've appreciated the ways that you've helped me. It's not your job to help me. You don't have to hold my hand. I have someone that I talk to about the things that are hurting me or that are bothering me at this time. This is what I'm doing about it myself. If I get on your nerves, we can talk about it, and if you get on mine, I sure will tell you," and let it rest with that.

Psychoeducation is one of the most helpful tools. Things that seem random or out of control need to be explained and understood because that's where your best prevention is. If you know that when you have a depressive episode you're going to be fatigued, you're going to be short of temper, you're going to be very quick to cry or become enraged, and that's something that your spouse or child or neighbor, for that matter, can know ahead of time, then they may be able to think about the kinds of modifications that they need to make so that they can cope with you better.

Hopefully, they will feel comfortable enough to share with you the kind of modifications they may need *you* to try to make, so that you can cope with them better, within reason and understanding of what's going to be possible. If they said, "We don't want you to get depressed," that would be an unreasonable request. But, instead they might say "If you're going to be that depressed and if you're going to be that cranky, give us some kind of a monitor. Tell us, do you want *us* to go to the show, or what time *can* we play the radio?" This is usually a conversation you want to have when you're feeling better rather than worse.

Also, you might want to tell the child "There may be some things that you can't say to me, sometimes, that you're frightened, or that you're worried about me. Maybe you would like to talk with somebody. Aunt Sarah has agreed to talk to you about it, because I've talked to her. She's talked to my doctor, and she understands. Dad understands, or whoever." Find the person in the family and/or community to whom the child can reach out at a time that they'd like to and give them your approval to do that. It might be better if you help them find the person, because then you could help that person have some understanding about what's going on, too. You might even want to think of more people than just your husband.

These talks can be very hard, and that's why I say it's often helpful to have a professional help you. Because I think a parent, particularly a parent who has been depressed, takes on too much of the guilt, for a lot of reasons, not the least of which is the depression. Sometimes just saying "I'm not feeling real well, honey, and it really doesn't have anything to do with you" may be helpful.

Children who have depressed family members are generally presumed to be at higher risk for depression, even if those family members don't live with them. There's almost a double impact—the genetic impact that may be transmitted, as well as the effects of living with a parent who episodically may not be available throughout the child's younger life. [The prevalence is] even higher in children who have two depressed parents. But by the same token that's not to say that every child of a depressed parent is going to be depressed. If you're worried about your children, I'd say, keep an eye out, but not a wariness out.

John Rush, M.D.

When you're ill, I think you should tell your kids "I'm depressed; I have an illness; I'm not able to function; I'm going to the doctor; I'm getting treated. It has nothing to do with you. You didn't cause it; you can't cure it." That's the key, because most kids will think, if their parents aren't feeling well, they did something bad. Inform them that you're sick. "You know I'm not myself. Here's how I'm not myself." That won't come as a news flash. "Don't worry. You didn't cause it, and I'm taking care of it, and shortly I'm going to be out of this mess."

Leslie Garis

I was afraid of insanity because that word was used about my father, that he's insane. That's a very frightening word, insane. I was always fighting that. And it was as if I was fighting my nature, the dark possibilities of life. It can turn out all right, or it can turn out not at all all right. My own experience of childhood was that it turns out not at all all right. You lose the house, you lose the money, the father dies. You hope not, as you're growing up. You hope that won't happen. But it does happen. The worst happens.

So, I didn't want the worst to happen for my children. I was hoping I could control it, and if I couldn't control it, then all was lost. I've always been prepared to expect that, that all might be lost.

I felt that I had to protect the children, and yet I wanted to talk to them about it so much. I wanted to sit down and take strength from them. But I avoided it except with my oldest, who was such incredible help. He was the one who made me see that I needed to go to a doctor. But the little ones, I just don't think they can understand.

I certainly don't believe that we have to keep from our children how difficult life is. I think they see that, particularly growing up in our family, with two freelance parents working at home. But one thing that I feel very strongly about is that we have to let our children be children for as long as they need to be. Having been somebody who was leaned on as a child, I think it takes a terrible toll as you get older. It's hard enough being a child without thinking that the one thing that you can count on, your source of strength, your parent, is in deep trouble.

When I got better, crazy things happened, like suddenly I got someone to clean the attic. The garage got done. Suddenly we just started getting organized. We started being able to do things, to function as a family. We've taken a day off and had bike rides. We've actually organized that, bought the bikes, taken the time. Those were things that before I could never have done. I would have just said "Oh, no, no, you go. I'm just going to lie down."

I had told my twelve-year-old that I had been very sad, and that I was taking medicine and that it helped me. He takes medicine for attention deficit disorder and hyperactivity, and I thought that if I told him that I take medicine, too, he would feel that taking medicine was a more commonplace and less frightening situation. Indeed, I think it did work that way.

I told him that I was going to be interviewed about depression, because he knew that I took the medicine. But, to my nine-year-old, I said the interview was about how women cope with writing and having children at the same time.

"Oh, you'll talk about me," she said.

"Maybe I will," I answered.

Then she went to Ben and said, "Do you know why Mommy is being interviewed? It's for her writing."

"No, it's about depression," Ben said.

So, my daughter came to me and said, "Ben said you're being interviewed about depression." Her lips were quivering, and tears started to roll down her cheeks.

"Well, both things are true," I said. "It's also about how you carry on with children." I told her that I had been depressed, but that I wasn't anymore, and that I took medicine for it. She seemed to be okay because I was out the other side. I said, "I was depressed when you were much younger, and I'm okay now." I think once she saw that I was okay now, and she knew that I was okay now, and I was talking about something that was in the past, she was okay, too. But it was a shock.

I worry very much about them suffering from depression,

yes. So, I keep them very carefully monitored. I don't worry about the oldest, Alex, so much. He's at Dartmouth now, he's happy. But the two others I want to keep track of forever. I just want to look at them and see if I start seeing things.

Rose Styron

You just have to observe so closely. And suddenly you see that this kid or this grown-up, whom you have known since he or she was born, is behaving in some different way. You have to stop, look, and listen. You have to listen very closely and not make assumptions.

I see my daughter, Susanna, reading every book that has come along on *Your Two-Year-Old, Your Three-Year-Old,* and so on. She's totally clued in psychologically in a way that I never was. Our generation didn't do all that. We were thrilled that Dr. Spock came along, so that we had something to hold on to, but that was as far as we went. But your generation is so clued in to everything that happens at every stage that on one hand I think your kids will never get into the trouble that our kids did, because you're looking at everything all of the time. On the other hand, I worry that you will see everything that happens to your child, or your child's responses to things, as part of a pattern that every child goes through at three or at sixteen or whatever, and maybe will not pay close enough attention to the fact that it's not the way they were behaving, or it's not the way things should happen. I can see a danger in that.

Even when you pay close attention, once your kids are adults you can't get in their heads, and you shouldn't get into their heads, and they don't want you to get in their heads, but it's very tough.

Pat Love, Ed.D.

When they were children, my depression must have affected them—the irritability and hostility, not being available, not being as much fun, too serious an outlook on life. I realized, I was doing fun things and I wasn't having fun. Because when you have children, that should be a wonderful time in your life, especially if you've planned your children.

But what happens is, whether we're depressed or not, they remind us of our own childhood. For example, I didn't get attention from my parents, and so when my children would come to me for attention that would reactivate that old wound, and I would be irritable about giving them attention. What that was really doing was re-creating a scenario that I had lived through as a little girl. That's why we have difficulty dealing with children, because they reenact our lives and remind us of our early pain. Now you are put in the role of dealing with that which you didn't have dealt with properly when you were the child. So all of that déjà vu, so to speak, is hard to deal with to begin with. And then if you don't feel good or are depressed, it's even harder to separate.

So, for example, when my kids would act silly, I would get upset. I wanted them to be serious because I was feeling serious, instead of just enjoying it and saying "Oh, isn't that funny!" and rolling with the punches. I wanted them to be perfect, don't rock the boat, don't make Mother anxious, because I already was anxious.

The depression prevents you from being rational and objective about it, saying "Wait a minute, these are just kids." That's what the depression does for me; it blurs the boundaries. I take things far too personally when I'm depressed. Everything is about me. I don't have any separation. If people aren't getting along here, oh shit, it's my fault. And that's the way it is with parenting. You can't say "That's Jimmy being eight years old. That's what an eight-year-old does." When you're clear, you can do that. But when you're in psychic pain, you can't be that lucid.

In order to help them, first of all, you ought to get help. Keep knocking on doors until you find it.

It's scary for children to think that their parents might be out of control—it feels to the child as though if your parent is depressed, your life's threatened—but they know it anyway, so it's better for them to get a reassurance. It's not like you're relying on the child, you really are reassuring the child. You can apologize, you can go back and say "You know, I was having a bad day and I realize I took it out on you." Even two- and three-year-olds understand apologies. Let them know that when people get down, they get back up.

Maybe it takes two or three generations to turn this depression around. Maybe we're the generation that has to medicate ourselves to give our kids some healthy experiences. Maybe the best parenting thing we can do is be willing to medicate ourselves.

Joan Rivers

Only my really good friends know. And even my daughter I don't show it to. You cannot take a twenty-two-year-old girl and burden her with "I'm so down, I'm so depressed, I'm so scared, I'm so worried."

I worry . . . I worry . . . I wonder maybe if it's genetic. You know, you always worry about that. I also worry how she could handle it, will she handle it, would she . . . ? Of course, you worry.

Susan Crosby

The kids knew from the beginning. I never lied to them. One time when Lindsay was at the hospital at Brockman, and he was finally leveled out, I took the kids out to see him. I had said,

"Your dad's really been through a lot. He has this illness, and that's when he gets kind of wild, and this stuff happens." I bundled them up in this ratty old rented orange station wagon, because Lindsay had sold my car. They were maybe two and three, just really little toddlers still. When Lindsay came out to the waiting room, he was really sad. His face looked like "My God, I can't go through this again, this is so awful, and what have I done?" And for him to see these two little faces looking up at him . . . Chipper had his parka on, and he's very blond and he's got very big dimples, and Chipper just looked up at him and he said the perfect thing; he said in his little voice, "What's the matter, Dad? Did you break your heart?"

And Lindsay said, "Yeah, Chip, I think I did."

And then they'd just hug him, and they would be glad to see him. We'd know it was a rough time, and we'd come back when it was over. I made sure they didn't have to see a whole lot of it.

It was real hard especially on Kevin when they got older. Lindsay would show up on the baseball field where Kevin was playing, and the other kids would point because Lindsay was so bizarre, he'd have his shirt off, you know, he'd be drinking a beer, cowboy hat on, and talking ridiculous, wandering in the field. Then the kids would point at Kevin and say "What's wrong with your dad, Kev?" One time, all the kids were in a huddle and we all looked over and there was Lindsay in the dugout just standing there, just lost. You know, he looked like a sick man, insane. Just lost. And Kevin would be torn. He would be so angry because his dad was out there and it was very embarrassing, very hard, yet he knew the pain his dad was going through. It was not easy on them. It was not easy at all. I've asked them often about it, and they're glad that we talked about it openly and always knew what it was.

What upset the kids even more than that embarrassment was other people that would take things. Kevin would say "I can't be around Dad. He'll hand things out and these people will take them." That hurt the kids more. They couldn't stand watching these people crowd in and take things. I think both my boys are very compassionate and very understanding, and they're not judgmental about people, you know? When you live like we have, you look beyond these things in other people.

Maybe, as Susan suggests, there are some strengths our children gain through living in the shadow of the dog. For myself, I still hurt remembering each cruel and thoughtless remark I made to my boys out of my own pain.

But I am learning new skills all the time, learning to not lean on them, learning to communicate better. I am learning that even when I am depressed, I must not exclude them from my presence and affection so completely that they feel abandoned. I am learning to interact with them the best I can at any given moment, trying to stay aware of and not exceed my limitations. My children and I have had some fun times in the kitchen together, and my three-year-old loves to help prepare a meal. But when I am depressed, I have no tolerance for the mess and the mistakes, and I cook alone. I am learning at least to find a moment to hold them, maybe to read aloud, to let them feel my touch, and give reassurance with my hugs as well as my words.

When I am well, and able to listen to and respond to their needs and desires, I try to make a special effort to do so. I ask "What would you like to do today?" putting aside my plans, allowing them to feel that at least some of the time their wishes can come first, their input can be valuable. With each new step I take, I too am reassured that children are resilient and that, as so many parents said, the best we can do for our children is to heal ourselves.

As I neared completion of this book, I asked William if I could interview him. To my surprise, he responded with interest. Although it was not easy to hear the effect my depression had had on my beloved boy, I learned, rather than guessing, what his experience has been, the limits of his knowledge about the disease, and most encouraging, the importance to him of being included in our conversations.

"What do you think it would feel like to be depressed?" I asked him first.

"Extremely overreactive and angry," he responded, describing the

*behavior that was most apparent to him. "Rage. Jumping and scream-
ing at someone for making an ordinary small mistake that anyone
could make."*

*"What would you do if you felt like you were depressed, or over-
reactive?"*

*"I don't know," he said at first, before coming up with a pretty
good suggestion for handling anger, if not depression. "I don't know if
this would work," he said, "but for one, get a good night's sleep and
then in the morning think of whatever you're mad at and all the ways
it's unimportant."*

*"Do you think you can tell whether I'm overreacting out of depres-
sion or I'm actually mad?" I asked.*

"No."

"What does it feel like when a parent is depressed?"

*"Terrible. Really terrible. It makes you feel like everything you do
is wrong and everything that happens that has anything to do with you
is not correct, because of how they're acting. They jump on you for small
mistakes even when everything is perfectly fine, or better than average.
For example, one time I was doing a school report that was one of the
best things I'd ever written, and you paid no attention to the rest of the
report but just visualized on two little mistakes and how bad they were.
You said nothing about the rest of the report."*

*Of course I felt terrible about an incident that I didn't even re-
member, an incident, however, that could have reflected my damned
perfectionism as much as my depression. I silently promised myself to try
harder to praise as well as correct.*

*"If you don't want to do something with me, I can go off and do
something by myself," he said. "But when you're angry at me, there's
nowhere to get away from you. I can't drive off and do something by
myself. You'll always be there, being mad at me.*

*I wondered what changes he had experienced since we started
dealing with the depression as a family and talking together about
what we could do to make it easier on all of us. Had he seen any
improvement?*

*"A lot," he said. "I can't remember the last time that you've done
anything crazy."*

"What else has changed?"

"*One thing: I've known what's going on, which has made it a whole lot easier on me. Like if you're on the fourth floor of a building and there's an explosion, you have no idea what's happening, but if you heard on the radio that there's a bomb in that building or a technical explosion, or something, you'd be less scared because you'd know what was going on.*

"*[When your parent is depressed], you never know what's going to happen. You never know when they're suddenly going to have some depression, because it's not like 'At this time I'm going to be depressed' or 'In thirty days I'm going to be depressed.' It's not that simple. I wish it was.*"

"*Is there anything you would like to know about the depression that maybe we've never talked about? Is there anything you'd like to tell other children whose parents are depressed?*"

"*I think I know all I need to know, or want to know,*" he answered. "*I just know enough that it suits me, but other people might want to know other things. I don't know enough to explain about it.*"

"*What would you say to parents who have depression?*"

"*I think that you should tell your kids as much as they want to know to make them less scared about it. Because going into fits of rage off and on can be very scary for some kids. I know it was for me.*"

21
Children with
Depression

*My first experience with depression may have been when I was twelve.
We spent that summer in Nantucket, and I felt a foreshadowing of the
romantic aloneness that would become intensely unhealthy in my later
teens. The fog, the sea, and the new independence I had to wander by
myself, wrapped in my own thoughts, allowed for pubescent brooding. I
discovered poetry. I discovered the pain of adolescent love.*

*I don't remember my feelings or behavior that summer as being
beyond the bounds of mental health, but those same thoughts and feelings intensified as I moved into my teens. The next summer I started
drinking, and by the next, doing drugs and sneaking out of our summer home to take a night train into Manhattan to carouse in Green-
wich Village. What they now call "acting out" became an art for me.
The September I was seventeen, I left school in the middle of the day
and ran away from home. And when I returned a few days later, I saw
a therapist for the first time.*

I don't believe my parents or teachers had any idea of the pain I was in or, I understand now, could even suspect such pain was possible in a child. In the late sixties, our culture still cherished the illusion that childhood was a happy-go-lucky time, without cares, without responsibilities. Even my first therapist, as good a friend as he was, wasn't able to touch the underlying illness.

Linda Freeman, M.D.

Talking about children being depressed is recent. Only since the seventies has depression in childhood been something that people write about and accept, something they will sit up and listen to you talk about at a professional conference. So obviously the research is very young. It's not possible to say "I met a child at four and now they're forty. I've observed that this is the outcome."

But the thinking is that it's continuous, that probably the younger the patient at the onset of the depressive illness, the more severe the disorder is.

Adolescents whose parents are depressed often will have their onset earlier, maybe around twelve or thirteen, versus fifteen or sixteen for depressed adolescents whose parents don't have the illness. So, there's some idea that genetic loading, or perhaps environmental factors of living with such a depressed person, may cause a more severe form of disorder when it occurs. There are some studies of children who continue to be depressed as adolescents, and some of adolescents who have continued to be depressed as young adults, but there hasn't been enough time yet to follow people all the way through the life cycle.

Still, we're talking about a pretty low incidence of this disorder in childhood. The community sample prevalence is less than 3 percent; in adolescents, maybe 6 to 8 percent.

Indications of depression in children include crying and sadness. They lose their ability to concentrate as well. Often a teacher reports home that Susie is not doing her schoolwork. You may hear comments that indicate that the child is getting down on herself: "I'm stupid, I'm ugly, nobody likes me anyway.

I don't want to go." Some children just have always had very poor social skills, but the depressed child isn't going to have been that way all his life. Change is what the parent will need to look for, for example, a change in the way that he behaves around the house. He may be less active or more irritable. So, it's like the child has a chip on his or her shoulder. She is very cranky. He flies off the handle very easily. Those kinds of experiences between the parent and child might be tip-offs. Less observable are the changes in sleep, or the changes in appetite, the child blaming himself for things that just don't seem to be that serious and/ or for which he's not to blame. Obviously, any child that comes up and says he thinks he wants to die, or she thinks she wants to kill herself, requires a good, hard look. Depression is not the only reason a child may say that, but it's a very common reason, so you'd want to pursue it further with a professional.

It is not uncommon for depressed children to somatize their complaints. When you don't feel good, and you are not an abstract thinking person, if you are asked "Well, what doesn't feel good about you?" you're not going to say "I don't know, I seem to have a low sense of my self-esteem." Maybe you feel anxious, you have some butterflies, and you say, "Well, I have a stomachache," because you're trying to use what thinking capacity you have, which is very concrete. As you know, anxiety can often give you a tension headache, and it's not unusual with depression that you'll have anxiety. If you're a child, you'll talk about your headache, not your anxiety. So, while the physical symptoms have to be taken seriously, there should also be consideration given that there might be a depression underlying it.

If a child has a test in school and says, "Gee, I really think I have a stomachache" and that happens about every third week when the teacher gives the test, that's a different situation altogether. I'm talking about a child who has frequent and chronic complaints that last a period of time, weeks to months. Frequently, kids will get referred to specialists by their pediatricians, because the pediatricians have had the child every week for different physical complaints for which they can't find physical causes. Then they'll say to the parent "You know, I think you better take this child to see a psychiatrist because I think she may be depressed."

You would probably start with the child's pediatrician. If you approach a professional who's either unable or unwilling to help you, then you should find another, and there *are* others. It may be useful not only to see a pediatrician, but other professionals such as child psychiatrists, psychologists, or social workers or other forms of counselors.

One of the things parents can do is try to understand, to talk about it. One of the problems that comes up for families is that often the circumstances that may have led to the child being depressed are not only the child's. For example, if we're talking about grief that has become severe, usually the child is not the only grieving person, so the parent might not always be available to do this kind of listening and hear this kind of pain. Let's say the child is suffering the kind of grief at a loss due to a divorce, the parent is suffering that same loss. It can be very difficult, and I don't think a parent should feel bad about that. Maybe the parent has a friend or a professional or a religious person that he or she feels close to or that the child feels close to that she could share some of this with, perhaps even as a threesome, or the child could have a person with whom he could talk about some of these thoughts and feelings alone.

At least initially, that's what we're going to do as professionals, too, unless there's some higher risk, dangerous factors like suicidal ideas or school refusal, in which case the child may need to be monitored very closely, maybe even in-hospital monitoring and treated with medication.

The depression will probably get better all on its own, within eight months in a child, but at what cost? The child is going to have, perhaps, failed in school, have lost friendships, and have disrupted peer relationships; the school may not want him back anymore. And all these things then feed back on lowering the child's self-esteem further. You have a school failure for one semester in class. The kids think you're a nerd. When you go back the next term, even though the depression might not be present the next term, all of these social factors are still lying there. So, before that happens, you want to alleviate the symptoms as quickly as possible.

Another problem is the kinds of behaviors that the child will get involved in during the depressive episode and the loss of the ability to learn and develop socially. These behaviors might include social withdrawal. That is not at all uncommon, in depression. Obviously, there's a very high association as the children get older, particularly boys in adolescence, with substance abuse, alcohol, and drugs. In younger children, there's a very high relationship with anxiety disorders, and all kinds of irritable behaviors where the child flies off the handle at people.

Conduct disorder is probably present in about one-third of depressed children. That is, oppositionalism, perhaps even destructive activities and other kinds of aggressive behaviors, vandalism, skipping school. If you can't concentrate, why go? Usually, if the depression is the real experience, then the conduct disorder or the behavioral disruption is going to go away when the depression goes away.

Jules Feiffer

I was a failure as a kid. I wasn't any good at it. I knew that life was going to change for me once I got to be an adult. As a child, I saw myself as a member of a class without any power, despite the fact that I saw how other kids could manipulate or boss around their parents.

My oldest sister was always fighting with my mother. But whenever I got into a fight with an adult I'd lose it, so there was no point in fighting. There wasn't an argument that I had with an adult even when I was in the right that my mother didn't think I was in the wrong, because grown-ups are automatically right and children are wrong.

I was not athletic and you can't be a boy and not be athletic in the Bronx and get away with it, or get away with a happy childhood. I was just biding time till I could be a famous cartoonist at twenty-five, till I could be Al Capp, or Milton Kaniff. I knew I had talent, I knew that talent would mature, I knew that talent would pay off sooner or later and that when I'm grown up that talent will work. But I also knew that I didn't have the talent which makes you a successful kid, which is good coordination and athletic ability, being big and strong. I was small and weak. I was just in the wrong job, which was childhood.

Linda Freeman, M.D.

All the same diagnoses are made in children as are made in adults —unipolar, bipolar, dysthymia, cyclothymia. But because children and adolescents think differently than adults do, the questions in diagnostic tests are going to be different. If you say to a five-year-old "What do you like about yourself?" he may say "Well, I like ice cream."

"Do you like yourself?"

"I like ice cream, I like roller skating . . ."

They don't have the same kind of abstract conceptualization as adults, so you have to say things more concretely. If you want to know about a child's self-esteem to help determine whether or not she's depressed, you'll say things like "Tell me, how do you like your looks? Do you like your hair? Do you like your eyes? Do your friends like you? Do they call you names?" Usually if a child is called names by her friends, that damages her self-esteem. She doesn't feel so good about herself. "Are you smart? Are you dumb?" You break it down into terms that she can understand. It's unlikely that you can go to a five-year-old or even a seven-year-old and say "Have you been feeling this way for at least two weeks?" and have him understand that. On the other hand, if you can date things to "Was it when you got out of school that you started feeling the worst? Was it around Christmastime? Was it around the time that Dad left?" then he can start to use some time anchors.

Obviously, interests are different for children. If you say to a child, "Well, are you not interested in school?"

"No." Is the child depressed? No; school is not what children are generally interested in.

"What do you do for fun?" you say to her.

"Well, I ride my bike."

"Oh, nice, how often do you ride your bike?"

"Oh, a couple of times a month." Now you've got a problem. If an adult rides his bike a couple of times a month, that may not be a depression. But for a child to ride this infrequently after she's told you that riding is one of the activities that she enjoys, you start to get the sense she's experiencing some loss of interest and pleasure in her activities.

Much of the diagnosis of depression has to do with how the person appears and moves. In an adult interview, I may move my hands, the other person may nod his head and that is the appropriate, physical level of activity for us. For five-year-olds, if they sat that quietly for half an hour, you'd start to wonder if there might not be some kind of psychomotor retardation, because normally they would have been much more physically active in that period of time.

A whole series of scales is used both for self-report for children and for examiners to use with children. Some of them use more physical characteristics: How their face looks, how sad do they actually look? Do they cry? Quietness isn't so much a symptom. Social withdrawal might be. Many quiet children still have friends.

Often what we've found is that a child is able to tell you about certain symptoms better than the parent is. For instance, the parent may put the child to bed and say that the child slept through the night. The child says, "Well, no, really I kind of fooled around with this toy and that and I haven't been able to sleep for quite some time." The parent isn't necessarily aware of this. Very often a parent is not aware of suicidal thoughts and behaviors, but a child is more able to tell you about his own experience.

We did a study once where we had depressed children carry beepers. Then we beeped them at various times during the day and said "Write down how you feel." Even children who clearly were depressed actually did have mood fluctuations during the day. So, it may be something that persists for three or four or five hours of the day, but not the whole day long. That's significant, too. If you think about it, outside of a major loss, the average normal child does not experience that kind of sustained sadness day after day for several weeks.

It's not at all unusual with depression that a child will refuse to go to school. I had a child who was depressed, a young girl in fourth grade, who had been humiliated by her teacher. She hadn't done her work the way she was supposed to; she had hidden it. The teacher made her stand up in front of the class and demonstrate the poorness of her work, and then said to the class, "Now, isn't she stupid?" The child never told her mother about it, she was so humiliated, but she refused to go to school for the next year and a half.

Now, when she came to the clinic, we said, "Oh, my God! This is a very seriously disturbed child," because school refusal is a very serious symptom in a child. Sometimes that's the beginning of a kind of psychotic illness, as well. And of course, at the evaluation she revealed that this had happened to her. And she was ashamed. For her, the direct intervention was to say "You don't have to go back to that school and face those children anymore." She also got further treatment for her depression, but I don't think we would have been as successful if we hadn't also helped her get into a new school placement.

If the child is unable to concentrate, it's probably unreasonable to demand that she complete all her homework in one sitting, for instance. Or that she complete it without some kind of supervised help, because [a depressed child is] distracted and unable to concentrate, and more easily frustrated. Sometimes it's just impossible to get all the schoolwork done. Then the parent or mental health professional may need to share this information with the teacher.

Sometimes there isn't really much a parent can do except to offer support and understanding while seeking professional care for the child. Understanding what the child's needs are, the parent may be able to help facilitate the child's structuring herself and doing the things that she can do to feel better. But making her happy isn't something the parent can do. There are some things you can do: You can share with her your joy of her existence and your pleasure in her company, but you can't make her happy. A parent may struggle to do that with a depressed child and may have that sense of helplessness, that there must be something that he or she can do. That might be what it takes for the parent to realize something is wrong: "I've done all the things that used to work, something is different here." If the special dinner or the trip to the zoo, or the project that the child always likes to work on with you, isn't something that's appealing to the child over a period of time, like a week or two, you may want to start thinking about getting some professional help.

Jane Doe

I was just a very sad child. I was very smart, very sad, terribly unacknowledged. Not too many friends.

I used to think that I was really lucky because one of my little friend's parents used to beat each other up and throw things. I think they were alcoholics as I look back, but I didn't know that at the time. I felt so lucky, so lucky; what a happy home I came from, because my parents just screamed and yelled and never hit each other. Of course, I had no privacy. I had a lot of trauma in the family at that time. It was a terrible time for me, a terrible, terrible time. I used to say I had an adolescence I wouldn't wish on Adolf Hitler. I never could bring anybody home after school, and in junior high and in high school I was horribly lonely. That is why I got married.

Mary Jones

I thought we were all Holden Caulfield, myself. What a miserable age!

Linda Freeman, M.D.

Psychiatry has definitely contributed to the idea that teenagers are "normally" obnoxious, rebellious, or as Anna Freud would have said, "adolescents in turmoil." Many modern psychiatric researchers have shown that the average adolescent is not in turmoil, miserable, hating their parents, totally opposed to their parents' values. In fact, that's a minority.

Some people will say 80 percent of kids simply go through adolescence without major problems. Only about 20 percent suffer through it. Out of that 20 percent, a high number of them have some kind of disorder. So if you see a child in school or at home who is obnoxious, who can't seem to get along with themselves, their friends, most certainly not with you, their parent, I think the parent should start to consider that it may be the signs of something more serious. Most normal adolescents really are just that, normal.

Many times, I'll have a parent come in, often at the child's insistence, and say, "Well, I just wanted to know, is this just hormones, or is there something wrong here?" I can guarantee to you right now when an adolescent is feeling that kind of distress, it's not hormones.

Every adolescent goes through the experience with their parents where they become more challenging or at least questioning of those notions that their parents hold. That's totally different, though, than being really oppositional and destructive.

Dick Clark

When I was about twelve to fourteen, I was a skinny kid with a bad complexion. I was very extraordinarily introverted. I would get home and close the door and stay there until I had to come out the next day. My brother would try to drag me out of this mood when he was home on leave from the war. My mother would console me and say "You're a nice-looking kid. Don't worry about it." But I had huge pimples all over my face.

I've always had a lot of sympathy for young people with skin problems, because it does dreadful things to your head. I just wanted to hide from everybody. I'd just eat myself into a hole, deeper and deeper, listening to the same records over and over again. I can remember to this day some of the songs I listened to most—[songs like] "Dreams" by the Pied Pipers and "I Can't Get Started with You" by Bunny Berrigan. I didn't think I would kill myself, but I think that I was down so far I couldn't see how to get up.

I had been very popular and in the public eye as the president of the junior high school, and all of a sudden I was a skinny and, I felt, ugly, unattractive guy going into a new atmosphere in high school, and nobody knew who I was. All of my armaments were stripped away. I wasn't a big hot deal anymore. I was ugly, a very, very simple reason for having the problem, but I was unable to cope with it at that point.

I'd never been as unhappy that I can recall for that length of time. I've been unhappy about the death of my parents, divorce, other things that can put you away for a while, but this was an extended period of time that I remember quite well. It frightened me.

But it wasn't anywhere near as serious as some of the things other people have suffered. I feel kind of silly building it up into more than it was. It seems frivolous. Everybody has lousy skin at that point in life. Nobody said, "Gee, you're ugly." Or "Gee, you've got pimples." It was something I built up in my own mind. I'll tell you an interesting aftermath of these efforts—I became the "professional extrovert." I became a popular kid and was in athletics, though not successful. I was a politician.

The problems that surround teenagers these days are far more serious than the problems we had in the forties, other than the war was going on. That was terribly serious. But the complications of life and the external circumstances that surround it make it tough. Otherwise, my guess is that probably the same things apply today as applied back then.

All this chemistry is changing in boys and girls and they're maturing and their hormones are going crazy and you would expect them to have some side effects. The other problem that goes along with that, and I'm a pretty good expert on that, is that parents don't understand any of the youth culture anyway. If the guy comes home with his hair zipped on the sides, long on the top, with his initials carved in it, that doesn't necessarily mean he's going to be a bad kid. It may be because that's what everybody is doing at that moment. I look at my own kids and their various hairdos and clothing and what have you and, you know, underneath it all, they're pretty normal people.

John Rush, M.D.

If you suffer from depression, tell your children that the chance of them getting this illness is far less than fifty/fifty, so they don't have to walk around their whole life worrying "Oh, if I feel sad, am I going to crash and burn?" It's not like Huntington's disease. If you have a parent with Huntington's disease, you have a fifty/fifty chance of getting it yourself. With depression, you're down in the 15 percent range. It's not zero, but it's not 50 percent.

And second, I would probably not even discuss the possibility of them having depression with them until at least they hit puberty, because most of the time, before puberty, you don't see it. I mean, it's possible, but the probability is low.

There are kids with bipolar illness that comes on at age five. There are kids with recurrent depression that comes on at age three. We have seen this, but these are uncommon.

The common scenario is onset somewhere between the ages of thirteen and thirty, and probably with the average around eighteen to twenty. College is a risk period, or a first job. Somewhere around the teenage years, I would tell them "I have a depression which is recurrent. As long as it's recurrent, then it's likely familial, so you have some risk for this. Don't worry; you had a risk for it anyway. You didn't pick your genes, but you got these, and so you have some increased risk. If you start to see these symptoms"—and then give them the symptoms of major depression—"and they really get you stuck, not just a few bad days, but you start not functioning and you start thinking about killing yourself, then, one, call me up; two, figure you've got a depression; and three, know it's treatable, and if you get it early, you can get rid of it. If you dawdle around and hang on to that thing for several years, now we have trouble treating it. It's like any other illness. If you get in early, you get out quick. If you get in late, it can kill you."

I would be sure to tell them it is highly treatable. If you want to pick a psychiatric illness, pick depression. It is the best outcome you can have. It's really good news. But the bad news is when it's not picked up and people fret about it.

You've got to remember that kids who feel lousy and are surrounded by the medications or drugs that are floating around in this society may decide to go out and experiment and try to self-medicate, just like adults. That doesn't make the depression better; it makes it worse. So one doesn't exclude the other at all, but typically, you will see the depression coming on first and then their involvement with the drugs and alcohol.

Which to treat first depends on how bad the substance abuse is. You want to treat the disorder that's causing the biggest problem. Most of the time, if it's just fiddling around or small amounts of substance abuse, yeah, treat the depression.

If it's serious substance abuse, big time, every-other-day cocaine or some such thing that's highly addicting and hard to treat, then you've got to put the person in inpatient [treatment] because when they come off of the cocaine, they'll have a depression for a few days or a week. They'll have a lot of difficulty staying off of it, and then you want to see if the depression is still there. If it is, then it's treated. So it's a matter of degree, which is "badder," so to speak.

As a parent, one of the first questions I had about my depression was "What about my children? Will they be all right?" And when I told my brother, he asked the same thing: "What about my son? Will he have it, too?" Of course there's no way to predict the future, but I do worry about my children's vulnerability to this disease. I worry very much. But after talking to Dr. Freeman, Dr. Kelsoe, and others, I feel somewhat reassured. The odds are not that great; I am doing everything I can; and by arming myself with knowledge, I will be equipped to help them, if they do encounter problems. And I can take care of myself, for their sakes.

The good news is that children are very resilient. I have learned that I can't beat myself up for how my illness may have affected or even damaged them in the past. But what I can do is remind myself that the sooner I get my own illness under control, the better I can help them cope with the stresses in their lives.

22

Old Dogs, New Tricks

Often as a society, or as a family, our treatment of our children and of our old people parallel each other. And as depression in children is beginning to be accepted as a reality, so is depression in the elderly. Until now, the behaviors associated with depression—withdrawal, lethargy, physical complaints, insomnia, and so on—have been chalked up to being natural consequences of aging. Loss of interest in previous activities? Naturally; they're getting old. They're not getting out and seeing people or doing things? Of course not; they're getting old.

Well, maybe it's not because they're old. Maybe it's because they're depressed, too depressed to visit friends and to do the things they enjoy. Are they depressed because they're old? Maybe. Or maybe because they're on medication for heart problems or blood pressure that causes depression. Or maybe they're suffering from Parkinson's disease, which is associated with depression. But the tragedy is that the pain of our older loved ones is being ignored. Instead of looking for the cause, searching for treatment, we simply expect and accept that their later years will be lonely and sad and filled with pain.

As I read over my husband's description of me when I'm depressed, I heard a friend of mine describing her elderly mother, whom she was afraid was demented. "There were times," Bill had said, "when your personal hygiene was ignored, several days at a time with no change of clothes, no makeup, no bathing. There was a lack of ability to concentrate—on cooking for example, or anything that followed a specific formula—forgetfulness, a greater-than-normal difficulty with punctuality, those kinds of things. I also saw a decreased interest in . . . social intercourse and activities, just kind of a reduction in living." Was the older woman demented? Or was she depressed?

Members of my family live a long time—both my aunt on one side and my grandmother on the other have lived over one hundred years—and they don't have ailments or, at least, they don't admit to them. I always laugh when a new doctor takes a medical history, because the only information I can give is that all my relatives died of old age. (When my sister-in-law asked my brother conversationally what my family's customs are regarding funerals, he answered succinctly, "We don't die.") For the most part, my own family experience is that people live almost forever, have a very good time, then die quickly, and with very little fuss.

Yet in the last year or so, it has occurred to me that one of my older relatives may suffer from depression. She has crying spells, she feels useless and lonely, even when she is surrounded by family. She is not psychotic; as far as I know, she is not suicidal. She is just miserable. She deserves better. Although it seems awfully late in life to stir up this particular hornets' nest, whether she has another decade to live or just a few months, that time could be happier.

But how can I broach the idea of psychiatric illness with as noble a woman as she is? How can I break through the veneer of self-sufficiency that she tries so hard to maintain? How can I traverse my fear of her anger, of her hurt, of her hurting me? How can I reach across the ages that divide us?

How can I not try?

I asked a locally prominent geriatric psychiatrist some general ques-

tions, fishing for information that would help me put my relative's problems in perspective.

"How do you know," I asked, "whether an older person is suffering from clinical depression or is reacting to normal losses? After all, her friends are dying off, she lives alone, her life is more restricted . . . ?"

"Depression," he said, "is not a necessary part of aging. Why, I know lots of active, involved elders who travel, and go out, who live rich, full lives, well into their seventies!"

"No, no," I said, "you don't understand my frame of reference. In my family, seventy is just middle-aged!"

How old is old? How long can we reasonably expect a rich, full life? And then what?

How much depression should we expect in the elderly?

Trey Sunderland, M.D.

There is often an assumption that the normal aging process is a sad time. I would quibble with that. Of course some sad occasions occur, such as a loss of loved ones, but there are also many obvious benefits, including decreased stress in lifestyle, increased flexibility and time for outside activities and socializing, the joy of grandchildren and the expansion of one's family, and hopefully the increase in one's status in the community as an older statesperson.

There are different stages of aging, just like there are different stages of younger adulthood. The current definition of elderly includes the "young-old," who are sixty-five to seventy-five years old, the "old," who are seventy-five to eighty-five, and then the "old-old," who are eighty-five and above. We no longer think of the elderly as just one group, because the pharmacology is different as we age, and in some cases even the illnesses manifest themselves differently.

The diagnosis of depression should only rarely be different from the diagnosis of depression in younger adults. The differences are minimal compared to the similarities. There may be more physical complaints such as sleep disorder, constipation, and some aches and pains in older people than there are in the younger population. So, it occasionally becomes difficult to differentiate treatable depression from the understandable sadness associated with physical decline, but the symptoms should never be ignored.

One of the great fallacies in geriatric psychiatry is that it's very hard to differentiate dementia and depression. Usually, distinguishing these two illnesses is quite straightforward. The complication comes when the two illnesses coexist. For instance, a patient can have a long-standing depression with the beginnings of dementia, or more likely one could have a progressive dementia with superimposed depression. For a researcher, this is a complicated situation, but from a clinical point of view there's really no diagnostic dilemma, because if a doctor notes a depression, he treats it. If the dementia remains, the patient probably had a dementia with depression; if the dementia symptoms resolve, the patient probably had what was called pseudodementia. In either case, it is incumbent on the physician to treat the usually reversible depressive symptoms.

Late-onset depression, which occurs by definition after the age of sixty-five, may be a slightly different illness than younger-onset depression. It may be associated with more memory impairments and the possibility of a higher incidence of dementia, but that's still a research question. Psychotic thinking is shocking at any age, whether you're five years old, fifty, or eighty-five. When psychosis is diagnosed in the elderly, it can be quite upsetting to the individual and the family and should be evaluated immediately and aggressively treated when possible. Now, psychosis or paranoia is associated with many things, not just depression or even schizophrenia. It can be associated with loss of hearing or any other form of sensory isolation, because people who can't hear or see well frequently get fearful and paranoid. Dementia subjects are particularly prone to these symptoms as a side effect of their dementia.

The pharmacologic treatment of the elderly is more complicated than with younger adults, because the average person over the age of sixty-five is on so many medicines to begin with. For instance, it was recently estimated that the average elderly person who has been in the hospital during the last year takes over six medicines or about eighteen pills a day. While the pharmacology is complicated, that shouldn't stop doctors from treating older people. In fact, you have to be concerned with the interactions of various medicines whenever you treat irrespective of the patient's age. So any time a psychiatrist or psychologist is evaluating a subject with a symptom of depression, the first question to ask is "Could this be a medication reaction?" It is not infrequent that the withdrawal of one or two medications may actually reduce or eliminate the depression symptoms. In other cases, there are usually a number of medication alternatives which are equally efficacious for the original target symptom that are less likely to cause a depression. They might be more expensive, and the expense of a medication, of course, is always a key issue for the elderly, but frequently the switch is worth it.

Regarding the over-eighty-five population, not much is known about using antidepressants. In fact, there are fewer than a handful of studies in this age group. Much more research needs to be done, but in the meantime there is no evidence that the "old-old" shouldn't be treated or that they would respond differently. Again, we should treat the depressive symptoms aggressively and never assume that depression is normal at any age.

John Kenneth Galbraith

As one gets older, anybody who doesn't think of the possibility of sickness and the possibility of death is immune to common sense. You're bound to think about it. And obviously when you get to be my age, you have two thoughts. First, "My God, Galbraith, you're eighty-three. How much longer do you have to live?" And second, "My God, Galbraith, how does it happen that you outlived everybody else?" And with the rarest exceptions, all of the people that I was with in my early career, including others that shared this enormous responsibility of running price control in World War II, they're all gone. I can think of only three or four that are left. And all of us who did share that experience, that was the peak of our power. My public power's been downhill now for nearly fifty years.

I accept it. I don't dwell on it, but I'm conscious of it.

If I had stopped everything when I retired as a Harvard professor seventeen years ago, if I had stopped all my life then, that would have been one thing. I shiver at the thought of that. But being a writer, I can keep on. There's no retirement. I'd always put a lot of my professorial time in on writing, I've always taught classes from twelve to one so it didn't interfere with morning or afternoon writing, or research, whatever I was doing. A writer can keep on going. Probably the quality diminishes, but you're the last person who notices that.

Jennie Forehand

"All your mother needs is a good spanking," her doctor said. "She is just spoiled." My dad did spoil her; there is no question. But "All she needs is a spanking"!

Mother's problems really had come to full head about four or five months after Dad died. He'd had an extended illness, four months in intensive care, that was really very difficult for all of us. Mother always had been a very vivacious person, but looking back, I think for the last three or four years before Dad died, she had been not nearly as upbeat as she had been before. I just wrote it off to slowing down because of age.

After his funeral, I thought that maybe she was jealous that the friends that they had had were not coming around as often. I thought she felt that maybe they had liked Daddy more than they had liked her. I tried to go down to Charlotte to see her as often as I could.

At first she would just do some strange things occasionally. She would hang up on me on the telephone. She was complaining and she wouldn't go out of the house.

I really had no idea what it was. She was just not doing the same types of activities and not interested in the kind of things the way she had been. She and my dad both had been really active people. She had always been really precise about how she kept records and how she kept the house. All of a sudden, that just went by the wayside. She was not being as communicative. She became very self-centered. People would bring her food, which is really appreciated when you are shut in. I will never forget a lady brought her some homemade brownies and a container of cottage cheese, because Mother has always liked that. And she didn't even thank her. She just slammed the door. Her friends were really upset about it and started calling me long distance, or stopping by while I was at home on the weekends. "Oh, I invited her to go out to dinner with us," somebody would say, "and then when we went to pick her up, she wouldn't answer the door."

So I went down and we took her to her family doctor that she had had for twenty-five years. I didn't know who else to take her to. This is the scary part of it, because here I am with access to anything and everybody. And I was doing what I thought was right. I didn't want to offend the family doctor. He checked her out and said, "All she needs is a good spanking." Then he said, "Well, maybe if we send her to [a respected] home for intermediate care, she'll get some extra attention there. She'll do some arts and crafts; she'll do activities. Maybe we'll just send her there for a little while, or maybe she'll like it and she'll want to stay."

We got her in the home where she and Daddy used to volunteer. After she got there, they said that they thought she needed to have a psychiatrist. So, she went to a psychiatrist and he put her on some kind of medicine. And it wasn't two weeks before she started doing some horrible things. They were having to strap her in the bed. She would stand up in the bed and jump up and down, really bizarre things.

She wouldn't go to the activities. Or if they made her go, she wouldn't participate. This was the first time in her adult life that people had been telling her what to do. She wasn't having any part of that. I was frustrated because I was trying to go down

there every other week, about an eight-hour trip. I have learned
so much since then. But I really wasn't sure what was happening
and I was just convinced that it was a wonderful place. It was the
home and they must know what they are doing. They were taking great care of her, but she kept complaining that she was not
getting her money's worth, because the rest of the people were
probably in there with other funding schemes and we were paying the full freight.

Then I started getting telephone calls from the nursing home
at night saying "Your mother is misbehaving. We don't know
what we can do with her."

One time, I was in a meeting on county business with some
psychiatrists who knew that I was practically commuting to
North Carolina and one of them said, "What is she doing?" I
described this bizarre behavior. And he said, "It sounds like she
is on Haldol."

And I said, "She is."

He said, "That is a side effect. Get her off."

So, I called, and they took her off of that. They put her on
something else, but then she started behaving in a different
mode. She was just bizarre. They couldn't control her. She
would run down the hall. I thought that maybe she was crazy. I
didn't know about side effects as I do now. So, when she started
doing this other bizarre behavior, I called the same doctor who
had warned me about the Haldol.

And he said, "Well, I bet they put her on Moban."

And I said, "Yes, that is it."

And he said, "Gosh, get her off of that."

Looking back, I guess my attitude had been like so many
people that I hear who have such faith in the doctors and in the
nursing homes. If I hadn't been as pushy and as aggressive as I
wound up being, she would be in the back wards of some mental
hospital today. They wanted to get her out of there. They
wanted to send her to the state mental hospital.

But here we had a top psychiatrist in Charlotte giving her
this stuff and not monitoring it. I have forgotten what the final
straw was, but she got kicked out. We took her home and we

took her off all medication. We tried to just dry her out. I had people lined up to go to her house and take care of her for eight hours a day and to take her out and do things with her because I wasn't there. So, we kind of dried her out and she got along. But she was still doing some bizarre things.

You could never predict. One day she would be just terrific and you could take her out to eat at a restaurant, but on other days she would go in her kitchen and pull the kitchen drawers out and throw them on the floor. And other days she would go into a catatonic state, and be rolling around on the floor for as long as forty-eight hours. Totally not there. Just totally out of it, just like hibernating, but rolling around on the floor.

I remember the one time she did it that was the most devastating to me. During the legislative session, I was flying to Charlotte every Friday afternoon and coming back on Monday morning. When I got there one Friday, she was so glad to see me. I had all these things planned for Saturday and Sunday. People had invited us out "if she feels like coming." She was terrific. We sat down and we talked for about an hour and the next thing that I knew she was down on the floor. She was rolling around and she didn't get up. Just in the middle of the conversation. And there she stayed for the next two days. She came to, to reality, about an hour before I was leaving for the plane to go back on Monday. The entire weekend. Here I am dealing with all sorts of legislative issues, like elder abuse. Now I could understand it. I was out of my mind. Very upset. I thought that it was deliberate, but it was not. There is no way, I know now, that she could control that.

Her doctor just thought she was being cantankerous. The whole time I really thought that she was controlling those catatonic states. One time a family friend offered to come and take her to the hospital for a scan. I called her that morning. She knew that she was going. Her keeper, her lady there, knew she was going. She was dressed. But when a friend came by to pick her up, she lay down on the floor in a catatonic state just like a kid saying "I won't go." And she pulled the piano bench over on herself.

But after a while, when he went over and very gently lifted her eyelids and told her it was time to go, she got right up and said, "Okay, I've been waiting on you."

I can see clearly why elderly are abused. Can you imagine if you woke somebody up after you've been waiting for them and all of a sudden they do that, wouldn't you be angry?

She would try to commit suicide.* The heat vents were in the floor and she pulled the grate up and tried to climb down, and it wasn't that big. She tried to stuff handkerchiefs in her mouth. She said she had five or six handkerchiefs in her mouth at one time; she was trying to swallow them.

My mother could not lift my briefcase sometimes, yet she lifted the end of her bed, which is very heavy. I couldn't lift it myself, but she could do that with some kind of a herculean strength that she got from this. Another time when she was in this catatonic state, rolling around, she pulled a TV set off the table. It missed her head by inches. This kind of bizarre behavior I have since learned is a form of depression. Most people think depression is just moping, but this is the real physical part.

The health care agencies sent different people each day to take care of her, and it was frustrating to her. One day she barricaded the front door and wouldn't let anybody in. Another phenomenon that occurred that may be a sign of aging, but that also happened to her at this time, was her inability to do things like replace a light bulb. She could not replace a light bulb. She couldn't use the key to get in the door. Simple things like that that she just couldn't figure out.

She would get something in her mind; she would have some obsession. Once she wanted to clean out her closet. She didn't just want to clean it out like you and I think of; she wanted everything out of there. All of her good clothes, all of her hats and shoes that were still terrific. She had the lady who was her nurse that day take them down to the Salvation Army, everything, to empty the closet.

---

* Suicide is more common among the elderly (primarily white males) than among any other age group. The elderly over sixty-five, who make up 12.5 percent of the population, account for 21 percent of suicides.

Another time she had this obsession that she thought she was poor. Well, she is not a wealthy woman; she is of very modest means. She wrote a letter to Medicare and asked them to please cancel and send her the refund. She had Blue Cross and AARP, but she wrote all of them and asked them to cancel. Luckily, I had changed some of the addresses on things so that they'd come to me, so she wouldn't do this. When she did, I got the check and called them back to reinstate her.

Throughout all of this, you could see her mind was working. There was just a gap. Later on, even through all this time, she could work crossword puzzles like crazy, even at the worst of it. But you couldn't read her writing.

I had just about declared her dead. I thought, "Oh, my gosh. Here in the same year, I'm losing my mother and my father." I really thought that she was just beyond help. If she committed suicide, I wasn't going to have a guilt trip over it, because I had done everything that I could possibly think of. But emotionally I just kept saying to myself "There's got to be a better answer and I'm going to find it." I guess that's one of the things my folks always taught me; just don't give up. You know you'll hit it.

From January through March, she was at home. Because I was having different people come into the house every day to take care of her, I left a yellow pad of paper there and I said, "I want a diary. I want to know what she has eaten. I want to know how her behavior was. I want to know what she did that day. Everything. Just write it down." I had no idea what a smart thing that was going to turn out to be.

I got a phone call at eight o'clock one morning in February. When the nurse got to Mother's house that day, she called me in Annapolis and said, "Your mother is not here." The door was wide open, and she'd left her purse behind. She has always been so frightened of her shadow even; the doors were always double locked. We live near a creek and I envisioned all these horrible things, because she had been trying to commit suicide in different ways.

It turned out that she had left the house at about four o'clock in the morning and had walked miles away from home, crossing an eight-lane highway several times. She had gone down to the railroad tracks. She said that she sat by the railroad tracks thinking that maybe a train would come. It didn't come so she went to a house where a friend had lived twenty years before and sat down on Mrs. Fermin's front lawn. A man driving by saw her sitting there and said, "I will take you home, lady, where do you live?" She gave him a fictitious address because, as she said later, "No self-respecting Southern lady would tell a stranger where she lived!" Here is this brain working.

The poor man must have driven around for an hour trying to find the street she told him she lived on. Finally, he had to go to work, so he left her on the front steps of a business, where she apparently went into a catatonic state. She wound up at the public hospital as an "unidentified white female." That little walk in the morning was the straw that broke the camel's back. Mother can tell that story vividly today. She remembers every bit of it.

Here in my position, I am supposed to be out there helping other people. I had access to the top health people in the entire state. The secretary of the Health Department was somebody that I was with for hours every day at Annapolis during the legislative session. I had access here in the county to the tops in psychiatry. In fact, we brought Mother up here to visit. I took her to a good friend of mine who is a psychiatrist, because I had great faith in him and he had a wonderful reputation. He didn't diagnose it correctly either. He just put her on some other drug. My faith in the medical community was shattered. Nobody knew what it was until down the road.

I have a neighbor who works at NIH, the National Institute of Health. And he didn't even know what I was going through. Later on, when I told him, he said, "Get her to Johns Hopkins."

I said, "What is at Hopkins?"

"Well, they got an NIH grant for geriatric depression," he told me. But there was a long waiting list to get into the program.

I went to work the next day and I said, "Who do I know to call at Hopkins?"

It was about the first time I had ever pulled a string, and it needed to be pulled. They called me back an hour later and said, "When do you want to have her there?"

She was there for a month. The doctors were so excited to have an example like her as a part of that program, because the bad reaction to the drug therapy was documented in this diary. So they could start on a clean slate with her. They never would have started her on shock therapy without first having done the drug therapy, but since that already had proven to be a failure, they just went right to this. Having seen a record of her behavior for the last two months, they didn't have to waste a lot of time observing her. That was where that diary paid off. Plus, I wrote a six-page history of her background to give to them. They started her immediately on shock therapy. At that point, I just trusted them. I said, "Everything else has failed. If you think this is going to work, terrific."

It was absolutely wonderful. So many people are afraid of shock treatment, but it's so different and so much better than it used to be.

She had seven shock treatments. She was under anesthesia, so she felt none of it. And her memory was not impaired except that she does not remember what happened at Hopkins. A lot of people talk of that as being one of the drawbacks. But she remembers everything: past, present, everything. I have not seen any downside. I know in past years hearing about people who have had shock treatments, who have lost their memory or who are not the same ever again. I think that electric shock used to be considered almost a medieval thing, just a terrible thing to do to people. And they did it in state institutions, almost as a punishment. But I am a terrific advocate for ECT because I saw the good that came from it.

People need to hear about stories like my mother's where they had tried everything else and nothing else worked, but this did. Now, a lot of patients with depression can be cured by drug therapy, but, boy, it was surely the wrong thing for Mother.

When she got out of Hopkins, it took her a little bit of time to adjust, but it was absolutely terrific. We stayed at my house for a couple of weeks, and then I took her back to Charlotte, because I knew the stigma of mental illness might be hard to get over. Every day we took a different group of people out to lunch to let them hear about what had happened and to let them see that she was her same self that they had known before.

We went out and we got some new clothes. I had all these people in to eat. She started going back to having her hair fixed every week. I took her on trips and I took her to see family. I took her everywhere that I could think of. She really loved it.

We went to the Methodist church that she had gone to for years. She had a Sunday school class with about two-hundred-fifty people in it that have all grown old together. They asked me to speak that morning, so I did and I told them what she had been through. And I said, "Don't ever stop with the medical people that you have here. It is wonderful to have confidence in your doctor, but if you're not getting the right results, go somewhere else. The relationship between the patient and the doctor is so important. We have been through doctor after doctor. I know that the expertise that all the doctors at Hopkins had was very important, but I can tell you that the warmth that her doctor showed to her as an individual was probably more important than his technical expertise. He showed her that he cared about her and she wanted to please him." And I said, "Whatever you do, you have to keep that in mind. Because I think that is the key to opening the door."

For fourteen years, I have done the budget of the Health Department in the state of Maryland. So, I think that I am probably one of the best-informed people in the legislature, at least, about what is out there for the public. Nowhere do I see treatment for this. I see people with some of these same symptoms who supposedly have Alzheimer's, but a lot of people out there tucked away, supposedly without promise, really have depression.

I don't know how you distinguish between the two, but knowing what I know now, I told my kids, "If I am ever in that situation, don't wait to try to distinguish. Just send me in for shock treatment and see if it helps." Because you don't know. I would risk it for the likelihood that it might be depression instead of Alzheimer's. Mother really lost a year of her life. And I lost a year of mine.

It hurts to see an older relative in pain, and it can be hard to know what to do. But any effort is worth it to salvage the remaining life of a loved one. Start by finding a quiet, calm time and place to talk. Express your love and concern, what you've noticed, what you suggest. "Emma, I love you and I feel so sad seeing you in pain. You seem so lonely. I notice you forgetting things, crying a lot, not eating. Let me go with you to the doctor and let's find out what's wrong." Of course, not all general practice doctors will take those complaints seriously. You might even want to speak to the depressed person's doctor ahead of time about what you've noticed and get a feel for the doctor's responsiveness.

"It's a myth," said Betty Davis, senior program specialist for the AARP, "that older people can't change. They can change just like young people. Sometimes it helps to remind them of the wisdom and coping mechanisms they have accrued over a lifetime of meeting adversity and to see that here [depression] is another thing they can overcome."

If your elderly relative is plagued by small ills, is withdrawing or losing interest in life, is emotionally unpredictable or vague and unfocused, don't just chalk it up to "age." As you would with a youngster, a sister, a mate, approach him or her with love and concern, offer assistance, and most of all offer hope.

23
Advice to the Players

Emotions are out of control, our lives careening away from us; we are riding a runaway train heading for a crash. In the black tunnel ahead lurks the panic. Although medications will help, and talk therapies will help, taking control—empowering ourselves to help ourselves—can be the brake that forestalls disaster. Taking action however small to help ourselves bestows on our psyches the belief that we are not helpless. Building on that strength, inch by inch, we slow the mighty engine of despair and emerge into the light.

 Unable to take medications, or while waiting for them to take effect, between appointments, or while searching for the right doctor, at times we may be without therapeutic help. Some of the people you've heard from in these pages have had frustrating, even frightening experiences with doctors before they found the help they needed. But they persevered, and they triumphed. And when asked what advice they would give, the answer was "Go for help. Keep asking questions. Be an informed consumer. Don't give up."

Meanwhile, by doing what you can for yourself, applying first aid for the mind, you may be able to hold off a deeper or an additional occurrence of depression.

Lewis Judd, M.D.

I happen to be a runner. I run five days a week, five miles a day, and I am certain that that makes me feel better. I know that when I'm not able to do it, I tend to get a little bit dysphoric and pessimistic about things, because I'm very used to it. We have learned that certain levels of aerobic exercise result in some changes in mood and a sense of well-being. Some mild depressions have been treated under double-blind circumstances with aerobic exercise and running, to some success. Severe depression, clinical depression, cannot. But as a part of my management of depression, I certainly prescribe that for people as a specific prescription. Not only do I treat them with medications, I treat them psychotherapeutically in ways that have been shown to benefit people who are depressed, and I will also prescribe for them within the limits of their cardiovascular capacity an hour of brisk walking or whatever each day during this period of time. It gives someone something to do anyway, but it's also very helpful.

As far as alternative treatments—acupuncture, yoga, Scientology—they never have been proven to be effective in the treatment of a mental disorder like depression at all. I don't think they are harmful necessarily, but I don't think they help, and I think that the danger is if they're extensively relied on, when there are effective treatments available and they're not used, that's really a tragedy.

Norman Rosenthal, M.D.

There are a lot of things that people with SAD can do to help themselves. They can get light therapy. They can get more natural light. They can just light up their houses. They can make their homes brighter; they can put white wallpaper on and light-colored carpet versus dark paneling and dark carpet. This makes a big difference. They can choose houses with large windows. They can trim hedges around windows so that they are not completely covered. They can exercise, which is helpful. Stress management is important. If this is a time of year when you can't handle stresses that well, see what you can do to modify it. Don't undertake big things in the winter if you know that is going to be a time when you can't handle it. Leave them for the summer.

Mary Jones

Get help. Get help. It is the only thing I ever learned about alcohol. It is maybe the only really important thing I learned in my life: Get help. 'Cause if you could fix it yourself, you would have fixed it by now.

Joan Rivers

It's important to say "You can get through it. I'm not saying you're not going to have it, but you can work through it. You must remember in the depths of it, that yes, you can work through it and you will get better. You must hold on to that thread. Even though you think it is, it's not that dark." It's like, when you've had a terrible love affair, and you say, "I can't live another day." But indeed you live another day, and a year later you say, "I liked him?!" And that's what you just have to keep letting [a depressed person] know.

    It was so important to me to hear my psychologist say "It's okay; you have a right." Just be aware that you have a right, but don't let it take over your whole life, that's the other thing. By him saying it was okay, I know it sounds so childish, it *was* okay. I didn't have to brood and think and constantly go "Poor me," and "Nobody understands," because there was someone who understood. You need one person who understands.

Pat Love, Ed.D.

Keep knocking on doors till you get an answer and feel better.
The good news is there's good health out there. The other thing
is that if you're not enjoying life, check it out. I think that's the
key. Is life fun for you?

Kitty Dukakis

I don't give advice because I've been in this place such a short
time. I just don't. I think if I had a close friend who came to me
and said, "What do I do?" I would say find the best
psychopharmacologist in your area who understands medications. Many hospitals have a team approach that can go through
a psychological workup with different kinds of therapeutic teams
and make a decision about who the best person is for you.

Jules Feiffer

Take it easier, I mean, lighten up, try to be easier on yourself.
Yes, it's every bit as bad as you think it is, big deal. So fucking
what? Just get on with it.

John Kenneth Galbraith

My advice would be to go and see a psychiatrist. Go and see a
counselor, absolutely. And now there's good medicine for it, too.
I don't see why people should go public with it. Tell them to
follow their own counsel on the matter. If they don't want to talk
about it, don't.

It was much worse for the generation that felt they had to
close themselves off from the world and couldn't talk about it.

And I feel very much more relaxed about the whole problem by having talked about it. Absolutely. You just have to tell them it is a real phenomenon, no question.

For myself, the common rules of good health, the kinds of things we all know, but don't always follow, can help head off or at least mitigate the effects of a mild depression. If I feel a little shaky, I make a few relatively simple adjustments—cut back on caffeine (and if I drank alcohol, I'd cut back on that, too), keep regular bedtimes, eat three meals of low-fat, high-fiber foods—salads, fruit, chicken, brown rice—and get some exercise. Depending on how badly I feel, these adjustments can take a little discipline or a lot. For me, the next level of self-help takes even more work: forced relaxation. If I can cancel all obligations that aren't imperative and take the time to sit in the hammock and stare at the sky, have my husband take the kids while I soak in a hot tub, or put on Bach and do a little needlework, the rest of my life will seem less overwhelming. And when these measures aren't enough, I obtain professional help.

24

Healing

Healing is more than just bringing a disease under control. Healing includes finding new strategies for dealing with stumbling blocks and encompasses thoughtful reflection of our lives, and putting depression in perspective. Healing requires acceptance of the past and hope for the future.

John Kelsoe, M.D.

The outlook for psychiatric illness in general is very bright. We are in an era where the understanding of these behavioral disorders as brain disorders is exploding. The tools which we now have available to us to study the brain and to understand these things are changing at an incredible rate. With the PET scanner, you can see that when the eyes are open, the back of the brain where the visual area is lights up. When the eyes are closed, it shuts down. Distinguishing what things are characteristic of depression is not entirely clear right now, but we are getting to the point where we will begin to be able to see functional brain differences in a scanner like that. If we understood what was really going wrong in the brain, we could devise drug treatments that were much more specific and potentially more effective. That is one area that has tremendous promise.

Another area of promise is in understanding the genetics. Although for at least fifty years we have had scientific evidence that some mental illnesses are hereditary, in the last ten to fifteen years molecular biology has developed the tools that enable us to figure out exactly what those genes are.

This has absolutely revolutionized medicine. Something that was absolutely unimagined years ago is the possibility to correct the genetic defect directly by putting the correct gene into a virus and then infecting the appropriate cells with that virus. The affected individual is now able to make the correct genetic product and the disease is cured. So I think that it is not impossible that one day someone who has a severe psychiatric disorder might be treated by giving them the correct gene.

The future is very bright and the possibilities are enormous in applying these new kinds of tools in psychiatry. When we can say "This is the gene" and know that for sure, then I think that has a tremendous impact on the public in terms of really believing that it is a biological illness. That is going to have a great beneficial effect on stigma and people's acceptance of behavioral problems and psychiatric disorders.

Jim Jensen

I'm never going to totally defeat depression, no. I have better coping techniques now, and I am getting some good medical attention from somebody who finally knows what the hell he's doing.

No more therapy, that's a waste of time. No. What my mother and father did, forget it. They did it and it's gone. What you've got to do, I think, is forgive. They didn't know any better, they didn't understand, they tried their best. Forgive them. You've got to forgive them so you can forgive yourself. And it's a big weight off your neck. Don't carry around resentments. They tangle you all up. You spend your whole day in resentments, ruin your whole day mad at somebody down the hall. Why? It's stupid. Oh, I did a lot of that, we all do.

The twelve-step program I'm in is extremely important. It's not a program for addicts per se. If they would start teaching this in the kindergartens, and keep teaching it all the way through school, we'd turn out human beings. We turn out great lawyers and journalists and scientists and everything else, but we turn out lousy human beings. Most of us don't know how to be human beings. Loving, giving, understanding, tolerant, forgiving human beings. I'm not talking about religion, I'm not talking about turning the other cheek, I am talking about spirituality, a trust in that power greater than yourself.

Step 11 and Step 12* are a guide, not only for addiction or drinking. Negative self-absorption is dangerous, but your only way out of it is not through another human being, but is to trust in a spiritual power greater than yourself. You will be taken care of, this negative thing will change automatically. It isn't that all you've got to do is believe in God. You have to have some medical help along the way, but you've got to bolster yourself up in many areas.

I'm more stabilized now than I've been in years. I certainly wouldn't touch cocaine again. I know that cocaine would destroy me. I've changed my lifestyle, too, somewhat. I'm more involved with people. I don't feel the way I used to feel. I'm more comfortable. You know, my work now is better than it ever was. I don't know why, but it is.

I wish I'd learned how to sail a boat. I need something like that. I need a kind of a hobby right now. I'd like to learn how to sail. That would be fun. And not to escape, either, but to go out

---

* Step 11: "Seek through prayer and meditation to improve our conscious contact with God *as we understand him*, praying only for knowledge of his will for us and the power to carry that out." Step 12: "Having had a spiritual awakening as the result of these steps, we try to carry this message to alcoholics, and to practice these principles in all our affairs."

with a bunch of people, you know? And have a party. That would be fun.

Jules Feiffer

I remember walking on this road or on the beach any number of times over the years, trying to figure out what the hell was the matter with me, why was I feeling so awful. A lot comes out when I walk. Suddenly I would hit on something, and I'd start laughing, because it was always so silly and so easy once I'd remember what it was that got me angry or got me upset or got me depressed. And once I had a name for it, once I had branded it, once it stopped being a mystery, I would start feeling better. In my case, what drives me nuts is a failure to understand what's going on within me. Even if it's very bad news, once I understand the nature of that bad news, I feel whole again and I can cope.

The cartoons have always acted as a kind of blow-hole for me. It's where air comes out and air goes in. When nothing else is working, it's my last grasp on holding on. Because it's a conversation between me and the reader. I do it once a week. There's no critic to say this isn't as good as your last one. I'm the only critic. In that sense, it's noncompetitive. And while I may put in a tiring day or two, I have something to show for it and it's in print immediately. So it's always been a restorative.

I keep figuring out new things to do with it. The more I do, the more I get interested in the work I've done before, so that rather than sapping energy it lends energy.

I don't think of my viewpoint as bleak, I think of it as a tough, ironic, unleavened view of the real world. Bleak means without any kind of way out or uplift, but I don't feel that way and I don't think the work shows that. The work is full of energy, and the energy presents a vitality, so even when the message might be considered bleak, the ambience isn't. People don't walk out of my plays depressed, they walk out of them charged and talking to each other, which is what I mean for it to be. So much of my life has been about work that I can't separate my emotional life from it. I don't know what emotional life it would be possible for me to have, if I didn't have this career. This has been my obsession in one form or another since the age of five. Yet for most of my life, I felt that there was a career and there was nothing else, that all relationships were not just second to what I did in my work, but way back there. And now what's most important is my family, and the career is secondary.

Everybody has looked for and been disappointed in looking for the parent figure. It's seldom our own parents, but the friend who will be the father or the mother, the agent who will take care of business for you so you won't have to take care of it. The producer, the publisher, the editor: your protector. And I've had actually a couple of experiences where I've met people who have come through in that regard. But never for very long, and never on a permanent basis. In the end, sad as it seems, you have to be your own parent, and you've got to do it for yourself. That doesn't mean there aren't people out there that are to be trusted, but you can't put your emotional being into anyone's hands but your own.

Over the short run, there's really very little to be done [to help ease depression]. Over the long run, it's the constancy of the relationship, the constancy of the family, it's the existence of that little child who is just a remarkable presence in my life, and the constancy of my older daughter, who is another remarkable presence in my life. And the oddity that at this age, I've got a family, and feel that I have roots, that there's something other than having a career.

William Styron

I don't think the depression is going to come back. But if it does, I'll just have to deal with it, and I'll know how to deal with it with considerably more insight than I did before . . . I still suffer from melancholia, because I think it's a condition of the personality. These seizures, such as I had, were merely a kind of gross manifestation, kind of an acute stage of the chronic illness that I'll probably have all my life only carried to enormous extremes.

I learned never again to joke about mental illness, [and I learned] to be respectful of people who are sort of strange. I learned how vulnerable the mind is. And I learned that the human spirit can really take a great deal and survive. I think it hardens the soul a bit, in the best sense. To some extent, it made me a little bit more tolerant to a lot of other things, although really I'm just as impatient with everyone. You don't emerge suddenly as some kind of remarkable new person, you know. That's a myth that somehow it converts you into a new luminous human being. But it does allow you to have certain toleration for other things that you didn't before, especially other people's mental distress.

Leslie Garis

Once you get centered in yourself, you realize what a miracle it is to stand and talk to someone. You get centered in yourself and you can connect to another person, you can come out of yourself, be in the other person, see the happiness, feel the entity of the other person which you can't feel when you're locked into the bubble that you were always in when you were depressed. You can enter into the joy of the existence of that person and how much you love that person. Before I would have need. I would need to be appreciated. I would need to be needed. I would need to be wanted. Once I came out of the depression, all of a sudden I was able to experience others purely for their separateness, their uniqueness, their own life force. I felt this wild surge of love, for my friends, for my children, for my husband. Before I was only experiencing it sideways or off stage; suddenly I was on stage in life and feeling the real emotions that they're feeling.

Also, my libido came back. When you're seriously depressed, you're unable to experience pleasure, and I became able to experience pleasure again. It's widely reported that taking Prozac lowers your libido, but I had pretty much zero libido before. It seems to me that if you get undepressed then you can experience those things again.

I always will be on Prozac. It's fine. It was not fine at the beginning. When you're in such a state of anxiety, the idea that you also have a disease is just one more thing to be anxious, upset, and depressed about. However, as I came out of it, I began to think of it like diabetes or a thyroid condition, which I'm perfectly able to accept. What's so terrible about that? I'm so lucky to be healthy. I'm so lucky not to be in a wheelchair, to not have disabilities that so many thousands of people live with.

Rona Barrett

At one point, I am positive, I had a chemical imbalance. I didn't take any drugs to get back into a more normal sense. For me, finding a greater understanding of myself, knowing who I am and what I am gave me the ability to restore the self-esteem that for a moment I had put under wraps. I also learned a lot about compromise. The art of compromise is one of the finest traits that anybody could teach himself or herself. When you can't look in the mirror any longer, then you know the compromise is too great and you must get out. To thine own self be true. All those stupid clichés. But it's a cliché because it holds a great deal of truth.

Now if I feel depressed, I can get out of it in a very short time, like minutes, seconds. I say to myself "Stop that. Stop that, little chatterbox! Stop it! No need. Go away . . . bye-bye!" All of us have that little internal person that sits there saying "Oh, Rona. You shouldn't be doing this. Rona, why are you doing this now? Don't do it, Rona. Be careful, Rona." Rona has to turn around and say "Shut up! Nice to hear from you, good-bye." It does work. It absolutely works.

I had allowed the depression to take hold and to run my life. If it isn't a chemical imbalance, you must realize that you are responsible for what you do to yourself. What depression really is expressing is the negatives of your life saying "Ha-ha, I gotcha now! I'm the ruler, I'm on the playing field. I've got more of your time. I've got more of your body!" That's not true; you can stop it. My own philosophy has always been: You can be whatever it is you want to be. Only you can stop it!

Years ago after my attempted suicide, I kept asking myself, "Why, why would these people do this? Why? What did I do that was so wrong?" How do you have a thirty-year career and you never get sued once doing the kind of work you do, and then you get sued by some very rich man who has nothing to do with show business, and another bunch of rich men decide "Aha, let's get Rona! She's too weak to fight back." There were lessons to learn from that chapter. I did. I changed. Now I'm a fighter, a survivor!

James Farmer

Making a speech, I find to be therapeutic. I am at home on a platform. I am at home with a large audience. I am not at home in a committee meeting or with people sitting around a table, in a round-table discussion. I am not at home there, because that is more one on one. I prefer solitude to that. But I have solitude; I am alone in "the lonely crowd." The actor in me comes out, I guess. The son of a preacher. The person who started to be a preacher. Also in the traveling and speaking are a lot of accolades. And the ego eats that up. And the applause at the end. That's good.

Rod Steiger

I have a problem with a mental disease, called depression, which can return at any time maybe, because of chemistry in me I don't understand. You just have to watch yourself, you have to take your medicines, and you have to be more intelligent about yourself. You have to keep moving when you begin to feel like you don't want to move. You have to occupy yourself, get out of the house. You have to learn all those things, go for a swim when you don't want to swim, go for a walk when you don't want to walk. It's easy for me to say that, but by and large I can't do it half the time. I used to play tennis. I do so little exercise now, all I do is swim every once in a while. I'm just trying to make myself swim for twenty minutes three times a week.

I know all the intellectual things. Have the courage to keep moving. KEEP MOVING, that's what my license plate on one car says. The other plate says COURAGE. Don't stay in bed. Get out. Now that I'm better, if I feel a little unhappy or uneasy or I feel what I call the cold water begin to fill up and my legs turning to icy concrete, I head for the swimming pool, exercise and get the endorphins up, get them going. I exercise for a half hour, twenty minutes, and I feel better.

The medicines keep you in control and you're able to command yourself. It keeps the depression away from you. But every once in a while a bubble gets through and you have a day and a half where you feel terrible. I saw signs of it again, crying for no reason. I'd wake up in the morning, calling for my wife to hold me, lay on top of me and give me a feeling of strength and closeness. Sure enough, we did a blood test on this ever-changing chemical machine and found that something had changed in my system so I had to increase the dose. That's one of my big fears, that it will return. And there's no guarantee it won't. And there's no guarantee it will, you know.

Pat Love, Ed.D.

A few years ago I realized I'd reached all the goals that I'd ever set out for myself. I asked myself, "What is there to have in life, anyway?" I sat down and I drew a chart of the different areas of my life that were important to me and started working on balancing my life. I started (1) having more fun, (2) being creative, (3) really enjoying things altruistically, (4) thinking about spirituality, (5) getting a good handle on my feelings, and (6) feeding my mind. I got pro-active about each one. If I'm having a bad time in my relationship, I'm still taking care of the other areas of my life, and that helps to keep everything in perspective.

And laughter helps a lot.

Susan Crosby

There is a happy ending. My kids and I are okay and we're surviving and we will continue to live a life. Families need to know that that will happen, that the whole world does not fall apart if the worst happens.

I was wondering if [we could learn to] catch somebody in Lindsay's situation at an early age, start treatment and be aware of what's going to come up and know how you have to handle it. In those last six months, Lindsay was talking about wanting to work with teenagers who had bipolar disorder. He wanted to talk to them and show them how important it was to stay close to the doctors and be aware of all the new medicines. He wanted at least to pass on what not to do.

We all like to think we're here for a purpose, and if it gives only an idea of things not to do and what happened in this generation, and let's not repeat that, and let's educate, then that will make me feel good. I want to be one of the people carrying the banners demanding more investigation. We hadn't talked about writing it or doing it on film, but I know this was what he [would] want done. And I'm going to see that it is done.

Joan Rivers

I believe in closing the circle. Edgar must have been so alone, God, that last night. . . . I just wanted to go to the hotel room in Philadelphia where he died and let him know that (a) it was okay, (b) I was still here, and (c) if there was anything still in that hotel room that wasn't [at peace] to put him at peace.

Three weeks after he killed himself, our daughter Melissa had had the courage to go back to Philadelphia, which is where she went to school. I have such respect, it was so hard for her, and she did it. Now it was a year later, and she was graduating with honors. It was all part of a weekend of great festivity and great happiness, and I thought, "Let's just go back and visit Daddy on the weekend." She didn't want to do it, but I thought it was important to go there for a minute and have a real closure. I'm not Catholic, but I brought a Catholic priest whom I knew, and I asked him to say prayers, to just bless the room. Somehow, it made me very serene about the whole thing, and it was very nice.

Kitty Dukakis

[Last] September, I was beside myself with anxiety about whether or not I was going to go through another period, but I haven't. I don't feel flat, although I don't have the same level of energy that I had before. I still spend too much money on clothes and other presents and things, and that's a part of me. I'm in school. Before, I had gotten to a point with the amphetamines where I didn't think I could do anything intellectual without them. I studied without them last week for the first time since I was an undergraduate at Penn State, and I think I did all right; I think I did well. I also have an ability today to follow through on stuff that even during my manic, feel-good periods just was not possible.

I go through periods of sadness when it's appropriate. I think I'm more in tune with issues that I need to work on than I've ever been before. I'm more honest with myself. And I feel good.

Dick Clark

I began to concentrate as my mother had done on what people think of you as a human being, not what they see in a quick look:

"He's got brown eyes and brown hair and is medium height." That's clearly unimportant. She'd learned that very early, and it made her very popular. I learned to concentrate on the other person, not on myself. And it works well in television, it works well in business, it's a good life experience. That was, in retrospect, the greatest thing that I could ever have learned at that stage in my life.

The one single thing that pulled me out of that depression probably was the death of my brother, December 23 of 1944. We didn't hear about it until some days after Christmas because of communication problems. I was the sole surviving kid in the family, and I realized that I couldn't be a burden to my mother and father as I had been. I had to get out and get going, since I was the one who had to carry on. As a matter of fact, we all had that philosophy. My mother and father and I cried a great deal the day we heard of his death. Then the next day, she went around her chores, my father went to work, and I went to school. So that probably is what snapped me out of it. Something bigger than I was.

I still have mood swings, but as you mature and get older you are somehow able to level them out, because you do look around, and if you're not totally in the depths of depression, you can relate to the fact that you don't have it so bad. No matter how lousy it looks, it's really not that bad.

Joan Rivers

You must go for help. You cannot do it yourself when you're that depressed. Even if you go for help and it doesn't seem like it's helping, it's still helping. Part of the help is that someone is there to at least share it with you. Nobody else wants to hear it. When my therapist said "You're totally correct, everything has fallen apart, your life is a shambles," that was tremendously important in the healing process. Someone gave me the right to feel the way I was feeling. . . .

But oh, I always have to go on. I'm the breadwinner. You

have to go forward. Especially when my husband went into such a depression after the Fox firing, I was the one that said we must keep moving. The same thing after the Broadway show. And what has saved me both times is I've made myself work, I've made myself get up, I've made myself make the phone calls, I've made myself go to the luncheons. It doesn't stop the depression. It's a lot like exercising, I've found. You work your way through the pain. You know what they say, "If it's burning, that's good, so keep going, keep going." And it's the same with depression— just keep going.

Jane Doe

I never blamed the world, I always blamed myself. I am still battling with low self-esteem, à la Gloria Steinem, our generation. And that rage that I carried is coming out a lot now. I hope I am going to let go of it someday.

I can see that my life choices were really determined by this damaged immune system. Now I have overcome it. Thank God for Prozac.

Now I really see the reality. The main thing is to feel that you are like everybody else. Like you have the same chances, the same ups and downs, and not to live in fear of the moods, the terror of those moods and the distorted thinking. Because you know at some level of your being, if you are a smart person, that that is real distorted thinking, but it still affects your judgment and your life. I still have depression when things go bad, when I am worried or something. But it is normal-life depression. The distorted thinking is gone. The paranoia is virtually gone. And if I get any little zings of those things then I can say to myself, right on the spot "Listen. Come on. That is paranoia, go change your activity, be active. Go wash the dishes, do something." And I'm cheerful. I'm smiling. My behavior with my friends has changed dramatically. I am sharing more. I am feeling nurtured by them. I can take in what they have to give me. Now I feel in the community of women, I feel like an equal. I share what's going on in my love life and so forth.

I can be self-deprecating and see my faults in being bossy, in being this and that. With friends there is a little bit of tension about something sometimes. But it takes the edge off of it, if I suddenly am getting too bossy and I can tease myself. I always thought that I never had a sense of humor and now I discover that sometimes I'll say things that will make people laugh. It is *Awakenings*. It really is like that film to a lesser degree, waking up and feeling normal! Waking up and not feeling depressed. I am aware of it every minute of every day.

Judith Belushi Pisano

I don't see that I went through something any harder than anyone else. If anything, I think I've been blessed. I know I went through some hard times, but as they say, "If it doesn't kill you, it'll make you stronger."

I'd like to think that it didn't take a traumatic death in my life to make me be at the place I'm at today, but of course, that's what I have and what I am, and I feel good. I feel good. I try to give a little bit back to people if I can, by just responding to others or by saying to the people who write me "I hear you, and I wish you well."

Keeping journals and writing about it was very important to my healing because it made me go through it consciously. Most of my emotional life before that I was going through unconsciously. I just didn't see the value in being clear with why I do certain things, as opposed to just reacting. The various twelve-step programs are helpful guidelines through the same kind of a process. I was doing that before I ever heard of them, just by instinct, except I was skipping step one, which is to give yourself up to the higher power.

You just have to take that leap of faith. I don't remember the day or the moment, but I had to jump over the part of my mind that said "There's no explanation, so how can we believe it? I'm too smart for this." I said to myself, "Well, let's just assume I don't understand some level of this. And then open up to it." And that's really when things started to change for me. Now I'm much more happy.

The biggest influence for me spiritually was *A Course in Miracles,* which is a book which offers a lesson a day for a year. It offered a view of things that with my leap of faith made perfect sense to me.

That was several years after John died. Before that, I was reading a lot, studying. *Zen Way, Jesus Way** was probably the first book I read where I started to see a connection between Eastern thought and Western, although they're very different.

I've come to a good place. You can go through this, you can be really depressed, you can be really down, you can think that life isn't worth living. But if you do hang in, if you just hang in, have a little faith—and faith's a hard thing to have, especially when you're depressed—but if you can just hang on to a thread of something, you'll come around. You will come around.

Sometimes, heeling the black dog of depression involves more than reining in the disease. Mending relationships, realigning our self-images, reordering our finances are all part of putting our lives back together once the depression is under control. Each person you have read about is on a different part of that path to wholeness.

* By Tucker N. Callaway, published 1976 by Charles E. Tuttle Co., Inc.

25
Ad Astra
per Aspera

Pain is a mechanism for growth; it carves out the heart and allows more room for compassion.

—Betty Sue Flowers

I had a dream, a new version of the apocalyptic nightmares that had haunted my depressed mind. The setting was familiar: the bleak landscape erratically lit by distant flares; the ragged and despondent refugees stumbling through rubble; the derelict buildings as insubstantial as memory. Darkness and despair hung heavily throughout like a fog. In what had once been an armory, I sought shelter from the night. A carpet-bagging impresario had filled the cavernous hall with displays of danger and disorder—an amusement hall of the apocalypse. Larger-than-life sculpture of twisted forms and violent scenes, circus acts choreographed not to divert but to disturb, multiple video screens, performance art and atonal music surrounded me, vague and disturbing, darkly ambiguous, Felliniesque. I made my way through the daunting

hall, each step dragging more slowly, until I reached the far door.
There I crouched on the ground, hugging my knees, overwhelmed. But
as I looked back across the obscure arena I had just navigated, a new
certainty freed me from this bleak vision. I rose to my feet. "No," I said
to no one, to everyone, to the hall, the performers, the impresario him-
self. "No, this is not what life is. Even in this place. There is light.
There is beauty. There is Hope."

I started this book with the image of a black dog, a conve-
nient code word for a fearsome idea. Making the intangible experience of depression corporeal made it seem more manageable.
Now I see the task is to deal with the dog and move on, to make
peace with depression however I can—not to wallow in it, but to
accept the reality of it; to change the vocabulary and the way I
think about it so I can live with it more comfortably. The dog
that opened this book may have appeared in my mind as a
Rottweiler, but now that it has been befriended, I see a black
Lab, not so much tamed as transformed. Although it still de-
mands attention, much of the time it lies quietly at my feet,
softer, gentler, familiar.

My original hope in writing this book was to describe depression for those who have never suffered its effects, but throughout
my interviews I heard "Nobody understands. . . . You can't understand unless you've been there." And that may be true. As
many times as I nodded, saying "Yes, yes, that's the way it is," I
was rendered speechless at the depths of pain, or at the denial, of
others.

It is hard to find shared experiences among people who *do*
understand, who *have* been there, because we are each in our
own rooms, in our own houses. We each put on a smiling face
for the world and each suffer in a private hell. But talking to
others, sharing experiences and philosophies will strengthen us
all, and I have found through these interviews greater acceptance
of my own depression.

In a sense, this book was the beginning of a support group.
For our own sakes, to help us gain a better understanding of
depression in our lives, we need to talk about our illnesses among

ourselves. For the sake of those who have yet to know that they have a treatable disease, we should talk about it with others.

We need to open the national dialogue on depression as well. In spite of the DART* program of the National Institute of Mental Health and other recent efforts, along with various publications, there are still too many people with undiagnosed and untreated depression. Although most of the people in this book have been able to obtain the services they needed, thousands if not millions throughout the country have not. Many families have seen loved ones confined to custodial care in a state hospital with little hope of ever leading a full and productive life; medications that could treat the illness are out of reach financially, competent intensive talk therapy is unavailable, electroshock therapy seems too frightening.

"The public health issue of depression has a profound impact on the United States," Dr. Lewis Judd told me, "not only on the overall health of the people, but on the economics. . . . We calculated that depression is costing San Diego alone, each year, $200 million. [People in the work force] are not being treated, are disabled, and suffering and dysfunctional from depression, and [the companies] don't even know about it. We can demonstrate that appropriate treatment and early recognition could save enormous amounts of money for corporations. By picking up a depression very early, recognizing it early and treating it appropriately, a dollar spent in prevention saves ten dollars in treatment.

"It's rare that you walk through an airport where you don't see a sign on high blood pressure, but you don't see that on depression," Judd continued. "The major corporations are reluctant to provide the sign space, or the television time, because of the stigma of mental illness.

"At a time when we know more about depression than ever, at a time when we can diagnose it reliably and treat it successfully, it's ironic that the options for people getting treatment are

* Depression Awareness, Recognition and Treatment, a program aimed at educating primary care physicians, mental health professionals, patients, and the public about depression.

increasingly remote and difficult. The trend in the insurance industry is to exclude more and more and to have fewer and fewer
benefits for mental disorders like depression. In terms of outpatient or ambulatory treatment, only 2 percent of all the health
insurance medical plans in 1992 has coverage for someone who's
suffering from a depression [that is comparable to that available
to] someone who is suffering from diabetes. So people are largely
going untreated at this point in time. It's a scandal, and something ought to be done about it.

"What will come out of this will be a hue and cry across the
land to the people who are making decisions that people are not
going to put up with this any longer. If you have a depression,
that's a health problem and it must be treated. . . . The country as a whole has to start taking responsibility for the mentally
ill and to realize that each person's mental health affects the nation."

In writing this book, in dealing with depression, in fighting
for change, I have learned the importance of not giving up, even
when it seems all odds are against you. Don't let anyone tell you
that what you feel isn't real, isn't serious, or isn't really depression. If you have the symptoms of depression, if for an extended
time you've lost interest in or can't face the activities that you
usually enjoy, seek help. If the way you feel or act doesn't match
up to the neighbor or the cousin or the talk show guest who had
depression, that doesn't mean you're not suffering; there'll always be someone less or more depressed than you are. When a
doctor prescribes the wrong medicine, when your family is less
than patient, when talk therapy doesn't seem to help, or when
your pastor tells you to pray for forgiveness, remember: There is
help; there is hope.

For some, expectations of "conquering" depression are un-
realistic. Instead of fighting the truth, make space for it in your
life, not by caving in, but by finding ways to adapt. Making space
may mean acknowledging that if you've had depression once,
you may be vulnerable to it again. It may mean being aware of
what it feels like and knowing when to go for help (two weeks
without relief, or if you're having suicidal thoughts). Making

space may mean adapting your routine to account for medication side effects or accepting that you may be on medication for the rest of your life. Making space for depression does not mean being defeated by it; rather it means working with whatever it has brought you.

When you're ready, ask yourself: In what ways has depression served you? Dick Clark's empathy with teens, Rod Steiger's greater emotional depth and range, Pat Love's broader understanding of family members, and even Mike Wallace's softened edges have enriched each of their lives in unexpected ways. In large part, the point of view depends on the ability to see depression as a gift rather than a curse.

Of course, part of the anxiety and dread of depression is the out of control feelings, that "storm in the brain" that blocks all possibility of sunlight. In the depths of a despair that by definition murders faith, courage may have to suffice. Keep slogging. Even if you don't believe it at the moment, remind yourself of the existence of good. Reassure yourself: "I once enjoyed X, I will again. *This disease* may have turned the spigot off of love, but it will come back on."

I used to pick up Bill from work each evening and launch into the day's litany of failure. "I never made it to the bank today. . . . I meant to call about the carpets. . . . I couldn't find the ticket for the dry-cleaner's."

"Tell me about what you *did* do," he'd say.

"Well, I almost made it to the grocery store, but . . ."

The habit of negative thinking dies hard. In the throes of depression, just getting out of bed is an accomplishment. I learned to give myself tiny, accomplishable goals. I would make very specific lists of things to do, ordinary things that otherwise I couldn't tackle: get out of bed, get dressed, brush teeth. Then when the day was through, I could report, "I did ten things on my list." And no matter how small, Bill would say "Good for you." (It was years before I started to celebrate my own achievements, without the congratulations of others.)

Some days that "Good for you" was all that kept me going. What else can you say to a depressed friend? Say, first of all

"I care about you; how can I help?" Say "Are you seeing somebody? Here are some names, do you want me to call? Shall I
come drive you there?" Say "I'll call you later to see how you're
doing." Say "This will pass." Say "I love you, no matter what."

Writing this book became a vehicle for looking at depression in a
wider frame of reference, not just medically and psychologically,
but philosophically. I found new perspectives on old problems.

For example, after I was diagnosed and successfully medicated, I felt very angry about all the years I had lost. I directed
that anger toward my parents, for not getting help for me
sooner, and toward all the psychologists and psychiatrists I'd
seen, some of them much beloved, who had failed to diagnose or
treat my depression. I realized later that one had diagnosed it but
hadn't treated it effectively. He had been my most beloved guru,
and I felt utterly betrayed. I was hurt and I was very angry. But
gradually I gained a new perspective and saw that my anger was
directed unfairly. I learned to say "Well, he did what he thought
was best, and I can't hate him for that." Maybe I had a right to
be mad—at life, at circumstances. But the fact remained that
when I was experiencing terrible depression in my teens, teenage
depression had not yet been recognized. And when I was being
treated by my various therapists, the medication that saved me
was not yet on the market. I absolved them from blame and the
burden of anger lifted.

Still, I think how different my life would have been if I had
known earlier and received appropriate treatment. My schooling
would have been easier; I imagine I could have made more of my
gifts, studied better and more, considered a wider range of careers. On the other hand, if I had not followed the path I did, it
would not have led me to Bill, the wonderful careers I have had,
and the experiences I've enjoyed.

I am reinterpreting my experience with depression, looking
back with forgiveness, looking forward with curiosity. I see that
it is not just how you treat your depression that matters, but also
how you label and explain your experience. For some the lesson
may be that depression allows you to confront weaknesses in the

system—in your worldview, in your psychological makeup, in your family life, or in your body—and to repair what is repairable; for others, that it enables you to feel empathy for the suffering of others.

Dr. Betty Sue Flowers gave me a great gift during our interview, in offering a new way to look at the relationship among my life, my depression, and my work. She reminded me that while no one else can teach you the lessons you were sent here to learn, they are waiting for you to discover on your own. "Or," she said, "you could choose the [belief] that when you signed on to come down to this earth, you said 'Okay, what I want to do is relieve suffering in the world. That's what I'm here for. So at a certain age I'm going to go through major depressions, and it's going to be hard in some ways. I have to put myself through this training in order to have the gifts that I can give.'

"When you signed up for it, they told you up there, 'Are you sure you want to take on multiple depressions? Because you're going to forget that you signed up for this when you get down there.'

"And you say, 'No, I can handle it, I'll never forget this, I know what I'm doing.' But we all forget.

"Maybe that's what you're doing: You're using [these difficulties] to change lives and people through writing this book."

I have always found strength in beliefs that ascribe a purpose to suffering—to deepen one's faith, to learn the lessons missed in previous lives, or to enhance our understanding of other people's trials. I believe I have resolved satisfactorily the medical issues of my depression; I continue to work on the psychological issues, and I see before me the stimulating prospect of further exploration of the spiritual.

I continue to learn new ways of dealing with my illness and its effects on my family. I am learning not to look over my shoulder, anxious about the next episode. There are still repairs to be made to my relationship with Bill and perhaps with the children. I continue to worry about their vulnerability to depression: I must learn not to be hypervigilant, while reassuring myself that I will be able to recognize nascent problems.

As research advances, new questions and challenges will arise. The connection between substance abuse and depression continues to be investigated. When I started this book, the debate was raging: Was depression a side effect of substance abuse, or did depression lead to the abuse, and how do we tell the difference? By the time I finished, a clearer idea of the genetic link between the two was emerging. We will see more information on, and most likely acceptance of, alternative theories about and therapies for depression. Nutrition, exercise, massage, and yoga are found useful for mild depressions already, and the relationship of depression to women's health and hormones is being researched with vigor. Now, as we grope toward a national health plan that includes equitable treatment for mental illnesses, even the U.S. government has started to study Americans' uses of alternative treatments.

There isn't an end to this story. New medications and combinations of medications come on the market, new talk therapies evolve, new controversies keep the conversation lively. We learn more every day about causes and cures of depression. And, as a society, we become more tolerant of those who are different, more understanding of those who are in pain, and more hopeful of a healthy future for us all.

Epilogue

May 1993

The boys run laughing and squealing in from school while I'm deeply immersed in my work.

"Hi, guys!" I call to them, smiling as I put my papers aside. It has been a good day's work. "Well, I guess we'd better hit the market, eh? Do you have homework, William? Oh! Look at your painting, Jack!" I grab a recipe off the fridge and my keys from the counter. By the time we get home, Bill has called to say he'll be late, and it's already time for Jack's bath.

"Tell you what, how about frozen waffles for dinner?" It won't hurt them once in a while, and I'll have time to sit with them while they eat without hurrying. I'll worry about feeding Bill and me later.

"Can I help cook?" Jack asks, dragging his step stool over. Although it slows me down, his clumsy efforts amuse rather than frustrate me. And by the time Bill arrives, the boys have eaten and bathed, and we're ready for our recently initiated family reading time.

These things hardly seem worth telling to the well, but they are a major accomplishment to the depressed, and I revel in the miracle of the mundane. Maybe that is one of the gifts of depression.

Medication hasn't made me into an ideal mom, but more days than not I feel capable, and loving, and within reach of that ideal. And on the other days, I don't castigate myself for falling short. Mistakes are made, things are left undone, but I'm able to handle even the larger crises, when the smallest used to be debilitating.

I still think my son plays his tapes too loudly, but when my youngest tap-tap-taps with his fork, when the dishwasher runs, when the radio comes on unexpectedly, I don't jump out of my skin. My muscles don't ache from the effort of holding myself together. My brows are unknit, my chin relaxed from its pout, my face feels smooth, open. My eyes feel awake, the view no longer obscured by a translucent film of pain. My skin feels alive, tingling. I relish the feel of my brush through my hair, the variety and subtlety of my meals; I am a sentient and sensuous being once more.

It is spring, a season when I have experienced some of my worst depressions. Looking back through my journals, I see agonizing entries dated April 20, 21, 22, whatever the year.

Now it is already May, and I am still well.

I find I am able to experience the present more fully, without exaggerated regret for the past nor fear for the future. I am able to slow down, to allow conversation with William, to make love with my husband, to work through a financial crisis without panicking (and discover I can tell the difference between the disease of depression and the state of depression!), to survive the scheduling and planning and attending of many end-of-school activities as well as professional and social commitments, without being overwhelmed and falling apart. I am able to enjoy the moment I am in, to lie in the sun relishing the gradual warming of my skin, to watch ants rebuilding their nest, to laugh into Jack's eyes, bright and shiny with humor and love.

I am filled with hope.

Biographies

RONA BARRETT is a former gossip columnist and entertainment reporter who pioneered the form before the advent of Barbara Walters specials and *Entertainment Tonight*. She has been married happily for more than twenty years. Barrett is the author of several books, including the best seller, *Miss Rona, An Autobiography*. She is now enthusiastically involved in several careers, including video distribution and stone-fruit farming.

ANN BUCHWALD, who at the time of this interview was married to Pulitzer Prize–winning humorist Art Buchwald, retired from her career as a literary agent after heart surgery. She is the author (with commentary by Art) of *Seems Like Yesterday*.

DICK CLARK, America's ever-cheerful perpetual teenager, was himself an insecure and unhappy adolescent, but the support of his family eased his burden. Shy by nature, Clark managed to become a professional extrovert, launching *American Bandstand* from a Philadelphia TV studio in 1956. The show subsequently moved to Los Angeles, where Clark remained host until 1989 and earned the nickname "America's oldest teenager." Throughout the run of *Bandstand*, Clark diversified his emcee duties and entertainment business holdings, branching out into the production of numerous award-winning series, specials, and movies. He is also the author of several books, including *Rock, Roll and Remember, Dick Clark's Guide to Good Grooming*, and many articles on teen problems.

DENTON COOLEY, M.D., is known to the public as a gifted cardiac surgeon. He admits to only two "major disappointments" in his life: his devastating financial troubles resulting in bankruptcy, and the suicide of his fourth daughter, Florence. A pioneer in his field, Cooley has won dozens of awards for his work and authored numerous articles on surgical heart procedure and medicine.

SUSAN CROSBY, Hollywood producer and a former Miss Alaska, was married for nearly a quarter of a century to crooner Bing Crosby's youngest son, Lindsay. Of Bing's four boys from his first marriage to Dixie Lee, eldest Gary is now a recovering alcoholic and the author of a book about his father. Less than two years after younger brother Lindsay committed suicide, Dennis followed.

SUSAN DIME-MEENAN is the executive director of the National Depressive and Manic Depressive Association. She has bipolar disorder.

JANE DOE is a professional woman from inside the Beltway of Washington, D.C. She believes she has too much to lose in the man's world of politics to come forward with her identity. Since one of the chapters of this book is devoted to the stigma associated with depression, her anonymous presence here makes the point that, as far as we've come as a society, we still have a distance to go in understanding and accepting this illness for what it is—a disease, not a character flaw.

KITTY DUKAKIS is a study in an individual's ability to meet adversity head on. To some, her name always will evoke memories of her two most publicized ordeals—her husband's loss of the presidency of the United States to George Bush in 1988 and her own ingestion of rubbing alcohol a few months later. She is recovering from both alcoholism and addiction to pills. She is the mother of three children, John, Kara, and Andrea, and daughter of Harry Ellis Dickson, a conductor with the Boston Symphony. She is the author, with Jane Scovell, of *Now You Know*.

JAMES FARMER became a familiar face during the 1960s on the front lines of the civil rights struggle alongside his contemporary, Dr. Martin Luther King, Jr. A former trade union official and founding member of the Congress of Racial Equality (CORE), Farmer led a perilous "Freedom Ride" bus trip to protest segregation across the South in 1961. Depression came some years later. A contemplative man of profound compassion and convictions, Farmer crawled from the wreckage of his illness to write his autobiography, *Lay Bare the Heart*, in 1985. Farmer has been honored with numerous awards in appreciation of his ongoing civil rights work. He is the father of two children, Tami and Abbey.

JAN FAWCETT, M.D., is chairman of the Department of Psychiatry and the Stanley G. Harris, Sr., Professor of Psychiatry at Rush-Presbyterian–St. Luke's Medical Center in Chicago. He is also the Grainger Director of the Rush Institute for Mental Well-Being. He is an expert on depression, suicide, and alcoholism.

JULES FEIFFER is one of America's most successful and enduring contemporary satirists, having found success as a playwright, screenwriter, and cartoonist. He is a 1961 Academy Award winner for his short-subject cartoon, "Munro," was named most promising playwright of the 1966–67 season by the New York Drama Critics, and won a Pulitzer Prize in 1986 for his cartoon work. He has two children, a grown daughter from his first marriage and a school-age daughter with his second wife.

BETTY SUE FLOWERS, Ph.D., a poet and professor of English at the University of Texas at Austin, is the author of several books, including *Four Shields of Power*, and editor of Bill Moyers's *Healing and the Mind*, *The Power of Myth* (with Joseph Campbell), and *A World of Ideas* (volume 1).

JENNIE FOREHAND is a delegate to Maryland's state legislature. She helped her eighty-year-old mother to complete recovery from a devastating passage through depression.

LINDA N. FREEMAN, M.D., is in the Department of Child and Adolescent Psychiatry of the College of Physicians and Surgeons of Columbia University. She is the author with Joanne B. Koch of *Good Parents for Hard Times.*

JOHN KENNETH GALBRAITH is as renowned among friends for his wit as for his intellect. He is an economist, educator, author, social critic, political activist, and diplomat. In his own estimation, he is a "a barely average" teacher (who nonetheless prodded students and provoked administrators at Harvard for a quarter century), and he ranks himself twelfth among the dozen leading experts on Indian painting. His writings range from a trilogy on economic theory that included *The Affluent Society* to a scathing novel on failed American foreign policies called *The Triumph: A Novel of Modern Diplomacy.* President Kennedy named Galbraith ambassador to India in 1961 and reported to confidants that it was one of his administration's best appointments.

LESLIE GARIS is a writer best known for her *New York Times Magazine* profiles. Daughter and granddaughter of writers, she is married to playwright Arthur Kopit and mother of three children. Currently Garis is working on a novel.

FREDERICK GOODWIN, M.D., is director of the NIMH. Previously, he directed the Alcohol, Drug Abuse, and Mental Health Administration. He is an internationally recognized authority in the research and treatment of major depression and manic-depressive illness. His contributions include research in the effects of lithium, and in drug addiction and alcoholism, with constant attention to the interactions of biological, psychological, and environmental factors in mental disorders. He has received many awards and honors including the Presidential Distinguished Executive Award, and is the author of numerous works including, with Kay R. Jamison, Ph.D., *Manic Depressive Illness* (Oxford University Press).

STEPHEN P. HERSH, M.D., F.A.P.A., is co-director of the Medical Illness Counseling Center, clinical professor of psychiatry and behavioral sciences at George Washington University, and on the medical staff of The Clinical Center of the National Institute of Health.

JIM JENSEN, CBS news anchor in New York City, suffered a very public battle against cocaine addiction and depression, triggered partly by the death of his twenty-six-year-old son, Randy, in a 1979 hang-gliding accident. One of the fastest-rising stars in television journalism, Jensen replaced Douglas Edwards in 1964 as anchor of the 11 P.M. news at Boston's WCBS and shortly thereafter replaced Robert Trout as the host of the 6:30 P.M. newscast as well.

NORMAN JEWISON is a former television actor, writer, and director who successfully moved into film direction and production in the 1960s. He is responsible for such Academy Award–honored films as *Fiddler on the Roof* and *Moonstruck*. In addition to *In the Heat of the Night*, his films with Rod Steiger include *F.I.S.T.* and *The January Man*.

MARY JONES is a pseudonym for a writer who has suffered from both depression and alcohol abuse. After returning from an alcohol treatment facility, she decided not to allow her name to be used.

LEWIS L. JUDD, M.D., is the Mary Gilman Marston Professor and chairman of the Department of Psychiatry at the University of California, San Diego.

JOHN KELSOE, M.D., is an assistant professor of psychiatry at the University of California, San Diego, with a special interest in the genetics of bipolar disorder.

PAT LOVE is a doctor of education in counseling as well as a licensed professional counselor and marriage and family therapist. The author of *The Emotional Incest Syndrome*, she has two grown children from her first marriage.

BARBARA L. PARRY, M.D., is an associate professor of psychiatry at the University of California, San Diego.

JUDITH BELUSHI PISANO is a writer/designer who was married to comic actor (and childhood sweetheart) John Belushi at the time of his death by drug overdose in 1982. Now wed to writer/producer Victor Pisano, she is the author of *Samurai Widow*, a book she describes as her own "journey through widowhood." In addition, she has written both *The Mom Book* and *Titters 101* in collaboration with Anne Beatts and Deanne Stillman. She also produced the video tribute to her late husband and designed jackets for all the Blues Brothers' releases as well as numerous other album and book covers.

JOAN RIVERS is a comedienne, talk show host, and author, as celebrated for the trials in her life—a rancorous feud with former *Tonight Show* host Johnny Carson and the shocking suicide of her husband, Edgar Rosenberg—as for her caustic wit and multiple visits to the plastic surgeon. Among her film credits are *Rabbit Test*, which gave Billy Crystal his first big-screen lead, and *Spaceballs*. Rivers is a Clio and Emmy Award winner, and her charity work includes time donated as chairperson for cystic fibrosis and for suicide prevention. Her books include *Enter Talking* and *Still Talking*.

NORMAN E. ROSENTHAL, M.D., along with Dr. Goodwin and others, first described seasonal affective disorder. He is the director of light therapy studies at the National Institute of Mental Health, and author of *Seasons of the Mind*, recently revised as *Winter Blues*.

A. JOHN RUSH, M.D., who holds the Betty Jo Hay Distinguished Chair in Mental Health, is professor and vice chairman for research in the Department of Psychiatry at the University of Texas Southwestern Medical Center. He chaired the panel responsible for the "Depression in Primary Care" guidelines for patients and doctors available from the U.S. Department of Health and Human Services (800-358-9295). He authored *Beating Depression* and other publications.

ROD STEIGER is an Academy Award–winning actor whose films include *In the Heat of the Night* (for which he won an Oscar and a Golden Globe Award), *Dr. Zhivago*, and *The Amityville Horror*.

ROSE STYRON is a poet and human rights activist who devotes much of her spare time to working with Amnesty International. She is the wife of novelist William Styron and mother to Susanna, Tom, Polly, and Alexandra.

WILLIAM STYRON is best known for such novels as *The Confessions of Nat Turner* and *Sophie's Choice*. Styron has won numerous literary accolades, including the Pulitzer Prize, the American Book Award, and great recognition in literary circles. He has been editor of the *Paris Review*. In 1983 he was jury president of the Cannes Film Festival. *Darkness Visible* is his account of his battle with depression.

TREY SUNDERLAND, M.D., heads the section on geriatric psychiatry at the Laboratory of Clinical Science of the National Institute of Mental Health.

MIKE WALLACE is a founding anchor of television's preeminent news magazine, *60 Minutes*. He and the *60 Minutes* team have won the George Foster Peabody and Emmy awards. Wallace is also the author of several books, among them *Mike Wallace Asks* and *Close Encounters*.

HARRY A. WILMER, M.D., is a member of the International Association for Analytical Psychology. He is the founder and director of the Institute for the Humanities in Salado, Texas, and author of numerous publications, including *Understandable Jung*.

FRED WRIGHT, Ed.D., is an assistant professor of psychology in the School of Medicine at the University of Pennsylvania and director of education at the Center for Cognitive Therapy.

Afterword

The interviews in this book were conducted between 1989 and 1993. Since then there have been changes in medical research as well as in the lives and psyches of the people interviewed. Therefore, I view this project as only a snapshot in time.

I realized early on that this book was merely an introduction to the topic of depression. Much has been left unsaid. My intention is to continue exploring the disruption of the parent/child relationship, from depression in infants and adolescents, through postpartum depression and menopause. I would like once again to interview medical experts and people in the public eye, particularly those who have had experience with child, adolescent, postpartum, or menopausal depression within their immediate families.

If you have suggestions or contacts that would help me in this pursuit, I would very much appreciate hearing from you. You may write to me in care of Doubleday.

Appendix 1

Liz's List

Liz Carpenter, author, mentor, former White House press secretary, is one of the most powerful personalities in my life. In the face of her no-nonsense manner, the strength of her beliefs, and her forceful physical presence, it's easy to feel intimidated. Behind all that, and over and around it, however, is a warmth and generosity and loyalty rare in anyone. As one man said, "She's the kind of friend you can call at two o'clock in the morning, just because you need a friend."

She's had her share of troubles, too, including the early death of her beloved husband, Les. Yes, she's had her share of the blues, but never crossed that line to clinical depression. I asked her what techniques she had found to keep the darkest clouds at bay. The next day she handed me a list, remarkably similar to the list of twelve self-help activities found in Rippere and Williams's study. Liz says:

"When you have the blues—try one or more of these remedies:

1. Do something for someone—a child, a friend, a mate.
2. Do something for yourself—a new hairdo, a new dress, a massage.
3. Do something for your home—garden, plant a tree, clean a drawer or closet to music.
4. Have eight people to dinner with your good china and best recipes.
5. Take three upbeat friends to lunch.
6. Plan a vacation.
7. Exercise—swim, dance, jog, walk.
8. Volunteer to work in a soup line.
9. Follow the AA formula of HALT—take positive steps to avoid being *H*ungry, *A*ngry, *L*onely, or *T*ired.
10. Confess your depression to a sensible friend or a sensible psychiatrist.
11. Join a cooking course, tennis club, church—or all three.
12. Sing—even if you think you can't.

Advice like this can go a long way toward lifting the blues. But people deep in a clinical depression are not going to find relief in self-help activities like these, if in fact they were capable of acting on them at all, and expecting them to "cheer up" or "snap out of it" can add to their pain. However, if you've had one bout of depression and can learn to recognize the symptoms early on, often you can avert a full-blown relapse by practicing good self-care and self-esteem–building activities like these. Looking at the list, it's pretty good advice for each of us, every day.

Appendix 2

Resources

The following groups can provide support, brochures, and in some cases referrals to support groups and mental health professionals.

American Association of Retired Persons,
202-434-2277

American Association for Marriage and Family Therapy,
202-452-0109

American Psychiatric Association, 202-682-6069

American Psychological Association, 202-336-5700

National Alliance for the Mentally Ill,
1-800-950-NAMI

* National Depressive and Manic-Depressive
Association, 1-800-82-NDMDA

* Contact these groups for especially helpful printed information.

National Foundation for Depressive Illness,
1-800-248-4344

*National Institute of Mental Health Depression
Awareness Recognition and Treatment Campaign,
301-443-4140. For brochures call 1-800-421-4211.

*National Mental Health Association 1-800-969-6642

*U.S. Department of Health and Human Services
AHCPR, 1-800-358-9295. Their brochure "Depression
Is a Treatable Illness" (# AHCPR 93-0553) is an
invaluable guide for people with depression.

In Canada, contact one of the 135 local branches of
the Mental Health Association or your Community
Information Center to find out about support services in
your area.

Appendix 3

Medical and Drug-Induced Depression

Medical Causes

Common medical causes of depression include thyroid deficiency, neurologic disorders, head injury, and cancer (even possibly before it has been diagnosed). Other medical causes include Addison's disease, Alzheimer's disease, cerebral ischemia, Cushing's disease, Huntington's disease, Parkinson's disease, hyper- and hypothyroidism, lupus, multiple sclerosis, nutritional deficiencies, pancreatic disease, rheumatoid arthritis, stroke, and viral and other infectious diseases.

Drugs

If at any time you experience depression while taking or after discontinuing any medication, inform your doctor. Some of the drugs that are known to cause depression are alcohol, amantadine, barbiturates, benzodiazepines, carbidopa, clonidine, cycloserine,

estrogen and birth control pills, levodopa, methyldopa, proprano-
lol, reserpine, vinblastine, and vincristine. Drugs that cause depression after discontinuing include amphetamines, cocaine and
other stimulants, steroids, and narcotics.

Many medications, although very valuable under certain circumstances, are not recommended as the sole treatment for un-
complicated depression. Antianxiety drugs, stimulants, and sleeping pills, for example, treat some of the most obvious symptoms
of depression without helping the disease. For more on this topic,
refer to the very valuable *What You Need to Know About Psychiatric
Drugs*, by S. C. Yudofsky, R. E. Hales, and T. Ferguson (New
York: Ballantine Books, 1991).

Bibliography

The following list includes works I have read in the preparation of this project, works that have been suggested by the people I interviewed, and works written by them.

Beck, A. T. 1976. *Cognitive Therapy and the Emotional Disorders.* New York: Penguin Books.

Beck, A. T.; A. J. Rush; B. F. Shaw; and G. Emery. 1979. *Cognitive Therapy.* New York: Guilford Press.

Berger, D., and L. Berger. 1991. *We Heard the Angels of Madness.* New York: William Morrow.

Blyskal, Jeff. 1993. "Head Hunt." *New York* magazine; January 11. On finding the right therapist. New York: K-III Magazines.

Carpenter, L. 1987. *Getting Better All the Time.* New York: Pocket Books.

Carson, R. D. 1986. *Taming Your Gremlin: A Guide to Enjoying Yourself.* New York: HarperCollins.

Dowling, C. 1991. *You Mean I Don't Have to Feel This Way?* New York: Scribner.

Duke, P., and K. Turan. 1987. *Call Me Anna: The Autobiography of Patty Duke.* New York: Bantam Books.

Edinberg, M. A. 1987. *Talking with Your Aging Parents.* Boston: Shambhala.

Fieve, R. R. 1989. *Moodswing.* New York: Bantam.

Found Inner Peace. 1992. *A Course of Miracles*, revised edition. Glen Ellen, CA: Found Inner Peace.

Gold, M. S. and L. B. Morris. 1988. *The Good News about Depression: New Medical Cures & Treatments That Can Work for You.* New York: Bantam.

Goodwin, F. K., and K. R. Jamison. 1990. *Manic-Depressive Illness.* New York: Oxford University Press.

Gorman, J. 1992. *The Essential Guide to Psychiatric Drugs.* New York: St. Martin's Press.

Herskowitz, J. 1988. *Is Your Child Depressed?* New York: Warner Books.

Klein, D. F. and P. H. Wender. 1988. *Do You Have a Depressive Illness: How to Tell, What to Do.* New York: New American Library.

Klerman, G. L.; M. M. Weissman; B. J. Rounsaville; E. S. Chevron. 1984. *Interpersonal Psychotherapy of Depression.* New York: HarperCollins.

Kline, N. S. 1974. *From Sad to Glad.* New York: Ballantine Books.

Meeks, J. E. 1988. *High Times/Low Times: The Many Faces of Adolescent Depression.* Summit, NJ: The PIA Press.

Miller, A. 1981. *The Drama of the Gifted Child.* New York: Basic Books.

Rosellini, G., and M. Worden. 1987. *Here Comes the Sun: Dealing with Depression.* Center City, MN: Hazelden Publishing Group.

Rosenthal, N. E. 1989. *Seasons of the Mind.* New York: Bantam Books. Revised as *Winter Blues.* New York: Guilford Press, 1993.

Rush, A. J. 1983. *Beating Depression.* New York: Facts on File.

Rush, A. J., and K. Z. Altshuler, eds. 1986. *Depression: Basic Mechanisms, Diagnosis, and Treatment.* New York: Guilford Press.

Seligman, M. E. P. 1991. *Learned Optimism.* New York: Knopf.

Steinbrecher, E. C. 1982. *The Inner Guide Meditation: A Transformational Journey to Enlightenment and Awareness.* Wellingborough, Northamptonshire, UK: The Aquarian Press.

Whybrow, Peter C. 1984. *Mood Disorders: Toward a New Psychobiology.* New York: Plenum Publishing Corp.

Yudofsky, S. C.; R. E. Hales; and T. Ferguson. 1991. *What You Need to Know About Psychiatric Drugs.* New York: Ballantine Books.

Index